C0-ATR-207

G. B. S. 90

# G. B. S. 90

## Aspects of Bernard Shaw's Life and Work

SIR MAX BEERBOHM
JOHN MASEFIELD, O.M.
J. D. BERNAL, F.R.S.
GILBERT MURRAY, O.M.
W. R. INGE
LAURENCE HOUSMAN
LORD PASSFIELD, O.M.
JAMES BRIDIE
C. E. M. JOAD
J. B. PRIESTLEY
ALDOUS HUXLEY
SIR WILLIAM HALEY
LORD DUNSANY
MAURICE DOBB
EDWARD J. DENT
VAL GIELGUD
EMIL DAVIES
ROY LIMBERT
DANIEL JONES
A. S. NEILL
SIR KENNETH BARNES
GABRIEL PASCAL
M. J. MACMANUS
J. C. TREWIN
S. I. HSIUNG
H. G. WELLS

Edited by S. Winsten

DODD, MEAD & COMPANY
NEW YORK—1946

PRINTED IN THE UNITED STATES OF AMERICA
AMERICAN BOOK–STRATFORD PRESS, INC., NEW YORK

To G.B.S.
ON HIS 90TH BIRTHDAY

Gilbert Murray

John Masefield

W. R. Inge

J. B. Priestley

Aldous Huxley

W. J. Haley

Maurice Dobb

Daniel Jones

Kenneth R. Barnes

J. C. Trewin

S. Winsten

## CONTENTS

# PROFESSOR GILBERT MURRAY, O.M.

## A FOREWORD

I AM in no fit state, writing in bed on a typewriter as old as myself and equally in need of repair, to send a worthy contribution to the *Festschrift* of G.B.S. But I could not bear to be left out while others are honouring one whom I admire so greatly.

Let me take a text. I dedicated my book on Aristophanes to "My old friend G.B.S., Lover of Ideas and Hater of Cruelty; Who has Filled Many Lands with Laughter and whose Courage has Never Failed——"

"Lover of ideas." Though I have lived much among intellectual workers, I doubt if I have known anyone who lived so vividly the life of the mind and cared so little for that of the mere body. The pleasures of eating and drinking count surprisingly little to him. No coarseness or sensuality ever shows its head through his overflowing wit. Even pain seems not to disturb him much. I once went to see him on Hindhead when he had just had a very bad accident, resulting in countless bruises, fractures and sprains. I took for granted that he would be in bed, but was told he was in the garden in a hammock. I went to look for him and saw no one, but presently heard a chuckle behind a large holly bush. Guided by this I found him, unconscious of my presence, unconscious of pains, swathed in bandages, writing away with his unbandaged hand and laughing with sheer enjoyment. Even as a reformer it is ideas that have interested him. Though he has a keen insight and eye for facts, he is not, I think, chiefly actuated, as for instance Miss

Rathbone was, by sympathy for human suffering; but more by the absurdity of the institutions that caused the suffering. He reforms by ridicule and hard logic more than by any appeal to emotion.

Of course one must never forget his extreme "hatred of cruelty," either to man or beast. He seems hardly to belong to our race of simian carnivores whose main pleasure or interest in life is what we call "sport," i.e., "huntin', shootin' and fishin' " and generally inflicting death and pain on almost every creature that can live and feel. He hates oppression of mankind in the same way; it is not that he particularly likes rabbits or foxes or the poor. But he cannot bear to see them ill treated.

As for his "filling many lands with laughter," that is too obvious to dwell upon, but there are two points worth noting. First, I doubt if there was ever in human history a great wit and satirist so singularly free from spite or malice. He can make tremendous attacks on actions or institutions which, rightly or wrongly, he considers cruel or unjust. But there is never the personal note; never the wish to hurt or to "get his own back," which one finds in almost all lesser satirists, and even in his great peers, Voltaire and Aristophanes. He is like those two, however, in a great quality which many wits and satirists lack; he has a real respect and appreciation for great poetry and art and music. Few scholars of his time have had a more close and intimate knowledge of Shakespeare. He has been always on the look-out, without envy or denigration, for contemporary genius; he rejoiced in Tolstoy, Ibsen, Maeterlinck, Rodin and was untiring in the help he gave to younger English writers. And of course I can never forget his generous and almost surprised admiration of Greek drama, even as obscured by my attempts at interpreting it.

His "courage never failed." I do not mean only that he attacked fearlessly all sorts of established beliefs and institutions which enjoyed great prestige and authority. He struck at Conservatism and Radicalism, at superstition and at science;

whichever seemed to him too dominant at the time, while now his devastating criticisms of "democracy" and the worship of "the common man" are particularly bold and valuable. But he has a much rarer quality; the courage, I would even say, the toughness, of genius. I can remember the time when his first comedies were written and published, and everyone thought them impossible for the stage. Kindly managers told him that he really had some dramatic talent; if he would only alter his absurd plays, or get some sensible person, with knowledge of the theatre, to help him to re-write them, they might actually be quite worth producing. I think I am right in saying it was twenty years before he had a play produced—*Arms and the Man,* by the daring Miss Horniman. It was an instantaneous success; and not long afterwards Shaw attained almost his present position as the most famous and most widely read dramatist in Europe. He had made no concession to his critics. He had just written on in the way that his genius chose to write.

With all his amazing brilliance he is one of the kindest and most generous of men. I would not say he was one of the wisest. His genius in practical affairs is analytic rather than constructive. He once wrote in defence of some article of his in the *Saturday Review,* the remarkable words: "Who am I that I should be just?" It was a true defence. It was not his business, or his gift, to weigh all the elements of a dispute, to sum up carefully and recommend the safest course. Officials and administrators can do that. Shaw's business was to show something that was wrong and not known to be wrong; to throw a dazzling light upon it and, even by exaggeration and unfairness, to compel people to see something which they were unable or unwilling to see.

In this book you will read about Shaw's dramas, his philosophy, his public work, perhaps even about his strange delusion that he, the most marked individualist and rebel of his time, is a good, obedient Socialist and could live in a Socialist world without forming a centre of revolution. I am content to have tried, however clumsily, to express my admiration and affection for my old friend, his unworldliness, his real greatness, his devotion to things of the mind, his incomparable wit and vitality.

*Jan. 5th, 1946*

## JOHN MASEFIELD, O.M.

### *ON THE NINETIETH BIRTHDAY OF BERNARD SHAW*

After these ninety years, he can survey
Changes enough, so many due to him:—
Old wax-work melted down, old tinsel dim,
Old sentimental clock-work put away.

There the old playthings with their lovers lie;
But he remains, the bright mind ever young,
The glorious great heart, the witty tongue,
Erasing Shaw, who made the folly die.

Is there a cranny in our old conceit
Unlightened by the brightness of his mind?
Is there a blinker, making many blind,
Unrent by him, to show that light is sweet?

Is there a mystery in life or fate
To which his spirit has not sought a door?
Is there a play, in all his pungent store,
Not touching home? unlinked with something great?

Honour him living, all Earth's brightest brains.
Let Ministers of Fine Arts, centuries hence,
Order him statues; let us have more sense,
And call a splendour great while he remains.

## S. WINSTEN

### *INTRODUCTION*

*They would not find me changed from him they knew,*
*Only more sure of all I thought was true.*

ROBERT FROST.

THERE are many things older than G.B.S. in Ayot Saint Lawrence, much older. The sycamore in the Park, serene and upright, always cocks a knowing eye at his co-mate when he passes.

"Conquered death?" asks the sycamore.

G.B.S. has much in common with the tree for he has rooted into Ayot. Though he has travelled and enjoyed his travels, the journeys from house to shelter and from shelter to house are those that give him the greatest pleasure. Here in this tiny village with its cobbled wall and Tudor dwellings the story goes that another bearded figure has been seen seeking an interview. Does he expect to meet him in the demolished abbey, the gothic windows of which light up in the moonlight? This corpulent gentleman, monarch, musician, Henry VIII by name, pillar of orthodoxy and morality, cannot stand the presence of a professional heretic. For here in the Rectory lives Bernard Shaw and letters have come to him addressed to Reverend George Shaw. He has often contemplated putting out a professional sign:

ORIGINAL THINKER
ESTABLISHED CREEDS AND CODES EXAMINED
ABLE TO DRAFT NEW CODES AND CREEDS

but he dislikes, as everybody knows, calling attention to himself. He prefers the quiet and unobtrusive life of routine. As I see him coming down the lane to us, he looks a Tudor figure who has survived wars, wars to end wars and wars to start new wars. Almost I can see Shakespeare following in his wake, glad that the last act of Cymbeline has been brought up to date by this *enfant terrible.*

GUIDERIUS: When I lived in a cave methought a palace
Must be a glorious place, peopled with men
Renowned as councillors, mighty as soldiers,
As saints a pattern of holy living.
And all at my command were I a prince.
This was my dream. I am awake to-day

and he finishes with:

Oh no, sir: give me back the dear old cave
And my unflattering four-footed friends.

"I thought," said William S. "you always preferred prose?"

Yes, Shaw is a man of diverse gifts. God has given him everything except the one thing . . . he wanted. But we shall come to that.

Has he in this picture post card village left the fawning, fickle human for the unflattering four-footed friend? Is he always singing to keep himself cheerful:

Blow, blow, thou winter wind
Thou art not so unkind
As man's ingratitude.

There is none of that, G.B.S. has been saved from cynicism not by the saving grace of laughter but by a realistic outlook.

After having gathered enough experience to last two or three lives, it is necessary for him to get away from things a little to think things out. The highest honour we can confer on this public-spirited servant is the Order of Solitude, for he can bear his own company and is not afraid of himself. For most people happiness is always round the corner, where two or three are gathered together, the more the merrier, for him it is to be found in G.B.S. He has watched men coming round to his views but he is still in a minority of one. We can only be thankful that his great gifts have been given to great causes: he has always defended the dog against the scientist, the sheep against the butcher, the artist against the philistine, the worker against the exploiter, the minority against the majority and the majority against the impostor.

* * *

It would be misleading to suggest that Ayot Saint Lawrence played any important part as a formative influence in the life of G.B.S. Before he set foot in this village his reputation had already been made in America and Germany and his name was even known in this country. In this village he is known as the man "Who came from over the hill," who does not hunt, shoot or attend church and is somewhat redeemed by the fact that he has a good garage and now even here his fame has penetrated through Vivien Leigh.

He puts himself down as a product of Squares and Circles: Fitzroy Square and Trafalgar Square, Fabian and artistic circles! For a long time art and economics did not mix. To the Webbs he was an artist, to William Morris, an economist. Beatrice could find no pigeon-hole and Mrs. Morris no words for him. Or as he puts it:

"I was highly obnoxious to Beatrice for the technical reason that I could not be classified. All her interest was in social organization. The complications introduced by artists were simply nuisances.

"I always felt apologetic with Mrs. Morris. I knew that the sudden eruption into her temple of beauty, of the proletarian comrades who began to infest the premises as Morris's fellow socialists must be horribly disagreeable to her and as one of this ugly ragtag and bobtail of socialism, I could not expect her to do more than bear my presence as best she might."

But he was such an easy, helpful person that it was not long before he was *persona grata* in both households: William Morris condescended to discuss art with him and the Webbs violently disputed economics. Mystic art and dismal science were the two parallel lines which met in him.

To Charlotte, his wife, he was just the genius with an infinite capacity for taking pains and giving pleasure. He was a horse for single harness and wanted some harnessing. The greatest tribute that can be paid to her is that she succeeded. Theory or no theory the marriage was a good practical proposition. She wrote: "A man wants to feel in his home that he is law-giver and deity." But if Bernard Shaw acted as the unacknowledged law-giver and deity in the outside world, at home he left everything to her except of course his writing. But even in this she broadened his vista by insisting on extensive travel. His home was in the inkpot and his heart was on the platform. I remember taking the chair for him at one of his meetings twenty years ago: a thousand people had gathered to listen to a lecture on drama. For two hours he held his audience with a serious thought-provoking address and, sitting by him, I could see the satisfaction on the faces of the listeners and the laughter which came at the turn of a thought and an original view of a familiar thing. Next day my duty took me to Ayot Saint Lawrence and there a native remarked: "Would you believe, I've never seen Mr. Shaw. I don't know what he does with himself all day." The charm of an English village is that a man, however famous as an artist or writer, can live there incognito. For, like Beatrice Webb, the natives must classify and codify and where could they place this strange figure? What can they say of this bearded man who at his age walks without a coat on a wintry day and whose head is high in the clouds?

* * *

There is nothing which escapes him. He may declare that his kingdom is not of this world, that he is at ease only with the mighty dead, that he belongs only to the great Republic of Thought and Art, but while in this silly, chaotic world he is interested in everything from diet to drains. He enters his shelter not to escape from life but to enter more fully into it. One evening when we were talking about titles of books, he thought the two best were Edward Carpenter's *Civilization, Its Cause and Cure,* and Henry Salt's *Seventy Years among Savages.* I suggested *Heartbreak House* would be a good third.

"None of us were defeatists," he answered decisively. "There is a way out of civilization and savagery."

"You are still convinced?"

"I've never changed my beliefs."

He came to the way out through music and poetry. He sang Mozart and read Shelley and having absorbed them was ready to enter his University, the street corner. Few people realize what the open air platform meant to him. Agitation became a full time job and he has never regretted it. It put him in contact with all sorts and conditions of men, transformed the supersensitive young man into the talker who could hold thousands. It took him out of himself so that he could talk about everything with the fullest freedom and learnt the way to people's hearts by laughing at everything. Never taken in by his own fluent tongue he studied hard and made himself a peer of the people he respected most: Webb and Morris. If one can hold a crowd against brass band and beer then it isn't difficult to split up into diverse characters and set them all talking. At least it wasn't difficult for G.B.S. For him the writing of plays was only the natural development of street corner propaganda. The magnificent theatre of to-day is after all the outcome of the open air Morality play, arising out of the desire to arrange somewhere where people cannot enter without a fee. And people were prepared to flock in their thousands to enjoy this devastating influence and give him ample means to afford the simple life he now leads.

Once when I was going to see him I found a small group peeping over the gate. "Is this where he practises the simple life?" one asked. They used to mean by simple life that a man left a routine job in an office or workshop or the Stock Exchange for the land. Like Tolstoy and Gandhi he was to live as frugally as a tramp, earn his keep by the toil of his hands and if not a cave, the log hut was to be his habitat. But Shaw is a man of to-morrow. He despises poverty and enjoys the comforts that this generation has effected. Creative thinking and working need a sense of security and leisure.

In many ways G.B.S. has been a most fortunate man. He was born in time to miss active participation in the deadly wars which robbed the world of much of its creative talent. He was old enough to place the world civil wars in due perspective and if his common sense irritated a hysterical people he could take it. He was lucky enough when young to be a revolutionary in England and not in Russia or Germany, for he eschewed honours and did not seek a martyr's crown.

His is a lover's quarrel with life. Having gained his reputation by being considered a dangerous and disreputable person the tendency now is to idolize him. But Shaw has not changed. He still denounces as vigorously as ever, he still thinks that we are a barbarous people, that we have a genuine dread of intellect in any form and are convinced that art though clandestinely enjoyable is essentially immoral. He wouldn't be in God's boots for worlds because the human experiment has proved an uncomfortable and disconcerting proposition. Scientist and theologian, teacher and philosopher, banker and butcher have always longed for his scalp as if he were the one who had endowed the human race with the evils he revealed.

* * *

It is difficult to understand how a man brought up as he was with music and poetry, with a wonderful view of mountain and sea, became the unromantic analyst of contemporary civilization. Listen to this description:

> "For brilliancy of colour, making rocks raining pools and herbage look like terrestrial jewellery, I have seen nothing like the heights above Sligo Bay. And for magic that takes you out, far out, of this time and this world, there is Skellig Michael, ten miles off the Kerry Coast, shooting straight up six hundred feet, sheer out of the Atlantic. Whoever has not stood in the graveyards at the summit of that cliff among those beehive dwellings and their beehive oratory does not know Ireland through and through. It is the beauty of Ireland that has made us what we are. I am a product of Dalkey's outlook."

This was written in his ninetieth year. He deliberately cast off his inheritance and set himself the antipathetic task of probing the ugly things of life and thus instead of becoming the idle singer with a sigh for the past, he became the busy prophet. From dabbling with ideas of a higher life which sought its inspiration in the Goethean motto: "*Im Ganzen, Guten, Schonen resolut zu leben,*" he quickly realized that the immediate problem of the day was not a personal one but the social one, that the personal welfare is of no use unless it is part and parcel of the welfare of the world. There is no doubt that he would have become successful in whatever he undertook if he saw reason for that work.

He saw no reason for writing verse himself because it would limit his thought and expression. He knew that the highest sentiments had been expressed in poetry but in his case it was a most laborious process to say something in rhyme. And yet as he himself says: "the beauty of Ireland has made us what we are. I am a product of Dalkey's outlook." So the poet in him led him to write plays in a prose which is as rich as any poetry. Listen to this:

> KEEGAN:
>
> In my dreams heaven is a country where the State is the Church and the Church the people: three in one and one in three. It is a commonwealth in which work is play and play is life: three in one and one in three. It is a temple in which the priest is the worshipper and worshipper the worshipped: three in one and one in three. It is a godhead in which all life is human and all humanity divine: three in one and one in three.
>
> *John Bull's Other Island*

Well may Bunyan say:

> A man there was, tho' some did count him mad,
> The more he cast away, the more he had.

* * *

He flung his first challenge at a respectable gathering who had come to glorify Shelley, by announcing himself as a vegetarian, a socialist and an atheist. A Shelley come to life! This was too much for the devotees, who at once dispersed. One can call oneself a socialist and yet make a fortune by exploitation, one can call oneself a clergyman and yet be an atheist, but one cannot call oneself a vegetarian without practising it. It is the one positive movement that demands complete surrender. If you eat meat you cannot be a vegetarian, which means that you have to give up the tastes and habits inculcated by parents, relatives and friends and most likely prepare your own meals. This suited G.B.S. to the ground. To be an atheist for him was only justified because he was a religious-minded person. He said as far back as 1896: "Pray what are the mysteries of religion? Are they faith, hope, love, heroism, life, creation; or are they pews and pulpits, prayer-books and Sunday bonnets, copes and stoles and dalmatics? Even the large section of the population of these islands whose religion is the merest idolatry of material symbols will not deny that the former are the realities of religion."

As to Socialism, he regards it as the greatest creative movement of all time because it can only be achieved by the effort of all of us.

* * *

Edward Carpenter told me that he thought Bernard Shaw a good example of the emerging type because he had a comprehensive consciousness. The human race had sent him forward to feel its way into a new life. In G.B.S. we had, he thought, the articulate man and there is no moving forward unless we know where we are going. When I was initiating G.B.S. into the pruning of trees, he said as he was vigorously cutting a branch to let in light and air; "I always liked trees, but now that I *know* them I can do things and not just gape in wonder. Feeling isn't enough and intellect isn't enough, what one needs is knowledge of the facts." Divest him of his creative genius and you still have left the Vestry man who probed into human need and faced up to fact, the man who learned painfully to work with others. It is easy to overlook the fact that much of his life was given over to the quiet, unrewarded work of public service. "When I became engaged in the local government of a quarter of a million Londoners, I found there was no public sanitary accommodation for women. When I moved in the matter . . ."

He was not taken in by pretty nomenclature or plausible explanation. The highest function that man can perform is to pick out the significant incidents from the chaos of daily happenings and arrange them so that their relationship to one another becomes apparent, thus changing us from bewildered spectators to men intelligently conscious of the world and its destinies.

"A world peopled by Shaws would be unthinkable," I can hear you say. It would be clean, orderly and purposeful and one would have to justify one's existence. The government would be in the hands of an equal number of men and women, elected by highly qualified electors and assisted by a panel of Aldermen all of whom, having reached the dispassionate and comforting age of a hundred and having proved their humanity by abstaining from meat, could keep the people well informed of the facts by publishing a weekly political What's What. The Town Halls would be glorified Sistine Chapels where the legislators instead of talking would sit in silence, waiting eagerly upon the Life Force for inspiration. As all the adult population would have more or less equal incomes there would be no economic bar to marriage, and men and women would be able to maintain themselves without selling their affections and their convictions.

"The evil resulting from the existing unequal distribution of wealth is so enormous, so incalculably greater than any other evil, actual or conceivable, on the face of the earth, that it is our first duty to alter it into an equal distribution."

It is a pity there are so few Bernard Shaws in the world. A thousand might have saved it.

* * *

I think he could do without people. Tolstoy turned away from the people of culture in disgust to associate with peasants but Shaw turned away from all people to associate with his own creations. Has he not created characters more alive and entertaining than mere human beings whom he describes as: "the only animals of which I am thoroughly and cravenly afraid"? The greatest and most enduring of all his creations is G.B.S. For this generation and the last G.B.S. is an institution, white beard, upturned moustache and penetrating eyes, part and parcel of our being, like the sky, ageless and secure. We expect a pronouncement on every conceivable subject and on every conceivable occasion and we expect the most tragic situation to be transmuted to laughter. In a world fed on barbarous superstitions, fabulous history, obsolete codes and the accumulated nonsense of centuries, the truth must sound a huge joke.

So he creates his characters, shades of himself, alive and obedient to his will. His disgust of social behaviour is such that it gives him joy to pull the strings, not to strangle but to set humanity laughing at itself. Over them all broods, in full view of the audience, this G.B.S., the compound of contradictions: the mystic atheist, the frivolous fanatic, the revolutionary tory, the millionaire toiler, the ancient youth, the living myth. He has his work cut out. Like Chirgwin, after a very difficult act, I can see him raising an eyebrow and hear him say (amidst applause of course): "Takes a bit of doing."

All we can do is to take him to pieces as children do a musical instrument to find the source of the music, to find his life force. We break him up into component parts and place each in a test tube with proper label attached ready for the experts to analyse: philosophy, science, drama, theology, economics, education, wit, music, art. A very solemn proceeding especially when it is found to one's dismay that he cannot be put together again. That must be left to the artist.

* * *

He would gladly have forgone all things to be known only as a painter. When a man has the gift of a painter, the qualification is so magical that one cannot think of him as anything else. Shaw endowed God with the gift of art, like a parent hoping that his only child will have the ability he lacked and longed for.

> "The world must learn from its artists because God made the world as an artist. Your philosophers steal all their bloated discoveries from the artists."

When it comes to art he cannot overflow enough. He recalls the lonely visits to the Dublin Art Gallery, his immediate responsiveness to works of art and later the penny a line criticism. If only the teachings of the Impressionists had penetrated the Dublin Art schools in those days, there would have been a Picasso senior! If he had remained a clerk he probably would have finished up by murdering somebody and, as he himself said to me, if he had become a painter he would have finished up by murdering himself. He realizes that the artist is the least wanted and most needed person in this chaotic world. Poor Max Nordau, a name completely unknown to the present generation, attacked the artist and came up against Shaw, with the result that Nordau was thrown precipitately from the pedestal he held in cultured Europe to oblivion. Nordau visited us many years afterwards and confessed himself a convert. He had been a hater of Art and now talked mainly about art, from the anthropological, from the biological, from the psychological, from every point of view except the artist's. He had brought his daughter with him whom he wanted to train as an artist and he sat down and read to us from Shaw's *The Sanity of Art*:

> "The severity of artistic discipline is produced by the fact that in creative art no ready made rules can help you. There is nothing to guide you to the right expression for your thought except your own sense of beauty and fitness; and as you advance upon those who went before you, that sense of beauty and fitness is necessarily often in conflict, not with fixed rules, because there are no rules, but with precedents."

"You see," he said to his daughter, "there are no rules and it is a great discipline."

As Shaw hadn't the benefit of the integrating force of painting, the white light of his vocation, he disintegrated into the activities of play-writing and philosopher. He had to find his joy in words. In a way he has been released from the slavery of his calling like a man on holiday running amok among the things that amuse him. But art is still the one and only string that pulls him, very delicately. His expression of religion is in terms of art as we have seen. "I've been threatened and blackmailed and insulted and starved. But I've played the game. I've fought the good fight. And now it's over, there's an indescribable peace. I believe in Michaelangelo, Velasquez and Rembrandt; in the might of design, the mystery of colour, the redemption of all things by beauty everlasting, and the message 'Art has made these hands blessed.' Amen, Amen."

I can hear G.B.S. say Amen and no other prayer would ever make him utter that word.

He has no use for evolution unless the creative element enters into it:

Don Juan in *Man and Superman:*

"Just as Life after ages of struggle, evolved that wonderful bodily organ, the eye, so that the living organism could see where it was going and what was coming to help or threaten it, and thus avoid a thousand dangers that formerly slew it, so it is evolving to-day a mind's eye that shall see, not the physical world, but the purpose of Life, and thereby enable the individual to work for that purpose instead of thwarting and baffling it by setting up shortsighted personal aims as at present."

His interest in economics springs from the fact that he is convinced that there should be none of the horrors of poverty, dirt and disease and that drudgery can be reduced to a minimum, that no person need work more than two or three hours a day so that there is ample time for enjoying the arts and for creative activity. "The players of the great game of economics of the future will have to be philosophers dealing with human conduct and destiny in the largest sense, international as well as national. The field of the political economist will be life and his instrument will be literature. The prophet of the race will be a political economist."

So it is with education. He hated the imprisonment of school where art and beauty had no place. "A complete public school and university training may leave its graduates so barbarously ignorant that when war comes they are found in all directions trying to close public art galleries."

This is his yard stick.

Well, G.B.S. has seen in his own lifetime, even before he reached four score and ten, the National Gallery spring into being, while bombs were flung over London, as a centre of national activity in art and music. People flocked in their thousands to listen to music, to keep in touch with contemporary art. For there is no doubt that the most permanently valuable education is the æsthetic education. "I like the state of continual becoming, with a goal in front and not behind. Then, too, I like fighting successful people; attacking them; rousing them; trying their mettle; kicking down their sand castles so as to make them build stone ones. It develops one's muscles." Here speaks the authentic artist.

You may say that it is well for him and for us that he did not become a painter. But beware. G.B.S. is ninety and there is time before the century to change his vocation. As he sits in the shelter he has the wind blowing his white hair and the sunshine streaming in, the birds are busy in the trees above and he still hopes to learn some things. There is so much to do. "So much to do," says G.B.S. as the days go by, "I am too young!"

Yes, so very much to do because so many come round to his views. Out of the chaos come questions: "Where shall I find happiness?" "Why should I and my children go on living?" "How shall I assuage this soul torment?" So he sits down and recalls his own moments of happiness. Only four such moments come to him in the length of four score and ten years.

Those moments were in dreams and waking was always a shock!

> "Killing yourself is a matter for your own judgment. Nobody can prevent you but you can always put it off to-morrow on the chance of something interesting turning up that evening. . . . My father was a failure: only his latest years (he was long lived) could be called happy. I am conceited enough to believe that it is just as well that he didn't dispose of me in a fit of low spirits. Life, happy or unhappy, successful or unsuccessful, is extraordinarily interesting. . . ."

Shaw has never sought happiness for its own sake and has found life extraordinarily interesting and his one advice is: get interested in something. In his own case everything absorbs him and the older he gets the deeper his interest. If G.B.S. has a grouse at all it is with Time for he would write a play, write a new treatise or preface, answer innumerable letters, advise politicians on the running of the world while at the same time attending to his trees, beside doing his accounts and seeing to his diet. The evening alone gives him an opportunity for relaxation, if one can call relaxation an agile interest in the activities of the world when he switches on the wireless late into the night, or listens to his beloved composers.

* * *

We are bringing out this volume not to remind him that he is ninety years old but because we are impatient folk and

We should honour while we can
The vertical Man.

We are only voicing the wish of the whole world, for is there a country where he has not been heard in the native tongue? We must break the tradition of England and honour the thinker and artist. The last birthday (celebrated twenty years ago) was ignored by the British Government, or to be more correct the only notice taken of it was the deliberate prohibition of the broadcasting of any words spoken by G.B.S. on this occasion. In those days the governing classes were proud of the way in which creative artists were neglected. Well, Molière was buried with the condemned criminals and Mozart died from sheer physical exhaustion, and there must be many an artist to-day who cannot find the means to do his work and who will be proclaimed as great after being buried in a pauper's grave: in fact the nation will derive honour from the very people it despised. In every career, no matter what brilliant talents, what industry, what artistic integrity, there also enters the element of good fortune. We like to think that the tribute we are paying to G.B.S. to-day is to his talent and not to his success. We can say this to our credit, that he was not made to drink the hemlock for uttering straightforward truths even if we had not the courage to take them seriously and act on them instead of pretending it was all meant to be laughed at. All human progress involves as its first condition the willingness of the pioneer to act as the fool. The sensible man is the man who adapts himself to conditions prepared for him, but the fool is he who persists in creating his own conditions. G.B.S., himself such a fool, has made fools of his contemporaries, for, however difficult and impossible it may seem, we mean to mould conditions to satisfy the modern conscience. There have been moments when men have shrunk from his terrible laughter, holding on to the romantic idea of living, but once they found themselves laughing they had to admit that an invincible force had appeared and cracked the surface of what had seemed to them an impregnable morality. What the fissures exposed sent a shudder throughout civilization and life seemed religiously, scientifically, politically not worth going on with, but Shaw's reply came as a clarion call: "So much the worse, not for life, but for what you call religion, science, politics, philosophy and the current practice of the art of living. There is something wrong with these things if they lead to nihilistic conclusions." Catastrophic wars and financial blizzards, civil wars and revolutions which sent many a philosopher to the end of his tether only intensified the previous convictions of G.B.S. and while humanity was in the throes of self-destruction, our laughing philosopher settled down in his shelter to confirm all his previous contentions and thus completed in his eighty-ninth year *Everybody's Political What's What?* And like all true conviction it made him magnanimous and humble in spirit though defiant in manner. For: "My *Everybody's What's What?* is only an attempt by a very ignorant old man to communicate to people still more ignorant than himself such elementary social statics as he has managed to pick up by study and collision with living persons and hard facts in the course of a life (long as lives go but too short for this particular job) spent largely in discovering and correcting the mistakes into which his social antecedents and surroundings led him. I certainly have not corrected them all. . . ."

Too short for this particular work . . . and yet G.B.S. has been favoured by nature, by fortune and by friendship more than any man.

* * *

We would say to G.B.S.: "Hitler broke one of your windows on your eighty-eighth birthday and you will forgive us if we raise a glass in honour of your ninetieth birthday. You have lived to see your work placed amongst the world's classics and have the satisfaction of knowing that young people will read you with the same delight as you, when young, read Shakespeare and Shelley, Bunyan and the Bible. In the same way as you are growing in the deeper appreciation of Mozart and Beethoven, so it must give you joy to know that you are now beginning to be understood. You will see from the contributions in this volume that we have tried very hard to retain our critical faculties but you have trained us brutally, subtly, with a thrush in your throat, as Mrs. Patrick Campbell used to say, to take you at your own valuation. You caught most of us very young and now that we have reached the years of discretion, in spite of ourselves very often, we have not changed our good opinion. That is a test indeed, not the test of mere time or flattery but of the maturing mind. Some of us wonder how it is you took the burden of life upon your shoulders and how you could transmute your indignation to laughter? Can it be that the plays which now lead us through laughter will one day lead us through tears? That would be the greatest tribute of all: that you brought art back to its original religious function and it gave satisfaction to the soul."

PHOTO BY WINDOW & GROVE,
LONDON

1879

THE EARLY EIGHTIES

WITH GRANVILLE-BARKER AT PICKARDS COTTAGE, 1884

THE ISLE OF WIGHT; THE YEAR OF "CÆSAR AND CLEOPATRA," 1898

HINDHEAD. THE HOUSE NOW CALLED ST. EDMUND'S COLLEGE, 1899

MR. AND MRS. BERNARD SHAW

BLACKDOWN, 1900

MAYBURY KNOLL, 1905

SIDNEY AND BEATRICE WEBB

AT HOME AT MAYBURY KNOLL, 1906

WITH KEIR HARDIE, 1910

IN IRELAND: DINGLE BAY: FIRST YEAR AT PARKNASILLA

BY THE FIRE, 1915

PHOTO BY STUDIO LISA

THE SITTING ROOM, AYOT SAINT LAWRENCE, 1938

PHOTO BY STUDIO LI[illegible]

IN THE GARDEN, 1939

PHOTO BY STUDIO LISA

THE HOUSE

THE CROWNING YEARS

M. J. MacMANUS

*Biographer of Eamon de Valera*

## SHAW'S IRISH BOYHOOD

### (I)

SEVENTY years have passed since Bernard Shaw invaded England. "Invade," of course, is the only possible word. There may have been no earth-tremors felt when the tall, thin, red-haired, keen-eyed youth of twenty walked down the gangway at Holyhead and set foot for the first time on British soil. No drums rolled; no guns blazed; the Fleet was not mobilized in the Irish Channel; there was not even a secret service agent about. All that happened was that a railway porter with a Welsh accent said: "Carry your bag, sir?"

So it happened that, instead of being repulsed, the invader was allowed to take the mail train to London and to proceed on his conquering way. That he was bent on conquest there can be no doubt. No Norman William ever surveyed the rolling Sussex Downs with a more possessive eye than that with which the beardless Irish stripling surveyed the flat English Midlands as his train thundered its way to the capital. Ireland was getting its own back. After enduring invasions for more than six centuries, she herself was sending out an invader; and one who was determined that he would not fail her. Nor did he. There had to be a good many reconnaissance flights; the land had to be spied out; the weak spots in the enemy's defences had to be carefully noted. Then came the full force of the invasion; then did citadels, seemingly impregnable, fall; then did time-honoured institutions crumble into dust. It would seem as if the innocent-looking travelling-bag which the Welsh porter had offered to carry must have contained an atom bomb.

(II)

How did Ireland shape and equip this champion bastion-stormer? From what secret armoury did his weapons come? In what *école militaire* did he receive his training? From the loins of what mighty ancestor was he sprung?

The last question must be answered first. The man responsible was no less a personage than Shakespeare's Macduff! Has not G.B.S. himself told us that he has traced his family's more remote origins to "the third son of that immortal yet unborn Thane of Fife, who, invulnerable to normally accouched swordsmen, laid on and slew Macbeth"? "It was as good," he added, "as being descended from Shakespeare, whom I had been unconsciously resolved to reincarnate from my cradle."

But that is going a long way back. Let us jump a matter of three centuries or so and land on one of the pleasant green banks of the River Boyne at a spot where it winds its placid way through the County Meath. The year is 1690 and the ballad-makers have immortalized the date:

> July the First, in Oldbridge town,
> There was a grievous battle,
> Where many a man lay on the ground
> And the cannons, they did rattle.

A Dutchman and an Englishman were fighting for a throne on Irish soil, and in the Dutchman's army, in addition to Hollanders, Danes, Prussians and French Huguenots, were two English cavalrymen, Sir Henry Ponsonby and William Shaw. Ponsonby was the son of a North-of-England man who had come to Ireland with Cromwell and who, after the Lord Protector in the course of that terrific visitation had dispatched the native Irish "to Hell or to Connaught," settled down comfortably on the fat slice of rich Irish land with which his services were rewarded. Captain Shaw was a newcomer, a Puritan from Hampshire, who had arrived "with a sword in his hand and a Bible in his boots." Dutch William won, saving Ireland from "popery, brass money and wooden shoes," and Ponsonby and Shaw, who had fought shoulder-to-shoulder at the fording of the Boyne, got further fat rewards in the shape of spreading acres in the warm, comfortable, well-wooded County of Kilkenny.

The Ponsonbys prospered and consolidated their fortunes—no very difficult matter in a time of forfeiture and settlements—took their place in the Irish peerage as Earls of Bessborough, managed the King's business in Ireland with complete efficiency, and gave their sons to the native Parliament, the Army, and the Protestant Church. Their neighbours, the Shaws, found in them patrons and protectors. Although they did not loom as large in Irish affairs as the great Ponsonbys, the Shaws lived a life of ease, comfort and security, a pleasant hunting-shooting-and-fishing life in the midst of rich pastures watered by the swift-flowing Nore. They may have been lesser gentry, but gentry they were, and part and parcel of England's faithful Irish garrison. Their sons, too, became, as generation succeeded generation, soldiers, politicians, divines, or members of the more "respectable" professions. One of them, Robert Shaw, entered the Irish Parliament, displayed his independence and integrity by refusing a bribe to vote for the Union, founded a bank which came to be known as "Shaw's Bank," and was created a baronet in 1821.

Another Shaw—Bernard—who was a first cousin of Sir Robert, left the old home in Kilkenny somewhere in the seventeen-nineties, took up law, married a parson's daughter in 1802, and died twenty-four years later, having begotten fifteen children in the interval, of whom eleven were living at the time of his death. Despite somewhat straitened circumstances, his widow carried on indomitably—helped by the wealthy Sir Robert who found her a cottage in a Dublin suburb called Terenure, not far from his own mansion at Bushy Park—and she brought up her eleven to believe in an Irish Protestant God, to remember that they were aristocrats to their finger-tips, and to revere the English connection. "There must," G.B.S. wrote later apropos of her hard struggle, "have been some terribly lean years before the children got on their own feet. Certainly my father left me strongly under that impression." Yet there was no actual poverty, for it was found possible to give the eldest son, William, a university education.

The third son, born on 30th December, 1814, was given the name George Carr. For him there was no university career nor is it likely that if he had been given one he would have gained very much from it. During the whole of his lifetime he was never seen to read anything more profound than a newspaper. He grew up to be a soft, easy-going man, with no sense of responsibility but with a heavily exaggerated sense of humour. His own misfortunes—and they were many—he regarded as some of the funniest things in life. He had a weak mouth, a pronounced squint—which Oscar Wilde's father, Dublin's most eminent oculist, vainly tried to cure—and a taste for the bottle. After losing his first job—a clerkship in an ironworks—he was pitchforked into a Government sinecure, but a few years later the sinecure was abolished and George Carr Shaw was pensioned off with £60 a year. Commuting the pension, he invested the proceeds in a small corn mill in an outlying part of Dublin called Dolphin's Barn. Then, at the not unripe age of forty, he married Lucinda Elizabeth ("Bessie") Gurley.

Bessie was the daughter of a County Dublin squireen who seemed to have stepped straight out of one of Charles Lever's early novels. He had short ginger whiskers which are said to have "embroidered his neck rather than covered his chin and cheeks." He could do anything with a horse, but nothing with money save squander it. When his wife died he handed over Bessie to an aunt for rearing. The aunt was a midget, a martinet, a woman of money, and a snob. She ruled Bessie autocratically, saw that she got the sort of education no Irish gentleman's daughter should be without—which meant that she learnt to make no use whatever of her talents or her hands—and determined that she should marry at least an earl. "My mother," wrote her son later, "was tyrannously taught French enough to recite one or two of La Fontaine's fables; to play the piano the wrong way; to harmonize by rule from Logier's *Thoroughbass;* to sit up straight and speak and dress and behave like a lady, and an Irish lady at that. She knew nothing of the value of money nor of housekeeping nor of hygiene nor of anything that could be left to servants or governesses or parents or solicitors or apothecaries or any other member of the retinue, indoor and outdoor, of a country house. She had great expectations from a humpbacked little aunt, a fairy-like creature with a will of iron, who had brought up her motherless niece with a firm determination to make her a paragon of good breeding, to achieve a distinguished marriage for her, and to leave her all her money as a dowry." But Bessie proved a grievous disappointment; she revolted against the tyranny of little humpbacked Aunt Ellen and failed to become a duchess, or even a countess. Instead, on 19th June, 1852, she married George Carr Shaw. She was twenty-two.

The couple found a home at 3 (now 33), Synge Street, Dublin, and there, within four years, they produced three children—Lucy, Agnes and George Bernard. George Bernard was born on 26th July, 1856. A few days later he was baptized at the near-by St. Bride's Church, where William George Carroll, who had married one of his maternal aunts, was rector. Another uncle, who had consented to be his godfather, having failed to turn up, the Rev. Mr. Carroll ordered the sexton to take his place.

There is no copy of the baptismal certificate in existence.

St. Bride's was taken over for secular uses many years ago and the other existing copy disappeared in the burning of the Four Courts in 1922.

## (III)

Dublin, unlike Gaul, is divided into two parts, locally known as North Side and South Side. Even to-day the South Side, which lies on the left bank of the river, is regarded as the more respectable. In the 'sixties it was respectability itself. There, in such exclusive residential suburbs as Ballsbridge, Rathmines, Rathgar and Terenure, lived at least ninety per cent of Dublin's well-to-do Protestant population. There, too, were to be found Dublin Castle, the seat of government, Trinity College, the two Protestant cathedrals, the National Gallery, St. Stephen's Green, fashionable Grafton Street and the very fashionable Shelbourne Hotel. To cross Carlisle (not yet O'Connell) Bridge and rub shoulders with the Catholic residents of the North Side was a thing that Protestant old ladies would no more dream of doing than their early seventeenth-century ancestors would have dreamt of venturing beyond the city walls into the country of the ferocious O'Byrnes or O'Tooles. The Viceregal Lodge, to be sure, was in the Phœnix Park (which is North Side) but that could be reached in a closed carriage by a roundabout route.

The Dublin that young Bernard Shaw first opened his eyes upon was in every sense a garrison city. It contained six large military barracks, five prisons which were even larger, and a vast "Depot" in the Park, where members of that very efficient semi-military body, the Royal Irish Constabulary, might be seen at bayonet practice a couple of times a week. Ireland was still lying prostrated from the effects of the Great Famine of '47, which had cost her more than a million dead, whilst nearly another million had fled across the Atlantic from a pestilence-stricken land. O'Connell and Repeal had passed away, the Young Irelanders were in exile, and Irish Nationalism had been reduced, in its most humiliating hour, to Sadlier and Keogh and "the Pope's Brass Band." But there were hidden fires burning; Fenianism was flowing through subterranean channels (it was to blaze out into open insurrection before young Shaw reached his twelfth birthday); and hardly a year passed in which the Habeas Corpus Act was not suspended. In 1856 Parnell was only ten years old and Gladstone, more concerned with Homeric literature than with Irish grievances, had not even begun to think of Irish Church Disestablishment or Home Rule.

Synge Street, of course, was South Side; no Shaw or Gurley would have lived anywhere else. But even in those days, when it was part of an outer and not, as it is to-day, of an inner suburb, it was not "good" South Side. With its five-roomed, kitchen-basement, yellow-brick houses and its location only a few hundred yards distant from the very ungreen banks of the Grand Canal, it could never have been anything except shabby genteel. The window-curtains might be clean and the door-knockers shining, but it was a street of city clerks, lower-grade civil servants, and not-so-well-to-do professional men. Number Three, Synge Street, was a world removed from the Big House at Bushy Park, Terenure—a mile or so farther on—where Sir Robert, soon to be succeeded by his brother, Sir Frederick, Recorder of Dublin, lived in ease and elegance.

## (IV)

"I have," G.B.S. has written, "no trace in me of the commercially imported North Spanish strain which passes for aboriginal Irish: I am a genuine typical Irishman of the Danish, Norman, Cromwellian and (of course) Scotch invasions. I am violently and arrogantly Protestant by family tradition; but let no English Government therefore count on my allegiance; I am English enough to be an inveterate

Republican and Home Ruler. It is true that my grandfather was an Orangeman; but then his sister was an abbess, and his uncle, I am proud to say, was hanged as a rebel."

That passage may help to explain some of the forces, hereditary and otherwise, that went to the making of Bernard Shaw; but it is very far from explaining everything. Shaw is no more a typical Irishman than Jonathan Swift or Theobald Wolfe Tone or Charles Stewart Parnell or Eamon de Valera. He is not even a typical Irish Protestant, nor was his upbringing that of a typically Irish Protestant home. On the other hand, he has very little in common with his Catholic and Nationalist fellow-countrymen; whoever it was said of him that "he was born on a bog and suckled on a shillelagh" was a thousand miles wide of the mark. Shaw never saw an Irish bog until he revisited Ireland for the first time some thirty years after leaving it, and shillelaghs had disappeared with Donnybrook Fair. Shaw is typical of nothing but Shaw.

His formative years were spent in an extraordinary atmosphere. The conditions at Synge Street had nothing about them of the rigid Irish Protestant convention: they were eccentric to the verge of anarchy ("anarchical," indeed, is Shaw's favourite description of them). Mrs. Shaw "went her own way with so complete a disregard and even unconsciousness of convention and scandal and prejudice that it was impossible to doubt her good faith and innocence, but it never occurred to her that other people, especially children, needed guidance or training, or that it mattered in the least what they ate or drank or what they did so long as they were not actively mischievous." (G.B.S.) As for George Carr Shaw, he went from one drinking bout to another, continued to disgrace himself socially, paid occasional visits to the Corn Exchange, and watched his income dwindling slowly but steadily. His drinking was not done secretly or convivially: he neither kept a hidden store nor did he find congenial company at the local pub. "He was," says his son, "a lonely drinker at the grocer-publican's. He was never carried out blind; drink did not affect him that way, nor did he drink enough to take him quite off his legs. But he was quite unmistakably drunk, stupefied, apparently sleep-walking, and, if remonstrated with, apt to fly into sudden momentary rages in which he would snatch something up and dash it on the floor." At other times when he had tippled too generously he would be moved to hilarity, and there was a comic occasion when he arrived home carrying a goose by the neck, mistook the gable wall for the front door, and was found outside laughing uproariously at his own blunder.

The social life of the Synge Street Shaws was severely circumscribed by the drinking habits of the head of the family. It was impossible to entertain a man who seldom arrived quite sober and who usually left quite disgracefully drunk. There was no welcome for him at Bushy Park House, where two butlers were kept, nor indeed at any of the other houses of the genteel Shaws. (Those who are interested in the wide periphery of G.B.S.'s uncles, aunts and cousins should consult that highly diverting—though not always accurate—book, *Bernard's Brethren*, by Charles MacMahon Shaw, an Australian cousin, which is interleaved and pleasantly embellished with such comments by G.B.S. as: "Rubbish!", "This is too silly," "Charles, you are a liar!") So the Synge Street establishment was thrown back upon its own resources and became self-centred and self-sufficient to an unusual degree.

There is no folk-lore about the boyhood of G.B.S. in Ireland —which is not surprising when we consider that he left it at twenty and that he has been away seventy years—but he himself has left plenty of material from which to reconstruct it, at any rate in its external aspects. Shaw has not indulged in autopsychology to any great extent nor given us his little world depicted, in the modern autobiographical manner, within the limits of his personal movements and intimacies. Intimacies, indeed, were very few, for in a household where "there was neither hate nor love, fear or reverence," each member of it naturally went his or her own way. The father tippled and laughed or raged, the mother, disillusioned from the beginning, soon devoted all her waking hours to what was to become her lifelong passion and her only salvation—music—and the children were handed over to nurses, governesses and apothecaries. Of intimate or emotional bonds between sisters and brother or between parents and children there appears to have been no trace whatever.

As a toddler, George Bernard was taken out by his nurse, who was supposed to bring him for walks along the canal banks or to show him the flowers in St. Stephen's Green. But she came from the slums, and it was to slum tenements or to slum public-houses, where she met her friends and relations, that he was taken. A Dublin tenement is a very unlovely place to-day; what it must have been in the 'sixties is rather awful to contemplate. At any rate, those visits left an indelible impression on the child's mind, instilling "a lifelong hatred of poverty, and the devotion of all my public life to the task of exterminating the poor and rendering their resurrection for ever impossible."

His early education was partly the work of his uncle, the rector of St. Bride's, and partly that of a governess, Miss Hill, who tried to give him a taste for poetry by reciting such lines as:

> Stop: for they tread is on an empire's dust,

an attempt which, he says, only moved him and his sisters to derisive humour. She also taught him to add, subtract and multiply, but failed to teach him division, "because she kept saying 'two into four, three into six,' and so forth, without ever explaining what the word 'into' meant in this connection. This was explained to me on my first day at school, and I solemnly declare that it was the only thing I ever learnt at school."

The school was called the Wesley Connexional (it is now Wesley College) but it was not by any means an exclusively Wesleyan establishment. It accepted pupils of all denominations except Catholics, and the majority of them, in fact, belonged to the still Established Church of Ireland. Shaw remembers it as a "damnable boy prison" and declares that his years there were a sheer waste of time. He went as a "day-boy," not as a boarder, which meant that he had his afternoons free, and he hated it with a hatred which has not grown any less in retrospect. "Lessons were set me which I had to learn on pain of punishment not cruel enough to effect its purpose with boys who like me were free enough at home to have something more interesting to do than poring over unreadable school-books; but I was not taught manners or loyalties nor held to any standards of dress or care of my person. Discipline was confined to silence and sitting still, which did not prevent me from carrying on furtive conversations or fights with the boy sitting next, who might be a friend or foe."

Shaw was no weakling at school and enjoyed his full share of fisticuffs in the playground and of juvenile gangsterdom in the streets. Untrammelled in any way by his "uncoercive" parents, he used his free half-day just as he liked, ignored his homework, and lied audaciously to his teachers when questioned about his negligence. His real education was being acquired elsewhere. At home there was a volume entitled *The Manners and Tone of Good Society*, and from it he learnt his table and company manners. And at home there was music—always music. His mother possessed an excellent mezzo-soprano voice, he himself and his two sisters could sing tolerably well, and there was, in addition to a piano, a profusion of other musical instruments always lying about. The front "parlour" at Synge Street was seldom silent of an evening and music came to play an all-important part—educative as well as recreational—in young Shaw's life.

## (V)

Suddenly a new figure appeared upon the scene, a man with the Victorian three-decker name of George John Vandaleur Lee. Lee lived in the next street and was a professional music-master. He was slightly lame, had black side-whiskers and a determined chin. His appearance at Synge Street was due to the fact that Mrs. Shaw had gone to him to have her voice trained.

Lee's impact on the Shaw household was terrific. From the day of his arrival nothing counted save music. He was an indefatigable organizer of concerts and amateur opera and Mrs. Shaw he regarded as a discovery. Being a man of talent as well as a born teacher, he succeeded in getting the most out of her voice and soon she was appearing in all his productions as his *prima donna* and chorus-leader. Rehearsals were held regularly in the front parlour at Synge Street, to the increasing annoyance of the neighbours. Although the music, judged by contemporary standards in Dublin, was good, the din must have been fearful. Brass instruments were fashionable in those days and even before the coming of Lee there were weekly concerts at which Uncle William played the now-forgotten ophicleide, George Carr the trombone, Cousin Emily (daughter of the rector of St. Bride's) the 'cello, and Aunt Charlotte the piano. It was enough to burst the walls of the little parlour asunder.

Something had to be done and the resolute and impetuous Lee did it. His brother with whom he shared a large house at Number One, Hatch Street, having died, he suggested to the Shaws that they should go and live with him. The proposal was accepted with alacrity, for the chaste flat-fronted Georgian house in Hatch Street—less than ten minutes' walk from Synge Street—was large enough to prevent orchestral rehearsals becoming a terror to the neighbourhood. Besides, the arrangement was economical. So the Synge Street days came to an end and a very odd *ménage à trois* sprang into existence.

Young George Bernard took his part in all the feverish musical activities of Number One, Hatch Street. He had a good ear and although until he was fifteen, when the family broke up, he could neither play nor read a note of music he "could sing and whistle from end to end leading works by Handel, Haydn, Mozart, Beethoven, Rossini, Bellini, Donizetti and Verdi." He was, in fact, though he got no formal training whatever, steeped in music, and it would be difficult to overestimate the part that it played in moulding his intellect and his character. Other children were given fairy-tales in their cradles. To George Bernard they came, kindling his young imagination, through the operas of the great composers. Not only was *Corno di Bassetto* in the making, but that delicate sense of rhythm which is evident in every line that Shaw writes was being acquired.

The Lee-Shaw alliance was productive of another result which brought the youngster some of the happiest days of his boyhood. Eight or nine miles to the south of the city, on Dalkey Hill, there was a cottage for sale, and Lee bought it as a summer residence for Mrs. Shaw. The hill overlooks Killiney Bay and is one of the loveliest spots in a lovely coast-line. There, for the first time, young Shaw was able to drink in natural beauty without stint and he drank it in greedily. He roamed over the gorse-clad hill-side until every rock and every goat-path was familiar to him; he looked across the blue waters to where Howth Head pushes its whale-nose into the sea; entranced, he lay on the grassy summit contemplating the curving silver shore of the bay down below; a bay that Dubliners are fond of comparing with the Bay of Naples, usually to the latter's disadvantage. On sultry days he would race down to a spot on the shingly strand known as the White Rock, strip, and plunge into the buoyant waves. It was on Killiney beach that he acquired the passion for bathing that he retained until he was nearly eighty.

A mile and a half to the north lay Kingstown Harbour, snug

within its breakwater, one of the gateways of Ireland, its waters dotted with the white sails of yachts, its skies blotted out every now and then by the smoke of the Holyhead steamers. And, in a direct line to the east, some seventy miles beyond the mists of the Irish Channel, lay the other great island—John Bull's Own—an island that had given him his ancestors, an island that claimed all the allegiance of the class from which he was sprung, an island that was beginning to enter more and more into his waking dreams.

## (VI)

Two important events happened when he was fifteen. Lee went to London where he was followed shortly afterwards by Mrs. Shaw, who decided that she could earn a living there by teaching singing; George Bernard finished his schooling and got his first job.

The home was broken up. The youngest girl, Agnes, who had been ailing for a long time, was taken to the Isle of Wight, where she died in a sanatorium: Lucy went to live with her mother in the Fulham Road. The furniture at Hatch Street and the cottage at Dalkey were sold and George Carr and his son removed to lodgings at No. 61, Harcourt Street.

The whole current of George Bernard's life was transformed by these sudden, sweeping changes. Although his afternoons were no longer free his evenings were entirely his own. His father, now elderly, had at last conquered his drinking habits and was, in fact, a rabid teetotaller. But the saving effected by his abstinence was more than offset by the almost entire disappearance of his income. The little that now came from the corn mill was barely sufficient to meet the Harcourt Street landlady's weekly demands.

The job that had been found for George Bernard was that of junior clerk in an estate-agent's office in Molesworth Street. Molesworth Street—South Side, of course—was, and still is, very respectable. Even to-day, with its Grand Lodge of Freemasons and its many buildings dedicated to Church of Ireland uses, it is what is called in Ireland "black Protestant." The world that the new junior clerk found there was—to him—as alarming as it was strange. The monotonous daily routine, the endless preoccupation with figures and forms and ledgers, the sensation of finding that he had suddenly become a cog in a wheel—all that was disquieting to a youth who had come straight from an "anarchic" home. On the other hand, he saw wider horizons opening out. Argumentative from birth (his continual Why? Why? Why? as a child had nearly driven his father mad) and armed with a questing mind, he now found himself in a position for the first time where he could pit his wit and his knowledge and his theories against those of other young men. More often than not he had the best of the argument. In many things he was better informed than most of his fellow-clerks. Shakespeare and Bunyan, Byron and Shelley, these and a host of the other immortals he had read and re-read and his literary taste and æsthetic sense had matured with phenomenal rapidity. He could discuss art with a more than juvenile assurance, for he had taken to roaming through the halls and corridors of Ireland's National Gallery, which even then was one of the world's more important lesser collections, and to studying the masterpieces so nobly housed there. And when it came to music he could, of course, leave them all "standing."

One subject constantly cropped up—religion. In a typically Shavian piece of exaggeration G.B.S. has declared that "he was a free-thinker before he knew how to think." Actually, he was brought up to be a good little Irish Protestant and as a child he went to church and Sunday school and sang hymns and said his prayers, and learnt that all Catholics went to hell when they died. His early reverence for the Bible was so great that one day when he was buying a pennyworth of sweets in a little shop near Synge Street and saw the shopkeeper tear a leaf out of a battered copy of the Holy Book to wrap them up in, he was so horrified that he half expected to see the man struck by lightning. "All the same I took the sweets and ate them, for to my Protestant mind the shopkeeper, as a Roman Catholic, would go to hell as such, Bible or no Bible, and was no gentleman anyhow."

It was his father's peculiar method of imparting religious instruction that first undermined his belief. George Carr kept up the custom of family prayers until his son was about ten and would often read out Bible stories for the boy's edification. But having done so he would, on occasion, moved by his love of anti-climax, hurl the book across the room, exclaiming: "It's all a pack of damned lies!" So G.B.S., as he tells us, grew out of his early beliefs as he was promoted from petticoats to knickerbockers: "the rest of my development was in a family atmosphere so sceptical, Bohemian, anarchic, and on its educational side æsthetic, that in my teens I was a professed atheist, with no reverence whatever for the Trinity, but a profound and lasting respect for Michael Angelo and Raphael, for Handel, Mozart and Beethoven." The whole theological structure which he had been brought up to believe as the most permanent of all things crashed to pieces one summer's evening as he was wandering under the stars on Dalkey Hill. "I suddenly asked myself why I went on repeating my prayer every night, when, as I put it, I did not believe in it. Being thus brought to book by my intellectual conscience, I felt obliged in common honesty to refrain from superstitious practices; and that night, for the first time since I could speak, I did not say my prayers."

The "boy atheist," as can be imagined, created something of a minor sensation in Protestant Molesworth Street. His fellow-clerks, whatever they believed, were rigid respecters of the conventions and they were not a little shocked to hear a red-headed youth of fifteen or sixteen boldly proclaiming that there was no God and describing the *Origin of Species* as

"Revelation." When he calmly dissected the Thirty-Nine Articles and threw them in their faces with smiling audacity, there was little that they could do about it, for although he was younger than any of them he was more than their match in knowledge and quick-wittedness. He quoted Shelley and Tom Paine and Mary Wollstonecraft at them, and there was no reply. All that they knew of Shelley was "Ode to a Skylark" which they had read in their school-books, and of the other two they had never even heard.

As time went on they left his convictions—or his lack of them—alone and were content to regard him as an uncommonly bright, provocative young man, with whom it was not safe to try an argument. At his job he was thoroughly efficient and his starting salary of eighteen shillings a month had increased by the time he was nineteen to £80 a year. He had mastered the problems of ledger work without any difficulty; he had changed his sloping schoolboy hand to the distinctive upright one we know to-day in order to achieve greater legibility in the cash-book; and although when his seniors were out he was not above conducting an amateur operatic class in the back office he was sufficiently well thought of by them to be given the post of cashier when it fell vacant.

Yet he was far from happy. The estate office might not be such a "damnable prison" as the Wesley Connexional School, but a prison it was for all that. His very success alarmed him; for he was making good in a job and an environment that had few attractions for him. Art was his only religion and it was shut out by the walls of his office. He wanted freedom, he wanted scope, he wanted escape from the routine and the narrowness of Molesworth Street into a vastly wider world; and he knew that he would not find that world in the Dublin of the 'seventies.

Already, although he did not know it, he had a means of escape in his hands; for did not Thomas of Ercledoune foretell the day when the grey goose-quill would rule the world?

When those noted revivalists, Moody and Sankey, visited Dublin in 1875, they created quite a sensation amongst the Protestant populace and young Shaw was amongst the big crowd that thronged to hear them. Having listened to their profound oratory and noted the reactions of the audience, he went home and composed a letter which he sent to the editor of *Public Opinion*. The editor, little aware that his unknown correspondent—who simply signed himself "S"—was a mere youth of eighteen and a half, printed it. It is worth giving in full:

*Sir,*

*In reply to your correspondent "J.R.D." as to the effect of the "wave of evangelism," I beg to offer the following observations on the late "revival" in Dublin, of which I was a witness.*

*As the enormous audiences drawn to the evangelistic services have been referred to as a proof of their efficacy, I will enumerate some of the motives which induced many persons to go. It will then be seen that they were not of a religious, but of a secular, not to say profane, character.*

*Predominant was the curiosity excited by the great reputation of the evangelists and the stories widely circulated of the summary annihilation by epilepsy and otherwise of sceptics who had openly proclaimed their doubts of Mr. Moody's divine mission.*

*Another motive exhibits a peculiar side of human nature. The services took place in the Exhibition Building, the entry to which was connected in the public mind with the expenditure of a certain sum of money. But Messrs. Moody and Sankey opened the building "for nothing," and the novelty, combined with the curiosity, made the attraction irresistible.*

*I mention these influences particularly as I believe they have hitherto been almost ignored. The audiences were, as a rule, respectable; and as Mr. Moody's orations were characterized by an excess of vehement assertion and a total absence of logic, respect-*

able audiences were precisely those which were least likely to derive any benefit from them.

It is to the rough, to the outcast of the streets, that such "awakenings" should be addressed, and those members of the aristocracy who by their presence tend to raise the meetings above the sphere of such outcasts are merely diverting the evangelistic vein into channels where it is wasted, its place being already supplied; and as, in the dull routine of hard work, I think it would be well for clergymen, who are nothing if not conspicuous, to render themselves so, in this instance, by their absence.

The unreasoning mind of the people is too apt to connect a white tie with a dreary church service, capped by a sermon of platitudes, and it is more likely to appreciate "the gift of the gab"—the possession of which by Mr. Moody nobody will deny—than that of the Apostolic Succession, which he lacks.

Respecting the effect of the revival on individuals I may mention that it has a tendency to make them highly objectionable members of society, and induces their unconverted friends to desire a speedy reaction, which either soon takes place or the revived one relapses slowly into his previous benighted condition as the effect fades, and although many young men have been snatched from careers of dissipation by Mr. Moody's exhortations, it remains doubtful whether the change is not merely in the nature of the excitement rather than in the moral nature of the individual. Hoping that these remarks may elucidate further opinions on the subject,

I remain, sir, yours, etc.,

S.

The writer of that letter, as remarkable for its maturity and ironic content as it was for its pungent, antithetic style, was obviously not destined to spend his days poring over ledgers and totting up rental accounts. Apart from his yearning for freedom, the youth must have been conscious of his own talents; conscious, too, that before he found an outlet for them a complete break would have to be made. Within less than a year after the publication of the letter he had come to a decision. He gave a month's notice, and in the first week of April, 1876, he stepped on the Holyhead boat.

It was good-bye to Ireland—but there were no tears. Ireland had given him something: his sharp wit, his unconventional ideas, his realistic sense of life, his knowledge of music, his horror of poverty, his love of beauty, his contempt for shams, his brogue; maybe his red hair and his grey-blue eyes. But it held no links the breaking of which cost a single pang. He was young, the world was before him and his eyes were on the future. Yet, as the boat ploughed its way through the waters of Dublin Bay he must have looked back—as everybody looks back—at the country he was leaving. And the last things he saw were Killiney's curving strand and the White Rock where he used to bathe and the summit of the gorse-clad hill where he had spent his happiest days and where, under God's stars, he had renounced God.

## (VII)

How would Shaw's career have shaped itself if he had been content to live in the land of his birth? It is an interesting, if unprofitable, speculation.

Had the national spirit not been at its lowest ebb; had the tempest of the Parnellite movement come in the early 'seventies instead of the 'eighties to sweep away despair and lethargy; had the Celtic Renaissance, with its new creative impulses, arrived thirty years before it did, making Dublin one of the great cultural centres of the world; had Douglas Hyde and the Gaelic League been there to show Ireland her hidden antique treasures of song and folk-lore: had any of these things happened, the genius of Shaw might have found more than one outlet at home. But Yeats and Synge and the Abbey Theatre were still a long way off; the Gaelic cultural heritage was still the close preserve of scholars; James Joyce was unimagined and unimaginable; and the Ireland in which G.B.S. grew to young manhood had little or nothing to offer the artist. But even if it had it is extremely doubtful if it would have held him. Shaw is a natural Citizen of the World (although, characteristically, he has in recent years taken out Irish citizenship) and nothing less than the world is big enough to be his province.

Yet Ireland is proud that through all his days he has insisted on remaining an Irishman and to-day it associates itself with men of light and learning all over the world in sending him felicitations on the occasion of his ninetieth birthday. No longer can he say, as he said with rueful cynicism forty years ago, that "the word 'Shaw' conveys nothing to my countrymen save a well-known brand of Limerick bacon." A lot of water has flowed under the bridges of the Liffey since then. The country that is no longer John Bull's Other Island has taken him to its heart; his books are a distinguished part of the Irish library; his lightest utterances are read with interest. Within the past few years a Bernard Shaw Society has sprung up in Dublin (all Ireland chuckled to see it helped on its way by what a Connaughtman would call "a left-handed kick" from the man in whose honour it was founded!). Bernard Shaw is "news" in the land of his birth as he is everywhere else.

There have been times when his irreverence has shocked us and when we have winced under the lash of his tongue—for he has, as we say in Ireland, "a tongue would clip a hedge"—but we are not behindhand in admiring his genius or recognizing his standing in the world of intellect and letters, nor have we forgotten how, at some vital and terrible moments of Ireland's recent history, when many who might have spoken were silent, the voice of Bernard Shaw rang out, clear and courageous, in her defence. But, Ireland apart, Irishmen will join wholeheartedly in saluting a very great man, a man who has waged incessant war against oppression and injustice, who has always been ready to defend the weak against the strong, who has ruthlessly exposed sham and hypocrisy, and who has never once lent the support of his pen to a mean or unworthy cause.

## LORD PASSFIELD, O.M.
## (SIDNEY WEBB)

### *"EVERYWHERE I GAINED SOMETHING"*

HIS ninetieth birthday cannot go by without a word from a very old friend of his.

I met him about the year 1888 and we have been friends ever since.

I have travelled with him in many parts of England, France, Belgium, Holland and Germany. Everywhere I gained something.

Now after sixty years my memory fails me.

# LAURENCE HOUSMAN

## G.B.S. AND THE VICTORIANS

I REGARD Bernard Shaw (and my regard for him is very great) as the most devastating influence that has befallen my country, from the 'nineties of the last century up to the present day. And the devastation that he has wrought has been almost entirely beneficent. I cannot think of anybody whose non-existence would have made a more profound intellectual difference to this transitional age of ours—if a negative can be thus stated as a positive—than would the non-existence of G.B.S. Had God, in mistaken mercy, decided not to inflict on us the gibes and ruthless common sense of this brilliant Irishman, we should have been—if not a different people (made up of all classes)—a very different "upper middle class," and a very different intelligentsia.

The Victorian age had produced an order of society, social, moral, and political, with which what we were then accustomed to call the "educated class" was far too sufficiently satisfied. It had its virtues, but those virtues were infected, and so rendered less valuable, by a large number of inhibitions, shams, repressions, sentimentalities, insincerities, on which, so far as it was conscious of them, it rather prided itself. Along with these went a curious streak of stupid callousness. The educated class did not see much use in the "lower classes" being better educated, nor was it much concerned that they should be better housed or better fed. There were among us genuine hard-working Christians who were concerned about these social deficiencies, but they didn't cut much ice: institutional Christianity—though we had hardly yet found it out—was losing its hold on conscience and conduct: and church-going was no longer the accepted mark of respectability which, in small country towns, had made it advisable even for doctors to put in a fairly regular attendance.

Against all those social deficiencies, and smug pretences, G.B.S. started in the early 'nineties to deliver the withering blast of his wit.

After a decade of sprightly journalism, *Widowers' Houses*, produced by the Independent Theatre in 1892, was the nest-egg which he deposited before a jeering public, to be followed later by that amazing series of dramatic productions which have made revolutionary history for the English theatre, and have forced us to a general recognition of Shaw as our greatest dramatist since Shakespeare. That does not mean that he is now, or has ever been, the most popular playwright of the day: lesser playwrights secure longer runs and more crowded houses; but it does mean that a writer who has never been afraid of ridiculing our most cherished conventions, and exposing our pet hypocrisies, has forced us to recognize the magnitude of his dramatic and social achievement, and—what is even more important—admit that his criticisms of our national defects were not only diverting but just. And it is really very much to our credit that we have been able to do so. Shaw, the Irishman, has conquered us largely by taking expert advantage of that very English characteristic of ours—so good that it almost amounts to a virtue—that we, more than any other nation on God's earth, are willing to laugh at ourselves.

It was by his wit more than by his wisdom that Shaw conquered us; had he not forced us to laugh we should never have listened to him. By forcing us to laugh, he kept us in a good humour while he was saying the most outrageous things to us; and because he said them amusingly, we were of a mind to discover on reflection that a great many of them were true. And by having so many of our pet notions reduced to absurdity our minds were changed for us—so much so that I believe the difference between the well-educated mind of the twentieth century and the less well-educated mind of the nineteenth century to be very largely of Shaw's production. That change was already in full swing before the war of 1914 came to account for so many of the other and greater changes that followed.

But behind all the wit there was wisdom too, and an intense seriousness of purpose: under his mask of laughter, Shaw was out to kill the shams of a form of society that had had its day and outlived its usefulness. If one can ascribe conscious prenatal purpose to the vital energy which took up its abode in him ninety years ago, Shaw was sent into the world to wipe up the Victorian age; and without him it would have been less wiped up than it has been.

I am myself a Victorian, and am conscious in my bones of what he has done to me: for better or for worse I am not the man I should have been had Shaw not tackled me, before I made his personal acquaintance, while I was still in my twenties. Let me own frankly that I began by disliking him; he was constantly offending my taste; and taste is often a protective extra skin which we have acquired from our parents, or have put on, to keep us from disturbing thought about things which are unpleasant. Sometimes he offends me still by his gratuitous exaggerations—not of facts, but of phrases; using, for instance, that worn-out cliché about grown-up lack of intelligence over things which "the mind of any child of ten could master." But I can still remember the characteristic Victorian statement which came out of my mouth in his hearing (the first time we ever met) at a small social debate, that, if the working class were paid better wages, they wouldn't know how to spend them properly, and how jovially he felled me to earth for it, and made it impossible for me ever again to defend an unjust wage system by that sort of argument.

It is worth noting, I think, that in his fight for the recovery of right values, in a social order which had become so mentally and morally defective under its veneer of Christianity, Shaw (though much more a Christian in principle than most of us) was entirely secular in his method of attack on the social conscience; and it was not until he wrote his preface to *Androcles and the Lion* that he openly championed Christianity against the charge that it had become a proved failure, and declared that it had not failed because it had never yet been tried, and that it was about time that it *was* tried. It was a case of the Humanist once again (as has happened before) coming to the rescue of Christian realism from the cold formalism of otherworldliness.

If Christianity is not to have its feet firmly planted in this world, defiantly and practically—irrespective of whether there is another world or not—its truth goes, and it is not worth having. And in this connection I would like to put on record what Shaw wrote to a friend of mine, in the course of the war which is now nominally over. The world, he said (I am not quite sure of the actual words), was passing through a period of hatred which would lead us nowhere and do no good to anybody. "Men must learn," he went on, "to be kind and just to those whom they very properly hate." That is not an ideally Christian statement, but it is much nearer to practical Christianity than anything which our Ruling Powers are prepared to accept as good guidance in their present devious attempts at peace-making.

In the essential kindliness of Shaw's heart, and the occasional cruelty of his tongue, I find a curious mixture of the characteristics of two of the great teachers of history—the whimsical benevolence and wisdom of Socrates, and the sharp, biting wit of Voltaire. To most people, especially to those who have read *The Adventures of the Black Girl in Her Search for God,* his likeness to Voltaire is more apparent. But though much more latent the likeness to Socrates is there also.

## J. B. PRIESTLEY

### *G.B.S.–SOCIAL CRITIC*

THERE is one good reason why it is very difficult for me to write a critical estimate of Shaw as a social critic or as anything else. I belong to the wrong generation. If I were older, much older, I could see him as a contemporary. If I were younger I could stand farther away from him. But Shaw, like Wells, dominated the world in which I grew up. They were there, doing their best work, when I arrived. My father was a Socialist schoolmaster with a passion for reading, and my boyhood was spent in Bradford, which was one of the early strongholds of the Labour movement. If my parents had regarded Shaw as a dangerous revolutionary or a self-advertising clown, then I might have discovered him for myself. But naturally he was among their heroes; and his plays and prefaces and pamphlets were there for me to feed upon; with the result that for at least thirty-five years I have taken his wit and wisdom for granted, like so much starshine and sunlight.

The consequence of this is that while my admiration and gratitude, warmly coloured by my affection for a glorious character, have remained as a solid foundation, I have probably spent more time in my own mind disagreeing with him than I have agreeing with him. Because I am a Socialist, too, and was converted by him long ago, then I look for points of difference. Because his plays were among the earliest I saw, I do not want to write the same kind of plays but insist upon doing something quite different, and even deplore his influence upon many of my colleagues in the theatre. (This is because the Shaw method without the Shaw mind does not make for good drama.) Probably I agree with seven-eighths of his magnificent social criticism, but it is upon the remaining eighth that I tend to concentrate all my attention. His influence upon people of my sort has been so immense, so all-pervading, that in order to prove—if only to ourselves—that we too exist as social critics or creative artists, we have had to break away deliberately from this Merlin of our time. He can have anything he likes from us as a birthday present. But a critical estimate? Why, we hardly know how to begin.

The Victorian Age was filled with giants and junk. The last Victorian giant was a red-bearded Irishman, who put a match to the junk and then sauntered away, chuckling, fully aware of the Mephistophelian effect of the leaping flames. Some explosive and combustible materials were to hand, of course: many supplied by Marx, and others by Samuel Butler and Ibsen; but it was Shaw himself who tossed them into the dust-heap and then struck the match. He had hammered out for himself a superb debating style, which was equally suitable for dramatic speech or polemical essays, and never too far from the stage or the platform; a style with a challenging and provocative tone in it, good enough for anything except dubieties and fine shades, in which its author had no interest. He had developed, too, a manner of his own, the importance of which seems to me to have been overlooked. It is a manner that apparently carries provocation almost to the point of insult and yet in fact is never really offensive. The blows rain down on us, but we never bleed. Somewhere behind the abrupt attack is a smiling magnanimity, just as behind the hammering and smashing style there is a voice that is enchanting in private talk and irresistible on the platform. And again, like all great masters of theatrical comedy, Shaw realized early that however hard the argument may be driven and the points pushed home, comedy demands an atmosphere of golden good nature, of mild and pleasant sunlight, an artificial world in which nobody is going to be badly hurt. Indeed, it might be charged against

Shaw that there are times, particularly during the more recent and more tragic years, when he mistakes this artificial world of comedy for the real world, in which men bleed and scream and welcome death as a deliverance. Thus, a manner perfectly adapted to the conditions of Edwardian debate may not be quite suitable for a later age of sudden arrests and concentration camps. But this is merely to say that he is not faultless. The diamond may have a flaw, but it is a diamond.

Throughout his social criticism Shaw has from first to last made the very best possible use of two ideas, using them like a pair of bulldozers to clear a road through a jungle. The first idea is still not sufficiently understood and appreciated. The second one is now part of our inheritance, and thousands of useful persons, from medical officers of health to young literary critics, make use of this idea themselves without even knowing that it was Shaw who originally showed us the way. And both ideas are alike in this, that they are at once Socialist or Communist and fundamentally religious. And they are evidence that Shaw possesses the outlook and temperament of the man of religion. He is in fact a prophet, and though he may have been addressing the London County Council or the Fabian Society, rehearsing a play at the Court Theatre or the Malvern Festival, debating with Belloc and Chesterton or scribbling witty postcards in Hertfordshire, he has always been a prophetic figure on the old plan, bearded and passionate and single-minded in the desert, living a spare life on locusts and wild honey and awaiting a new revelation from the God that he prefers to call the Life Force. And if this is overlooked, then he cannot be properly understood.

The first idea, which is common to both Early Christians and Late Communists, is that theory and practice must correspond. We must not keep belief and action in two separate compartments. Beliefs that do not directly inspire definite action are merely so much humbug. A man who professes to think one way and then acts in quite a different way is either a fool or a rogue. It is dishonest to condemn slaughter-houses and then call for steaks or chops. It is hypocritical to lead what you imagine to be a cultured spiritual life if you are doing it on money wrung out of exploitation and swindling. Our great-grandfathers wept over the deaths of Little Nell and Paul Dombey but objected to equally small children being taken out of the mines and factories. Victorian novelists pretended to blush and tremble at the very notion of prostitution, and then went cheerfully out on the spree with women of the town. Men were pious church-wardens on Sunday evening and commercial pirates and cut-throats on Monday morning. Delicate fine ladies, who turned pale at the sight of a limping poodle, allowed their fellow-women to work themselves blind and idiotic for them. The manufacturers who often turned the Midlands and Lancashire into a black stinking hell eagerly acquired Pre-Raphaelite pictures of Arthurian knights and dim swooning princesses. There was one code for the drawing-room and another code for the foundry and the mill. Men prayed for peace while initiating moves that would inevitably lead to war. They hung coloured silks over the iron machinery of society. And what was not cant and humbug was so much ignorance.

All true religion has sharply demanded a correspondence and consistency of theory and practice, thought and action, just as all pseudo-religion has always tried to escape from them, taking refuge in "ideals." These are convenient because they are not in this world and can be kept nicely floating in mid-air, where they make no real demands on anybody and allow men to feel that they are at heart noble creatures while actually behaving very badly. Thus, the Russian intellectuals of the nineteenth century never stopped talking about their ideals, but it was not until there came an end to this pleasant chatter and the Bolsheviks took over that Russian society was genuinely transformed. It is this idealism, which belongs to pseudo-religion, that Ibsen attacks; and Shaw, who has always had the single vision of the genuine religious type, followed him. He asked the Late Victorians, who were his first audience, to stop talking about their ideals, to break down the division between theory and practice, to take a long, hard look at their society and then not to sigh over it but to change it. His single vision enabled him to see the connection between the things that had often escaped the misty double vision of his contemporaries. While much must be allowed for his wit and style, the fact remains that some of his best effects were obtained simply by telling the plain truth. Thus, you have only to read any genuine military history to realize that making war successfully is not a slapdash romantic affair but a grim organizing job on a large scale, in which a cool head will be worth much more than a hot heart; and out of this plain truth he made his glorious comedy of *Arms and the Man*. Being a dramatic critic in the 'nineties, when a conventional unreality and bogus romanticism still nourished the theatre, Shaw had a grand opportunity to discover how much nonsense and humbug people were still ready to accept, in theory but not as guides to action; and into this rickety hot-house he let in a roaring east wind. Nevertheless he was not, as was often imagined, himself entirely unromantic. His impulse was often more truly romantic than anything known to the people he shocked. He was not playing Sancho to their Don Quixote, but was far nearer than they could ever be to the Don himself.

The difference is that he knew a great deal more than Don Quixote. In fact he knew that what other people imagined were giants were actually windmills. Where they saw huge threatening figures, he saw sails and wheels going round. He had learned from Marx to observe the structure of society. He added economics to literary genius, just as Wells added biology to literary genius; and in each instance it was this immense bonus that gave each man so much force and originality. This brings us to his second idea, the one that may be said now to be part of our inheritance. It is the conception of the community as a living whole. (This again is a truly religious idea, and may be found among all the prophets.) Most of Shaw's thinking is done in terms not of persons or groups but of the community as a whole. He is, so to speak, standing farther back, taking a wider view, observing the movement of the whole contemporary mass of men and women. It may be objected that too often his generalizations are too large and sweeping, that he over-simplifies too much, that he presses great names into his argument often in the most unscrupulous fashion, that he performs platform tricks where they are unwelcome. But the breadth of his outlook, together with his frequent flashes of insight, would make us forgive faults far worse than any of his, if only because in reading him or hearing his dialogue we seem to be breathing exhilarating mountain air and to be looking down upon the world from a great height. We are with the wittiest and most magnanimous of the major prophets. But the outlook, the vision, the tone, are still those of a genuine prophet: Man is seen against the stars, and is even now being judged.

It was this that gave force to Chesterton's shrewdest thrust at Shaw. Chesterton said: "He has always had a secret ideal that has withered all the things of this world. He has all the time been silently comparing humanity with something that was not human, with a monster from Mars, with the Wise Men of the Stoics, with the Economic Man of the Fabians, with Julius Cæsar, with Siegfried, with the Superman." But the same argument could be used against every founder of a religion, against every genuine prophet, all of whom declared emphatically that humanity as they found it was not good enough, that God demanded something better. And Shaw's acceptance of Lamarckian evolution, his belief that the outward development of living creatures corresponded to an inward growth, that new needs acquire new powers to satisfy them, made this endless comparison, this withering of things as they are for the sake of things as they might be, essential to his outlook. It is true that often he affects a deliberate coldness, a chilling austerity, but this to my mind is merely an overplaying of a character part, assumed as a protest against an early Dublin-operatic environment and then against Victorian cosiness and muddle-headedness. I think too that, reacting against the complacent nonsense talked by the politicians about democracy, he has always tended to overrate the wisdom of the outstanding individual and to underestimate the collective common sense of ordinary people. He has never lived under a severely authoritarian regime, and if he had he would have been one of the first to challenge and denounce it, at any cost; and perhaps owing to some failure of imagination, or an unconscious trick of identifying himself with the Cæsars and dictators, he seems almost ready to admire such regimes for their own sake, just as he has always understood the weaknesses of democracy better than he has appreciated its virtues, many of which—including the benefits of reasonably free speech—he takes for granted.

Already some of his early plays have lost their challenge as social criticism, or at least as topical social criticism, and are now enjoyed as pieces of excellent stage-craft in the all-too-rare comedy of intellectual high spirits. I wish he could see these delighted audiences (who arrive at the playhouse tired and worried and hungry, not like the well-fed easy-going folk for whom he wrote originally) and could hear their shouts of laughter, for that would be the best birthday present of all. These play-goers of our grim time who enjoy his wit, his stagecraft, his philosophy, may still be unfamiliar with nine-tenths of what he has meant them to understand; but nevertheless I think that most of them have already absorbed or have even been conditioned by a good deal of his social criticism. They bring it with them to the playhouse, like another and much vaster programme. Much of what now seems to them common sense was once considered merely a part of Shaw's "paradoxical clowning." (And the critics who denounced him for it now seem quaint period figures.) Some of the air we breathe now has G.B.S. in it, a little mountain oxygen that has somehow penetrated the fog. And where this mountain air comes from there is nothing small, nothing mean, nothing vindictive and cruel; it knows the sun of wit and wisdom and great cleansing winds of doctrine.

# A LETTER FROM H. G. WELLS

16th April, 1941.

My dear G.B.S.,

I was going to write to you to-day—our minds move in sympathy. I saw Major Barbara on Monday and I found it delightful. You have given it fresh definition. Andrew Undershaft might have been better cast with a more subtle face. As it is he seems to be astonished at himself throughout. The house was packed. Moura and I got the last two seats and you could not have had a more responsive audience. They laughed at all the right places. Mostly young people in uniform they were. That old Fabian audience is scattered for evermore. I firmly believe that we are getting the young. We shall rise again sooner than Marx did and for a better reason.

Pavlov was invincibly like you. You will probably be confused by posterity. He talked almost as well. But he wrote damnable prose. I was never educated by any sort of schooling. I left school at thirteen. Afterwards I did biological work at the Royal College of Science, but the nearest I came to "Materialistic Mechanistic Science" was a half-year in the Physics course at Kensington. It bored me so much that I learnt Latin and German and matriculated while it was going on. It is a pity you never had a sound dose of biology. Still, you do pretty well as you are.

This getting old is tiresome. I don't feel old in my wits but my heart seems to falter and I have phases of brain anæmia when I forget names and all that small print stuff. I've written a Guide to the New World Order and I am writing a novel. So get on with your play.

Whatever happens now we have had a pretty good time.

Yours as ever,

H.G.

# A LETTER FROM SIR MAX BEERBOHM

Dear Mr. Winsten,

I like your idea very much. "I suppose that the world itself could not contain all the books" that have been written about G.B.S., and I think it is high time that a book should be written to him. I wish I could be among the writers of it. But I think that no great man at the moment of his reaching the age of ninety should be offered anything but praise. And very fond though I am of G.B.S., and immensely kind though he has always been to me, my admiration for his genius has during fifty years and more been marred for me by dissent from almost any view that he holds about anything. I remember that in an interview published in Frank Harris's "Candid Friend" G.B.S., having commented on the adverse criticisms by his old friends Archer and Walkley, said, "And Max's blessings are all of them thinly disguised curses." I remember also a published confession of my own that I was always distracted between two emotions about him, (1) a wish that he had never been born, (2) a hope that he would never die. The first of those two wishes I retract. To the second one I warmly adhere. Certainly he will live for ever in the consciousness of future ages. If in one of those ages I happen to be reincarnate I shall write a reasoned estimate of some aspect of him and of his work. But now I merely send him my love.

Yours sincerely,

Max Beerbohm.

# C. E. M. JOAD

## *SHAW'S PHILOSOPHY*

### NATURE AND SOURCES OF SHAW'S PHILOSOPHY

THERE are two senses in which a man can be said to have a philosophy or to be a philosopher. First, there is the sense in which a man may seek to present a coherent and comprehensive view of the universe as a whole, of the status of human life within it and of the way in which in the light of that view and granted that status human life ought to be lived.

Secondly, there is the sense in which a man may be the dispenser of wisdom in memorable thoughts and sayings on a vast number of topics of secular importance—on money, God, love, marriage, desire, death, ambition—wisdom which may, as in Shaw's case, spring from and be informed by the coherent and comprehensive view; or, as in that of Dr. Johnson, be unpervaded by any synthesizing conception of the meaning and purpose of life as a whole. (I don't mean that Johnson did not advance such a conception, merely that it has little to do with what he has to say on money, marriage, the navy and so on.) Shaw is a philosopher and has a philosophy in both these senses. In this chapter I shall be concerned only with the first of them, the sense in which he is the exponent and part originator of the philosophical doctrine called Creative Evolution.

Although this philosophy outcrops sporadically throughout the plays, its main deposits are to be found in two places; in the Preface to and the Hell Scene in *Man and Superman*, and in the Preface to and the five plays of the *Back to Methuselah* Pentateuch. Of these the latter is the more important, not only because when it appeared in 1921, Shaw's thought had undergone considerable development since the *Man and Superman* (1903) stage, but also because, as Shaw himself at the end of the *Back to Methuselah* Preface says of the 1903 presentation of his philosophy, "being then at the height of my invention and comedic talent, I decorated it too brilliantly and lavishly. I surrounded it with a comedy of which it formed only one act and that act was so completely episodical . . . that the comedy could be detached and played by itself. . . . The effect was so vertiginous apparently that nobody noticed the new religion in the centre of the intellectual whirlpool."

In what follows I shall rely chiefly on the exposition in *Back to Methuselah*, reinforced by reference on subsidiary points to *Man and Superman*.

### The Materialist Scheme

I will first say something of the background and sources of Shaw's theory of Creative Evolution. Shaw's thought runs back through Samuel Butler to Lamarck. The view that Butler expounded can best be understood in relation to the doctrine of Darwin. Darwin's doctrine was essentially biological, but it formed an essential part of the comprehensive materialist scheme of the universe which held the field in the latter part of the nineteenth century. Under this scheme the universe was envisaged after the model of a gigantic clock; somebody at some time or other had, so to speak, wound the clock up; in other words the universe had at some time got itself started—the materialist could not, of course, explain how but as nobody else was in this respect in any better position his inability was not a distinctive objection to materialism—and thereafter it functioned indefinitely through the automatic interaction of its parts. Life was one of the parts, a product of the operation of the same physical and chemical laws as governed the behaviour of non-living matter.

Under the influence of certain rather rare physical conditions—materialists were never tired of emphasizing the paucity of the areas of the cosmos in which the conditions favourable to life obtained—matter had become conscious, conscious as it was sometimes put, of itself. Matter's consciousness of itself was life, and life's subsequent development was governed by the same material conditions as had given it birth. One day when these conditions no longer obtained, life would finish its pointless journey with as little significance as in the person of the amœba it began in. Meanwhile, its status in the universe was that of an outside passenger travelling across a fundamentally alien and hostile environment in which what was mindless and brutal conditioned and determined what was spiritual and akin. Causation in other words operated universally from the less living as cause to the more living as effect; within the living organism from the body to the mind and within the mind from the less to the more conscious part of it.

This was the scheme in which Darwin's discovery of evolution, or, more precisely, of the laws of natural selection and the survival of the fittest through which evolution operated, played an integral part; integral, because in the attitude which it adopted to the phenomenon of life, in the explanation which it offered of the elaborate and varied process which beginning with the amœba had culminated in ourselves, Darwin's account postulated the intervention of no spiritual force or agency, no mind, no life and no god, but was content to rely upon the operation of those same material forces as had governed the planet prior to life's appearance.

More particularly, variations in species occurred. Either they were adapted to their environment or they were not. If they were not, they were eliminated; if they were, the variation in respect of which they were adapted and by reason of the adaptation obtained an advantage in the struggle for existence was handed on to their offspring and became stamped into the life history of the species, where it developed and intensified, until at last it represented a degree of differentiation which entitled biologists to say that a new species had emerged. So far, so good; but why did the variations occur? Darwin professed agnosticism; he did not know, although sometimes he attributed them to chance. But the question was, it was obvious, of crucial importance. If there were no variations, if no changes in species occurred, then each generation would be an exact replica of the preceding one and, short of new creations, the amœba and his contemporaries would still be the sole forms of life upon the planet. Variations, then, played an essential part in the machinery of evolution; they were necessary to get it started. Why, then, did they occur? It was here that the followers of Lamarck took the field.

### Lamarckianism

Variations in species, they urged, were due to the effects of environment. When the environment changed, living organisms must either adapt themselves to it or disappear. Those who were successful in effecting the adaptation survived and transmitted the adaptation in virtue of which they had survived to their descendants. These adaptations were mainly envisaged by Lamarck in terms of the growth of new organs and the gradual lapsing of old ones. Changes in environment led to new wants, new wants to new habits and new habits to new organs which were formed to minister to the habits. In point of fact, the difference between Lamarck's doctrine, so far as I have stated it hitherto, and Darwin's was not very striking. Why, it was asked, in the contemporary controversies, did the giraffe grow his long neck? According to Darwin's followers, long-necked giraffes were born by chance much as children with freckles are born by chance. They enjoyed a natural advantage in the struggle for food—they could nibble the leaves on the higher branches—and, therefore, were better placed in the struggle for existence than their shorter-necked contemporaries. Thus, the fittest survived but they were the fittest by chance; they had not become the fittest by design. According to Lamarck, the giraffes at a certain stage of their history, finding that most of the leaves on the lower branches on the available trees had been eaten, were under the necessity of either growing longer necks in order to reach the higher leaves, or of perishing of hunger. Those who successfully adapted themselves to the changed conditions by growing longer necks survived and transmitted the characteristic of long-neckedness to their offspring. Once again in the struggle for existence the fittest survived, but they were the fittest not by chance but by reason of their success in adapting themselves. But the process was, in Lamarck's view, no less automatic, no less determined than in Darwin's; in fact, it was more so. A change in the external environment, a change, it might be, in the climate determined a change in the living organisms which were exposed to it, or it did not. If it did not, the organisms died out. The scheme was thus so far at one with Darwin's in that it, too, abstained from postulating the action of any informing purpose of plan to account for the changes in and development of species; up to this point it fitted equally well into the prevalent materialistic scheme.

### Butler's Contribution

But suppose that the changes in living organisms by means of which they adapted themselves to changes in their environment were purposive, in the sense that somebody or something operating independently of the living organism, or perhaps developing in and through it, willed them; suppose, in fact, that changes in living things were not *always* the by-products of prior changes in dead things, but that at least sometimes they occurred independently, as the result of living things' desire to adapt themselves better to dead things and possibly to use dead things for their own purposes. If this were so, causation might sometimes at least operate from the animate to the inanimate, and the vital, in virtue of which animate matter was animated, instead of being merely a by-product of the material, might be in some sense independent of it, and, being independent, might be able to act upon it, use it, even enter into and inform it. Such, in effect, was the assertion of Samuel Butler, an assertion which he proceeded to work up into the sketch of a philosophy. It was of this sketch that Shaw proceeded to fill in the outlines, fully acknowledging his debt to Butler "in his own department the greatest English writer of the latter half of the nineteenth century,"—"when," Shaw wrote in the preface to *Major Barbara*, "I produce plays in which Butler's extremely fresh, free and future-piercing suggestions have an obvious share, I am met with nothing but vague cacklings about Ibsen and Nietzsche,"—and developed into the fully fledged philosophy of *Back to Methuselah*.

So much for a sketch of the background; let me now try and outline the philosophy, as it appears in its fully developed form.

## Outline of Shaw's Theory of Creative Evolution

Shaw postulates a universe containing or consisting of two factors, Life and matter. Admittedly he sometimes speaks of Life as creating matter as when, by willing to use our arms in a certain way, we bring into existence a roll of muscle, but the general view is that matter is, as it were, there to begin with. Thus, matter is spoken of as Life's "enemy." "I brought life into the whirlpool of force, and compelled my enemy, Matter, to obey a living soul," say Lilith at the end of *Back to Methuselah*. Regarding matter in the light of an enemy, Life seeks to dominate and subdue it. Partly to this end, partly because of its innate drive to self-expression, Life enters into and animates matter. The product of this animation of matter by Life is a living organism. A living organism, then, derives from and bears witness to the presence of both the two fundamental constituents of which the universe is composed; it is Life expressed in matter. Shaw suggests rather than explicitly states that Life cannot evolve or develop *unless* it enters into matter to create organisms; they are, in fact, the indispensable tools wherewith it promotes its own development. To put the point in another way, by means of the device of expressing itself in and through matter Life is enabled to enjoy a greater variety of experience, to accumulate more knowledge and greater intelligence and to develop a more intense power of awareness. To develop these faculties, to make these acquisitions may be described as Life's immediate purpose since they facilitate, indeed they constitute, the process of Life's development. Living organisms, then, are the instruments which Life creates to facilitate the process of its own development, and matter, though Life's enemy, is also, as it were, the whetstone upon which Life sharpens itself in order to further its own evolution. This office matter performs by reason of the limitations which it imposes upon Life's powers, thus forcing Life to make efforts to overcome the limitation and so to develop itself by the acquisition of new powers.

Yet the object of Life is to pass beyond matter: to pass, that is to say, beyond the necessity for incarnating itself in and concerning itself with matter. Until this consummation is reached, matter will continue to obstruct and limit life.

Life is also dependent on matter in the sense that each individual expression of Life, being dependent upon the body in which Life incarnates itself to constitute a living organism, terminates its separate existence *as an individual expression* with the death of the body, and, presumably, reverts to the main stream.

When the need for incarnation in matter has been transcended, Life's individualized expressions being no longer dependent upon incorporation in a body for their individuality will, we may suppose, become permanently individualized; will, in fact, be immortal. This conclusion is indicated in the dialogue between the *Ancients* and the *Newly Born* in the last play of *Back to Methuselah.*

> The He-Ancient: For whilst we are tied to this tyrannous body we are subject to its death, and our destiny is not achieved.
>
> The Newly Born: What is your destiny?
>
> The He-Ancient: To be immortal.
>
> The She-Ancient: The day will come when there will be no people, only thought.
>
> The He-Ancient: And that will be life eternal.

This, perhaps, is not as clear as could be wished, since it leaves it uncertain whether the immortality looked forward to will be the personal immortality of separate individual units of life, or will be merely the immortality of Life as a whole. If it means the latter—and this is, I think, Shaw's general view—then individuality, the individuality of the living organism, is a function of matter.

### The Method of Evolution

What is the nature of the force or activity which is spoken of sometimes as driving the evolutionary process forward, sometimes as identical with it? We cannot say or, rather, we can define it only in terms of its own activity. It is, to use an expression of Shaw's, "vitality with a direction," expressing itself in the will to create matter or to mould the matter which it finds but has not created. "The will to do anything," he writes, "can and does, at a certain pitch of intensity set up by conviction of its necessity, create and organize new tissue to do it with. . . . If the weight lifter, under the trivial stimulus of an athletic competition, can 'put up a muscle,' it seems reasonable to believe that an equally earnest and convinced philosopher could 'put up a brain.' Both are directions of vitality to a certain end. Evolution shows us this direction of vitality doing all sorts of things."

Now, the need for new tissue to carry out the will and to further the development of the vital impulse leads to the development of new organs in existing species and ultimately to the development of new species of living things. Shaw is here taking over from Butler and the Lamarckians, the view that Life's need for something sooner or later produces that for which the need is felt.

How, to revert to the classical example, does the giraffe get his long neck? "By wanting to get at the tender leaves high up on the tree, and trying until he succeeded in wishing the necessary length of neck into existence." In this quotation Shaw summarizes what he takes to be the doctrine of Lamarck. He proceeds to add in his own right: "You want, consequently, additional organs, or additional uses of your existing organs: that is, additional habits. You get them because you want them badly enough to keep trying for them until they come. Nobody knows how: nobody knows why: all we know is that the thing actually takes place. We relapse miserably from effort to effort until the old organ is modified or the new one created, when suddenly the impossible becomes possible and the habit is formed." The new habit and the new organ to be the vehicle of the new habit, are evolved because in the long run we need them or—for Shaw uses both modes of expression—because Life needs them in us. "If you have no eyes and want to see and keep on trying to see you will finally get eyes."

This, the method of evolution at the pre-conscious level, is still its method at the conscious, is still, in other words, the method of evolving humanity. Man feels a need and gradually wills into existence the faculty or organ which will enable him to satisfy it. The formula for this process is described in the first play of *Back to Methuselah*, as first desire, then imagination, then will, then creation. Here is a summary statement of it from that wonderful dialogue between Eve and the Serpent at the beginning of the first play[1]:

> The Serpent: . . . imagination is the beginning of creation. You imagine what you desire; you will what you imagine; and at last you create what you will.
>
> Eve: How can I create out of nothing?
>
> The Serpent: Everything must have been created out of nothing. Look at that thick roll of hard flesh on your strong arm! That was not always there: you could not climb a tree when I first saw you. But you willed and tried and willed and tried; and your will created out of nothing the roll on your arm until you had your desire, and could drag yourself up with one hand, and seat yourself on the bough that was above your head.

A point which Shaw stresses is the *abruptness* of the appearance of the acquisition, whether it takes the form of organ or faculty or awareness, in which the new evolutionary advance consists. There is a definite jump from the old level of behaviour and thinking to the new one: "The process is not continuous, as it would be if mere practice had anything to do with it; for though you may improve at each bicycling lesson *during* the lesson, when you begin your next lesson you do not begin at the point at which you left off; you relapse apparently to the beginning. Finally, you succeed quite suddenly, and do not relapse again. More miraculous still, you at once exercise the new power unconsciously."

The process of Life's development, as hitherto described, expresses itself mainly in the acquisition of new bodily habits and physical traits. But the same process continues at the level

[1] I heard Shaw read this aloud—he had written it during the day—on two successive evenings at a Fabian Summer School—beyond comparison the most impressive, dramatic occasion at which I have been privileged to be present.

of thought. We develop new powers not only of the body but of the mind, powers of insight, vision and intelligence because we want them, or because Life wants to develop them in us that we may more effectively implement Life's purpose as it is, or conceive for Life new purposes which it has not yet itself conceived.

Later, however, it appears that Life's entry in and concern with matter is a mere temporary phase of Life's development. Matter is entered into, only that it may be transcended; it is a ladder which must be scaled in order that, having arrived at the top, Life may pass on to something else. Thus, though the Ancients in the last play in *Back to Methuselah* have complete mastery over their bodies, and can create surplus arms and legs at will, though they also possess power over other bodies and can apparently kill with a glance, the exercise of these powers does not interest them. They are bored with the knowledge of matter, bored even with the manipulation of matter. Their attention is directed elsewhere, their interests lie in something else. In what else? Before I attempt to answer this question, there are one or two subsidiary developments of the main evolutionary theme about which something must be said.

### Digression: (1) On the Right Conduct of Life

As I hinted at the beginning, Shaw is a philosopher in both the senses of the word which I there distinguished. In his capacity as a dispenser of wisdom, he has contrived to let fall a great number of pregnant observations on the secular topics of human interest and concern from Marriage to Moderation and from Greatness to Gambling.

Many of these are collected in the *Revolutionist's Hand-Book* which is printed at the end of *Man and Superman*. All are more or less informed by the underlying philosophy—in the first sense of the word "philosophy"—of which they are the directly deduced corollaries. I have space here to mention only three topics which are of such importance both to the preacher and to his congregation that though, as I have hinted, Shaw's treatment of them is a corollary from his general position and could, therefore, with sufficient insight presumably be deduced from it, what he has to say on them may deservedly rank as an integral part of the Shavian philosophy.

These three topics are, first, the right conduct of life; secondly, women and genius, and, thirdly, art.

If we are instruments created by Life for the furtherance of Life's instinctive purpose, our *raison d'être* will be found in the fulfilment of Life's intentions in regard to us; not, then, in the pursuit of our own purposes. The furtherance of Life's purpose will consist in the being used up to the last ounce of one's energy and capacity in work that seems to one to be worth while for its own sake. Shaw's own talents and energies have been remorselessly used in the spreading of Socialism and the writing of plays. It is by the maximum expenditure of effort in the ardours and endurances of living and thinking that one will develop and improve one's initial endowment of faculty and accomplishment, thus returning them at death with interest—an interest which is to be measured by the degree of the realised improvement upon the initially given potentiality—to the general stream of Life of which we are the individualized expressions, with the result that when Life expresses itself in the next generation of living organisms, it will do so at a slightly higher level than it did before, because of the enrichments of acquisition and accomplishment that we have brought to it.

Now happiness will be found in the furtherance of the purpose for which we were created. Not unnaturally, since life will do its best to ensure the donkey's activity by dangling the carrot of happiness before its nose. Effort and endeavour, then, are the means to the happy and successful life and we shall find the recipe for happiness in not having enough leisure to wonder whether we are miserable or not. It is in the same vein that Shaw bids us "get what you like or else you will grow to like what you get."

Shaw's philosophy enables him to provide a new basis for the moral philosopher's traditional criticism of the life of pleasure-seeking. This, for Shaw, is a perversion of function, since it entails a diversion of effort to the pursuit of one's *own* concerns, and in the indulgence in one's *own* gratifications, when we should be engaged about Life's business. The life of the epicure, the hedonist and the egotist is, then, a kind of playing truant when we should be at school and Life pays us out for our apostasy by ensuring that, as the direct pursuers of pleasure, we shall miss the pleasure that we pursue. Hence, the aphorism, "Folly is the direct pursuit of Happiness and Beauty."

### Digression: (ii) On Women and Genius

I do not wish to suggest by this sub-heading that women are geniuses or even that women have genius. The intention is to present the genius whom Shaw assumes, by implication, to be essentially male in relation, a relation which is usually one of opposition to women. (Shaw does, incidentally, speak in connection with George Sand of the comedy afforded by the accident of the genius being "himself a woman").

Femaleness, in the creative evolutionary philosophy, is represented as being more primitive, in the sense of being more fundamental, than maleness. Shaw even goes to the length of suggesting that the initial form of life was female. Lilith in *Back to Methuselah* is represented as producing Adam from within herself. In the beginning, Lilith "who came before Adam and Eve . . . was alone: there was no man with her." She "sunders herself in twain" to give birth and is left at the end of the Fifth Play wondering whether in order to supersede human beings she must needs give birth again.

Already latent in the dialogue between Gloria and Valentine in *You Never Can Tell,* this conception is developed in the Hell scene in *Man and Superman.* Here Shaw conceives Life as working through woman to create man to carry Life to higher levels. "Sexually, Woman is Nature's contrivance for perpetuating Nature's highest achievement. Sexually, Man is Woman's contrivance for fulfilling Nature's behest in the most economical way. She knows by instinct that far back in the evolutional process she invented him, differentiated him, created him, in order to produce something better than the single-sexed process can produce."

So far, so good; but unfortunately (for woman) in giving man so small a part in the process of reproduction, she set free his energies for developing his vital inheritance by making acquisitions of which she had no prevision; as, for example, by thinking thoughts that she could not follow, by whoring after beauty that she could not understand, by desiring and pursuing things disinterestedly in and for themselves. For "how rash and dangerous it was to invent a separate creature whose sole function was her own impregnation! For mark what has happened. First, Man has multiplied on her hands until there are as many men as women; so that she has been unable to employ for her purposes more than a fraction of the immense energy she has left at his disposal by saving him the exhausting labour of gestation. This superfluous energy has gone to his brain and to his muscle. He has become too strong to be controlled by her bodily, and too imaginative and mentally vigorous to be content with mere self-reproduction. He has created civilization without consulting her, taking her domestic labour for granted as the foundation of it."

Man also invents "dreams, follies, ideals, heroisms" and, we may add, creeds and causes with which both to amuse and develop himself, thus further diverting his energy and attention from the performance of the purely biological purpose for which woman created him. But since woman is the vehicle of a more direct inheritance from Life, since she is biologically primary and man biologically secondary, woman succeeds in ninety-nine cases out of a hundred in bringing him to heel by turning him back to his specifically biological function, which means turning him from adventurer or visionary, first, into the worshipper of herself—hence romance—and, secondly, when the hook of family maintenance has been swallowed with the bait of sexual attraction, into a bread-winner for herself and children. And since getting a job means doing the work which the world is prepared to offer you and to pay you for doing, instead of the work which you want to do, the subsidence of the artist, the idealist, the revolutionary or the scholar into the breadwinner involves a struggle, a struggle between creativity and the thrill of beauty, curiosity and the pull of knowledge and, it may be, the vision of God on the one hand and the power of woman, symbolizing security, conservatism, common sense and earthiness in the interests of keeping the family together and the Life Force's pot boiling on the other. Thus, we are told that for a man "marriage is a heavy chain to rivet on himself." Woman "is born with the chain attached to her, and marriage is the only way open to her of riveting the other end of it into a man." In ninety-nine cases out of a hundred she succeeds. Woman is endowed by the Life Force with the faculty, or rather with the appearance of the faculty, of being able to share man's enthusiasms, respond to his ideals, echo his thoughts. But this apparent sympathy is only the bait on woman's hook. Once it is swallowed the feminine enthusiasms, the shared ideals, the "disinterested" interests, are discarded like a worn-out glove and the young man who would reform society, see visions, talk with God, finds himself reduced by his triumphant mate to the role of a breadwinner for herself and her children.

And so it goes for ninety-nine cases out of a hundred; but the hundredth case is the case of the genius. The genius is the repository of a special "potential" of Life expressly created for the specific purpose of carrying Life to higher levels by giving man a new insight into truth, a new concept of political association and moral obligation, a new vision of beauty, or a new refinement and subtlety of personal relationship. As Shaw puts it, a genius is a man "selected by Nature to carry on the work of building up an intellectual consciousness of her own instinctive purpose." He is, accordingly, the vehicle of as direct and purposeful an inheritance from Life as the woman herself, and will sacrifice woman in pursuance of his purpose as ruthlessly as she sacrifices the ordinary man in pursuance of hers.

Since the genius is by definition in advance of the existing level of evolutionary consciousness, being, in fact, a biological "sport" on the spiritual and intellectual planes, the work which he feels impelled to do is *ex hypothesi* work for which the world is not yet ready; for which, therefore, it is not prepared to pay. If he is a "sport" in the æsthetic field, if he is a Schubert or a Cézanne, he is usually allowed to starve to death in a garret in the usual way. If he is a "sport" on the moral or political plane, if he is a Blake, a Tolstoy, a Swedenborg, a Servetus or a Bunyan, or, Shaw would add, a Christ, he is usually persecuted with all the rigour of the law. In either event he is not a good husband, precisely because he is not "making good." What is more, he will be prepared without scruple to put his wife to the job of earning for himself and family the money which he is too preoccupied to earn himself. He will risk the stake and the cross; starve, when necessary, in a garret all his life; work his nerves into rags without payment; study women and live on their work and care as Darwin studied worms or Ehrlich bacteria; a sublime altruist in his disregard of himself, an atrocious egotist in his disregard of others. Here woman meets a purpose as impersonal, as irresistible as her own; and the clash is sometimes tragic.

Hence the clash between woman and the genius arises from the directness of the inheritance which each has from Life; or, if the phrase be preferred, the strength of the respective "potentials" at which Life is manifested in them. In the genius,

Life's purpose is to lift itself to heights of consciousness not previously achieved; in the woman, to safeguard and maintain the level which has already been attained.

### Digression: (iii) On Art and the Artist

Shaw's view of art has already, by implication, been touched upon. Art is a device by means of which Life achieves its purpose of lifting itself to a higher level of conscious awareness and the great artist is the instrument which it creates for the fulfilment of that purpose.

The method of Life's advance is envisaged in two stages; first, the great artist appears—an original thinker from this point of view is a special case of the artist—the representative of a new and original inspiration from Life. He embodies his vision in paint or sound or stone or words. Now, precisely because it *is* an original vision, the work of art in which it is embodied breaks the rules of composition, outrages the accepted concepts of form and style and taste, discards the hitherto accepted recipes for the catching and embalming of beauty and is, therefore, held to be a monstrosity of ugliness and disharmony. (Beethoven's Third Symphony, the music of Wagner, and the paintings of the Impressionists are examples especially cited by Shaw.) It challenges prevalent notions, flouts current prejudices, startles, shocks and flies in the face of popular morality. Hence, the life of the genius is usually poor, solitary and brutish and, since he is a genius in respect of only the hundredth part of himself, the remaining ninety-nine hundredths being an ordinary chap with a craving for human sympathy and affection, and a natural desire to win the world's esteem and to bask in the sunshine of popular favour and his wife's approval, the genius is usually the most wretched of men. If, however, his vision does, indeed, embody a new and original impression from Life, others will presently come to see things in the colours of the spectacles which he has tinted for them. The outrageous symphony or painting will be adopted as the accepted standard of orthodoxy and good taste and the heterodoxies of to-day will be enshrined in the *Home Notes* of to-morrow. This is the second stage, the stage in which the common consciousness of civilised mankind moves up to the level of insight at which the original genius first appeared. Thus, the genius is beauty's midwife. He does not create beauty but he brings to birth in sound or paint or stone the beauty which he has first discerned, so that ordinary men with their duller and grosser senses may presently apprehend for themselves the beauty which the work of art throws, as it were, into high relief. He makes wide and straight for the many the narrow path which he has been the first to follow.

Such, then, is the distinctive Shavian attitude to art and its function. It is a device, one of the most important, for refining and enlarging the awareness of men and women and so lifting Life itself to a higher level of consciousness.

This is a high function and Shaw's attack on romantic art, by which he usually means art directed to the glorification of woman, is the expression of his indignation at its perversion. Art, as Shaw conceives it, is very largely a male preserve. It is, of course, natural that woman should seek to induce the artist to be content to glorify her, instead of going about his proper business of raising the general level of Life's awareness and deepening and refining Life's power of insight. But to do this is, in effect, to use the power of art to stabilise life at the level which it has already reached, instead of raising it to higher levels. It is as if the artist were to rest on the oars of his predecessors' achievements, instead of striking out for himself. Rightly regarded, art should supersede sex and not glorify it. In this sense, *ne cherchez pas la femme*, Shaw tells us, is the clue to the motivation of great art.

But there another attitude is discernible in Shaw's work in respect of which, and in respect of the manner of his advance to it, Shaw's thought curiously reproduces Plato's.

Plato has a twofold attitude to art. He suspects it because it rouses the sleeping dogs of emotion which were better left to lie, strengthens the irrational part of the soul, and makes images of the things of the sensible world and so directs soul's attention away from instead of towards reality. But there is another strain in Plato's thought, a strain that comes out more particularly in the *Phaedrus* and the *Symposium*, which represents art as the medium in which the Form of Beauty is manifested and, therefore, as a window, one of the clearest, through which man's soul may obtain a glimpse of reality.

Whilst Plato tends to move from the first position to the second, the development of Shaw's thought seems rather to have been from the second to the first. In the last play of *Back to Methuselah* we find a comparatively lowly place assigned to art. With love, it is regarded as the staple occupation of the very young; the Festival of the Artists, staged at the beginning of the last play of the Pentateuch is, apparently, supported entirely by the "under fives." "Soon," says the Ancient, "you will give up all these toys and games and sweets."

The He-Ancient belittles art, very much as Plato might have done when advocating the expulsion of artists from the ideal State. "As you grow up," he says, "you make images and paint pictures. Those of you who cannot do that make stories about imaginary dolls." But who, he presently asks, would make statues and images if he could apprehend the originals? Who would want stories if he knew the facts? This thought is developed by the She-Ancient: "Art is the magic mirror you make to reflect your invisible dreams in visible pictures. You use a glass mirror to see your face: you use works of art to see your soul. But we who are older use neither glass mirrors nor works of art. We have a direct sense of life. When you gain that you will put aside your mirrors and statues, your toys and your dolls." Shaw does not here go to Plato's length and treat art as a will-o'-the-wisp leading men away from reality. It is, for him, rather a substitute for reality, a substitute accepted perforce by those in whom Life has not yet sufficiently developed to be able to achieve and sustain a direct view of reality itself.

The suggestion might be ventured that the artist may be regarded as one who has *had* the vision of the soul but been unable to sustain it, and so makes the work of art to serve as a memento of the original, which his vision once glimpsed, but can glimpse no longer. If this were true, the work of art would be an expression not of the inspiration which the artist has, but the inspiration that he had once but has failed to maintain. I cannot find any evidence for this suggestion in Shaw, although it seems a logical corollary of his view of art.

### Return from Digression. The Purpose of Life

What, then, is the reality of which the artist makes copies, but which the Ancients directly apprehend? Shaw never seems to have made up his mind. His philosophy envisages Life's evolution as the development of an ever more intense and penetrating power of awareness. Now, awareness must be directed upon something, this something being other than itself, and Shaw's thought seems to me to demand the inclusion in the universe of an element of static and immutable perfection upon which the consciousness of a fully developed Life Force might come to rest. Such an element is, indeed, postulated by other philosophical systems with which Shaw's has affinity. Thus, Platonic philosophers attain to a vision of the timeless Forms which, thereafter, they contemplate. Aristotle's God is engaged, at least in part, in working out mathematical problems, engaged, that is to say, in contemplating the static perfection of mathematical quantities and their relations. The reason for this demand is obvious; thought by its very nature demands an object; there must be something for thought to think about. This something must be other than the thought itself and, since the factor of change in the universe has been appropriated for the developing consciousness of the thinker in whom the ever-changing Life Force is expressed, the object, the thing thought about, must, one would have supposed, be represented as exempt from the changes by which the evolutionary process is itself pervaded.

Shaw comes within striking distance of this position without ever explicitly adopting it. It will be noted that in the quotation cited above, the She-Ancient speaks of a "direct sense" not of reality, but "of life," which suggests that Life's power of cognition in its latest and fullest development is directed upon itself. The speech of Lilith with which the play concludes, while contriving to give a fairly full exposition of Shaw's general view is, on this particular point, singularly uninformative.

What, we want to know, do the Ancients *do* with their developed consciousness? What does their thought busy itself about? What is it that it is the ultimate purpose of Life to know?

Such answer as Shaw gives is contained in the two following passages from Lilith's last speech:

> "After passing a million goals they press on to the goal of redemption from the flesh, to the vortex freed from matter, to the whirlpool in pure intelligence that, when the world began, was a whirlpool in pure force. And though all that they have done seems but the first hour of the infinite work of creation, yet I will not supersede them until they have forded this last stream that lies between flesh and spirit, and disentangled their life from the matter that has always mocked it."
>
> "I brought Life into the whirlpool of force, and com-

pelled my enemy, Matter, to obey a living soul. But in enslaving Life's enemy I made him Life's master; for that is the end of all slavery; and now I shall see the slave set free and the enemy reconciled, the whirlpool become all Life and no matter."

These passages embody the following propositions:

(1) That Life was originally a whirlpool in pure force;

(2) that it entered into matter, used matter and compelled matter to obey it;

(3) that by so doing it became matter's slave;

(4) that the object of Life's development is to put an end to this slavery by winning free of or conquering matter. It is not clear whether matter still remains, Life having, as it were, merely disentangled itself from it, or whether matter is ultimately eliminated by Life, so that it ceases to be;

(5) that redemption from the flesh having been achieved, Life will become pure thought.

But if, insisting once again that thought must surely be *of* something and that that something must be other than the thinking about it, we repeat the question, what, then, does Life in its ultimate expression think about, there is no answer. The system, in fact, in its ultimate consummation seems to deny the truth upon which Shaw has so often insisted in the course of its development. We are told that we must not think about and concern ourselves with ourselves but lose ourselves in what is greater than and external to the self. But if we are Ancients, these admonitions no longer apparently apply, for in the case of the Ancients thought, so far as one can see, is directed only upon itself. To postulate that it should be directed upon anything else would be tantamount to introducing into the Shavian universe a timeless, static element whether conceived as God, as Forms, as the Absolute or, even, as mathematical relations, which Shaw's thought, dominated by the conviction that the evolutionary process is all that there is, can never quite bring itself explicitly to admit.

* * *

I propose to conclude by indicating first, the respects in which the Shavian philosophy carries the doctrine of Creative Evolution beyond the point at which it was left by his predecessor, Butler, and, secondly, some of its more obvious weaknesses.

### Likenesses of and Differences between the Shavian and Butlerian Philosophies

A conscious, creative, immaterial force expressing itself in matter and using and moulding matter in the pursuit of its own purposes is the premise taken as the starting point of both Shaw's and Butler's philosophies. They show a common outlook on many subsidiary matters, for example, each writer is a great adherent of practical intelligence; each sings the praises of common sense. Shaw, like Butler, hates professionals, especially doctors, and tends to look at people from a biological point of view, recognizing in those organisms which are best adapted to the purposes of living the most valuable products of evolution. Moreover, for Shaw as for Butler, such persons are those who, while possessing no culture and few intellectual attainments, nevertheless exhibit a store of instinctive rule-of-thumb philosophy. 'Enry Straker and Alfred Doolittle are the lineal descendants of Mrs. Jupp in *The Way of All Flesh*, and Yram in *Erewhon*. All these very pleasant and amusing people know what to do on all ordinary and extraordinary occasions, but none of them could tell you how they know it or why they ought to do it. Like some fortunate bridge players, they play the right card instinctively, while others after much thought and travail as often as not produce the wrong one.

So far the outlook of the two thinkers is the same; but when we push our inquiries a stage further, a marked difference reveals itself. Butler regards the operations of the speculative intellect as a pedantic futility, and appears to look forward with equanimity to the merging of the practical intellect in unconscious instinct. There is nothing in his writings to show that he does not think man would be better off without the intellect altogether, and that its gradual supersession may be expected as the next stage in human progress towards the goal of evolution. For Shaw, on the other hand, the operations of the intellect *are* the goal of evolution. While for both the Force that animates the universe is a single, unified, unconscious urge, it is, in Shaw, an unconscious urge struggling for consciousness. He admires the instinctively successful and practical man, but only because it is in such as he that Life, by achieving a momentary equilibrium in the present, prepares itself for new achievements in the future. Shaw glories in life; he glories in it to the extent of maintaining that if we are to live properly we must live longer; but he only wants us to live longer, in order that we may think more. Thus the Ancients in the last play of the *Back to Methuselah* Pentateuch, having achieved a relative emancipation from the needs and exigencies of material existence employ their freedom in the unfettered activity of the intellect. What does the intellect do? It contemplates. It is this contemplation, the occupation and the delight of mystics in all ages, that Shaw seems to regard as the object of evolution; it is for this that the whole experiment of life was undertaken. Butler prepared the way for this conception, but he did not share it. He devined the meaning and described the method of evolution, but he gave no hint of its ultimate purpose. The system with which Shaw presents us in *Back to Methuselah* is thus a definite advance on Butler's work. It embodies a constructive essay in philosophy, which was probably beyond the reach of Butler's more negative mind; though it may be doubted whether, if Butler had not lived, such an essay could have been made. In this, as in so much else, Butler was Socrates to Shaw's Plato.

## Reception of Shaw's Philosophy

It cannot be said that Shaw's philosophy has won wide acceptance. For this his eminence in other fields is, no doubt, in part responsible. The English find it hard to forgive a man for making more than one reputation, and Shaw has made at least half a dozen. It is easy, then, to play down his claims as a philosopher on the ground that the man who was a great prose-writer, playwright, orator, wit, political thinker and public figure could not also be endowed with the profundity of the original philosopher, apart altogether from the time, energy and industry which the pursuit of philosophy demands. This criticism, the fruit of sour grapes, is, I think, negligible. Shaw's eminence in each of the various departments I have mentioned enhances and does not detract from his eminence in the others; for his thought, as I have tried to show, is remarkably coherent and the doctrine of Creative Evolution informs and unifies his doctrines on every other topic. Another reason for the comparative neglect of the more philosophical aspect of Shaw's work is the contemporary appearance of two divergent developments of the creative evolutionary view, that of Bergson in *Creative Evolution* and that of S. Alexander in *Space, Time and Deity*, which, though they postulate the same metaphysical background as Shaw does, depart in their development of this background in radical particulars from Shaw's. As they were presented to the world in the more orthodox trappings of formal philosophical writings, they tended to occupy the spotlight of philosophical scrutiny and criticism to the exclusion of Shaw. As one who has endeavoured, not very successfully, to provide a formal philosophical setting for Shaw's doctrines,[1] I can vouch from personal experience for the com-

[1] In *Matter, Life and Value* (Oxford University Press).

parative absence of serious attention which they have evoked. So much having been said by way of explanation and extenuation, it must be pointed out that there are manifest points of weakness upon which serious criticism, if it had, in fact, been accorded, could have fastened.

### The Difficulty of End or Goal

Of these the most important are: (1) The neglect, to which attention has already been drawn, to make provision for any end or goal upon which the developed consciousness of the evolving Life Force could be directed. Shaw presents us with a dualistic universe which contains Life and matter in which Life incarnates itself and through which Life develops. But if we ask, to what end does it develop, there is no answer. There is, that is to say, no element of perfect or changeless reality in Shaw's scheme, the apprehension and realization of which might be regarded as forming the purpose and goal of the evolutionary process. Shaw's cosmic scheme would seem to demand the inclusion of precisely such an element, an element of absolute value. Shaw might have said that Life evolved in matter, through matter and beyond matter to a knowledge of value. He hints as much, but never explicitly says it.

### The Difficulty of the Relation Between Life and Matter

(2) No satisfactory account is given of the relation between Life and matter. Life enters into matter, uses and moulds it. But how? We are not told. The traditional problem of the relation of Life to matter, of the spaceless to the spatial, of the animating spirit to the animated medium is not so much solved as begged. Sometimes Shaw speaks of matter as attracting Life. "What was wrong," says Pygmalion in the last play of *Back to Methuselah* "with the synthetic protoplasm was

that it could not fix and conduct the Life Force. It was like a wooden magnet or a lightning conductor made of silk; it would not take the current." The metaphor here is that of an electric current running down a wire; different kinds of wire can, presumably, take different potentials of current. More often we are simply told that Life or evolution "must meanwhile struggle with matter and circumstance by the method of trial and error," in order to rise above "matter and circumstance." It may, of course, be the case that the relation is ineffable and can only be prefigured in the language of metaphor and myth; but to many this fact, if fact it be, would seem so intractable and the relation which it conceals so unthinkable, that they would insist on demanding the abandonment of the dualistic scheme which requires it and substitute a monistic explanation either, like the materialist in terms of matter alone or, like the idealist in terms of Life or mind alone. The reflection that the unexplained relationship between Life and matter entails and includes the vexed question of the relationship within the living organism between mind and body, only serves to throw into high relief the enormity of the assumption that Shaw leaves as it were ungrounded. The two loose ends, mind and body, are never tied together, but are left dangling.

## The Difficulty of Free Will

(3) It is never clear how far, for Shaw, the individual is free. Is he merely a vehicle for the canalisation and subsequent development of the Life Force, or can he win some measure of freedom from Life's promptings? In the first event, he is a mere fountain-pen for conveying the stream of Life, no more responsible for what he does than is the pen for what it writes. It is fairly clear that Shaw does not mean this. For if the individual were not in some sense free, the admonitions and exhortations and injunctions of which Shaw's practical philosophy consists would be beside the point. To be told, for exam-

ple, that success in life consists in being used in pursuit of its purposes by the power that made you, clearly implies that it is open to you to resist being used in this way, open to you to follow your own purposes, in fact, to fail.

This, I have no doubt, is Shaw's view. We are, at best, imperfect instruments of Life's purpose. In particular, we busy ourselves with our own concerns instead of using ourselves up in Life's service, and although Life does its best to point out to us through the instrumentality of Shaw and other wise men, whom it sends into the world "to give conscious expression to its instinctive purpose," the way it would have us go, and encourages us to follow it by contriving that the life of direct pleasure-seeking will be unrewarding even in terms of pleasure, nevertheless, we do in fact all too frequently go astray.

Assuming, then, that we do have freedom, three difficulties arise. (a) First, is our freedom only a freedom to go wrong? Are we, when we go right, when, that is to say, we go about Life's business, mere automata, responding to the promptings and impulses that reach us from Life, whereas when we assert our own wills and go our own ways, when, in fact, we thwart Life's purposes, we are acting as self-determining individuals? This is a depressing view to take of human free will.

(b) If we are free, whence do we derive the energy which enables us to pursue a course divergent from Life's purpose in regard to us? Granted that we are instruments of life, how can the instrument turn against the hand that wields it? Is it, perhaps, the interposition of matter between the main stream of Life and its individual expressions that confers a measure of freedom upon the latter, much as a line of rocks lying athwart a river will diversify it into a number of different streamlets, each of which may pursue its own course, though *the energy with which it pursues* is that of the parent river. This suggestion, perhaps, is not unplausible; but besides making use of a metaphor which may well be inadmissible, it derives the fact of freedom from the interposition of matter which limits the power of Life over its individual expressions. Shaw himself never, so far as I know, tackles this difficulty.

(c) It may and has been urged that Shaw's theory provides a pitiably inadequate expression of the facts of moral experience.

## JAMES BRIDIE

### *SHAW AS DRAMATIST*

### *(including a Surrealist Life of G.B.S.)*

*When Leighton was President of the Royal Academy, a lady was praising him to Whistler for his wit, his personal beauty, his learning and his manifold talents. Whistler took a tug at his white forelock and murmured "Paints too, I'm told."*

ONE of the manœuvres of Army Psychologists is to ask a victim the difference or similarity between a horse, a penny and a piece of string. It is doubtful whether our knowledge of any of these objects is advanced by the answers they receive; but there must be some object in putting the question though I cannot, at the moment, think what it is. The trick of associating Shaw with Molière may evoke from this minor professional Dramatist at least an honester estimate of that great one than if the minor had racked his brains to produce a conventional critical essay. Anyhow I am not a Critic. I am a writer of compositions in which character expresses itself by contrast. I shall attempt the sort of thing I know something about.

The traditional first step is to examine what are called "the backgrounds" of the two men. This is the historical method of approach and it seems to be very popular.

George Bernard Shaw, so far as I can remember, was born in Dublin in 1856. There is a legend that he is of Scottish extraction and this legend also attaches to Molière. This does not carry us very far in our research, for the same legend attaches to nearly all great men and is very often true. Even if it is true in this case and Shaw is, in fact, the rightful Thane of Fife, it is quite irrelevant and need not detain us.

So far as I can remember without consulting works of reference, it was shortly after the Crimean War and the Indian Mutiny that Shaw's father found himself in straitened circumstances and emigrated to London with his family. Mrs. Shaw was what used to be called "well connected" and her relatives, if my memory is to be trusted, secured for Mr. Shaw, Sr., the post of Superintendent of Victorian Upholstery to her Majesty the Queen. The remuneration attached to this post was not large but Mr. Shaw and his forbears had been sufficiently long in Ireland to have absorbed the Hibernian attitude of mind to any sum of money that could be called a fortune. He sent little George Bernard to Eton. There is a popular tradition that, during his stay at that educational establishment, he was fag to the Duke of Connaught and that his skill in preparing hot buttered toast and in preserving the nap of his master's silk hat were to stand him in good stead in later years.

After leaving Eton, he is said to have gone to Oxford where he read History with the idea of being later admitted to the Bar. He read also the Classics and Metaphysics and was a member of the O.U.D.S. His promising academic career was cut short by the death of his father—by this time Sir George Carr Shaw, K.C.V.O.—and his appointment, at an early age, to his father's position in the Royal Household. He held this position for six years. He was probably responsible for the tartan decorations at Balmoral Castle and has been credited with the invention of the Osborne tartan, which made such a tasteful colour scheme for pencil cases and other simple gifts and mementoes.

Fate and the Hibernian temperament would not allow young George to remain for long in a sinecure office and in any state of comparative obscurity, however tempered by grandeur. We find him in 1877 resigning his post and investing his small savings in converting a Good Templar's Hall near

Shaftesbury Avenue into a Theatre for the production of stage plays. I believe that he went bankrupt two years later and took his Company for an extended tour of what were then known as the Provinces.

The tour was extended indeed. It lasted for seven years, presenting all the vicissitudes common to such enterprises. The plays of Shakespeare and others were performed in theatres, in tents, in sheds, in barns. These peripatetics came to a halt in Sligo, which, I need hardly remind you, is situated in the Dukedom of Shaw's old fag master at Eton. It happened that His Royal Highness was visiting the district at the time when Shaw's barnstormers were giving performances. A Command Performance was given before the Duke at the house of his host. The play was *The Merry Wives of Windsor*, and Shaw, if my memory serves me aright, took the part of Falstaff. The Duke was so delighted by the interpretation of the humours of the Fat Knight, that he endowed a Theatre Royal at Sligo, where, for four happy and lucrative years, Shaw entertained the simple inhabitants with Repertory. The plays were mostly adaptations from the Norwegian or the German and Shaw himself played the leading character parts.

This state of security was not to last. The Duke revisited Sligo; witnessed a performance, and formed the impression that Shaw was an atheist and a bad influence. He withdrew his patronage and his endowment and Shaw returned to London after fifteen years "on the road."

He opened at the Haymarket Theatre with *Ghosts* and *Widowers' Houses*. *Ghosts* was heartily disliked both by the critics and by the Public; but *Widowers' Houses* had a success of esteem mainly because of a very amusing performance by the author in the part of William de Burgh Cokaygne. The Shaw Theatre had arrived.

Yet, in spite of his efforts to improve the public taste by presenting the tragedies and dramas of Arthur Wing Pinero, Henrik Ibsen, Gerhart Hauptmann and others, the Public insisted on regarding Shaw as a comedian *pur sang*, and it is as a comedian he will go down to posterity, though his tragedy, based on the life of Jeanne d'Arc, was a success.

To the verdict of the Public, Shaw bowed his head and profited by this gesture. Yet the popular path he had chosen was not, entirely, a bed of roses. His thinly veiled attacks on Mr. Gladstone, Lord Salisbury, John Brown, the Archbishop of Canterbury, Sir Henry Irving, Arthur Roberts, Mr. Spurgeon, Mrs. Langtry, Lord Lonsdale, and Mr. Wilson Barrett aroused enmity in various quarters. On one occasion he was publicly beaten by Lord Alfred Douglas in St. James's Park; and acts of sabotage were, as they say, of daily occurrence in the theatres at which he was appearing. By way of a holiday he took a company to Cape Town during the first South African War; but, as he proposed to entertain the Troops with *Mrs. Warren's Profession*, the G.O.C. in C. returned him to Southampton by the first Union Castle steamer.

Probably by this time you have realized that I have got my protagonists a little muddled. I have an uneasy feeling that my account of Shaw's life has, in places, strayed from the path of strict accuracy. For example, he is not even mentioned in a recent biography of the Duke of Connaught. But, handy-dandy, as King Lear put it, most of these things might easily have happened to Shaw. Indeed, something very like them happened to Pocquelin. Pocquelin *was* a King's upholsterer after being a notable scholar in a fashionable establishment. He started an unsuccessful theatre in the capital of his country when he was twenty-one. He spent fifteen years in the provinces. He was, for a time, protégé of a Royal Prince. And his ENSA tour was cut short by the Authorities.

On the other hand, there is a tradition that Shaw learned his craft on the audience side of the footlights and commenced Dramatist only when he was well over forty.

At the same time, I doubt whether my peculiar blunder—

a blunder that could not have been made by anybody with a true historical sense—is really a capital mistake. Is an historical sense, after all, everything? Men of genius have a disconcerting habit of leaping out of their centuries. They even, from time to time, make History itself look a little foolish. Who to-day cares much what Mazarin said in 1658 or what were the views of Colbert on the Gold Standard or token payments? Fouquet was no doubt as important a man in his day as Lord Catto is in ours. But his day is done. The day of John Baptist Pocquelin is not done. Nor will it be surprising if Frenchmen are talking about Georges Bernard-Shaw long after they have forgotten the names of Mr. Eden, Mr. Bevin, and Mr. Stettinius.

There is another reason why the national, political, economic and sociological backgrounds of our heroes are of minor importance. They are men of the Theatre and the sanctions of the Theatre are curious and precise.

The Theatre is *insulated* against its times. We have only to read the Elizabethans and then to consider the extraordinary things that were happening in the world around them to realize the truth of this observation. The dramatist must, then, write matter that can be understood by his little world within a world. Hardly any other writer is in such a case. The novelist *does* meet an occasional human being who complains to him about rent restriction or boasts about passenger transport or tells him about penicillin. So we are able to measure his times against Dickens and Dickens against his times, Balzac against his France and France against Balzac. Even when Dumas and Scott write out of their own times they try for verisimilitude. We can picture a France and an era from the Musketeer novels and a British semi-civilization from Scott.

The dramatist is different. Actors talk and live nothing but Theatre. They might be monks in a Trappist Monastery for all the world means to them. They steal a gloss from the outside world; but Troilus and Cressida, Romeo and Juliet are, in essence, plays about rival Theatre Companies on the banks of the Thames. We learn nothing of Troy or of "fair Verona" from these plays.

This may be a disadvantage; but there is a corresponding advantage. Some playmakers acquire greatness from this very lack of the provincial touch. Their practical ignorance of the detailed daily life of ordinary individual human beings leads them to universalize the creatures. We do not see on the stage our butcher, our baker, our candlestick-maker, but a dressed up simulacrum of each, that is Man himself.

That is why Molière's plays are everybody's plays; for he was a Man of the Theatre if ever there was one. We should expect to find Shaw an exception to our rule. In point of fact we do not. Shaw had some contact with the realities of daily life, though it was the contact of a teacher, a prophet, a reformer; but the Stage Door always beckoned him. It was his avenue of escape. To say truth, real life was always a little too much for Shaw. It is said that in the Kingdom of the Blind the one-eyed man is King. Wells has pointed out, in a beautiful and terrifying short story, the fallacy of this idea. In the Kingdom of the Blind, the one-eyed man expects to be King, but finds himself merely an oddity and a resented oddity at that. So it was with Shaw till he escaped into the Theatre.

There is no complete oblivion for the man of genius. Shaw did take with him into the Theatre some of the detail and hurly-burly of the shops, villas and institutes. He did not become any the less a Socialist because he was living in a land of make-believe. Molière was caught younger, but he too had some detailed knowledge of people and things. He knew the court of Louis XIV with its caste system, its elastic moral code, its practicality, its intrigues, its economics and its habit of celebrating in vacuo. It is pleasant to speculate what Shaw might have picked up in the corresponding court of Merry King Charles. Shaw has a curious affection for that monarch probably because of the law that draws opposites to opposites. Charles was a loathsome-looking, cynical, treacherous, cowardly cheat, liar, thief, debauchee, vulgarian, hypocrite, quisling and plain scoundrel. Louis XIV was at least a gentleman who knew how to handle poets and artists. Charles was no gentleman and he corrupted poets and artists as he corrupted everything else in the country to which he came as an unmitigated curse. He might have corrupted Shaw and turned him into a Chauvinist like Dryden or a snob like Congreve. Happy is the dramatist who has no history.

We have taken a confused, nystagmoid, astigmatic glance at the backgrounds of these two writers. We have learned very little from this glance and I have tried to explain why it is unlikely that we ever could learn very much. We shall be on safer ground if we proceed now to a consideration of their work.

In so far as their backgrounds affect their work at all we find more or less what we might expect. That is to say, Molière has an easy confident grace in handling his material. He is completely at home in the Theatre. He knows exactly how to take liberties and how far he can go. It is agreeable to compare the risks he takes with his audiences with the most daring experiments of the most daring our modern experimentalists. In this peculiar kind of mastery he leaves Shaw panting far behind. Even in his latest majestic pattern plays (*Geneva* and *Good King Charles*) Shaw never achieves the superb confidence in his own hypnotic power that Molière shows in his most casual pieces.

I could, perhaps, make this clearer by discussing two plays about matrimony, one by Molière and the other by Shaw. Mr. Hilaire Belloc says of *Le Misanthrope*: "The supreme art of words is to produce a multiple and profound effect with simplicity in construction. There is hardly in this masterpiece one phrase which is not the phrase of convention or of daily use. Where the words are not the words that men used, or the sentences the sentences they used at the court of Louis XIV, then they are the words conventionally used in the heroic couplets of that day. And each character has a set of lines to declaim (not very much), and there is, you may say, no rhetoric, and there is, you may say, no lyric, no deliberate poignancy; one might venture a paradox and say that in *Le Misanthrope* there was no 'effect,' meaning no sudden, sharp, contrasted effect. This mighty comedy of Molière's represents no more than the simplest conjunction, the everyday business of a man who expects too much of mankind, who is in love and expects too much of the lady, who has a friend, a man who gives him good advice, and another friend, a woman, who herself would marry him willingly enough, and yet who advises him quietly and is more a support than a lover. There is hardly any plot—merely the discovery that the young widow for whom the Misanthrope feels such passion is a chatterbox and runs her friends down behind their backs for the sake of tattle. There is the fatuous mad versifier. There are the silly men of the world.

"Such are the materials of *Le Misanthrope*, common stones, and into them a man did once breathe such life that he made a thing standing quite apart from all his other creations, and something higher than any other had accomplished. What depths and further depths! What suggestions to the left and to the right! What infinite complexity of real character (and just that infinite complexity of real character exists in all of us), shines through those few pages, illumines and glorifies two hours of acting on a stage!

". . . It is not single lines; it is the whole river of the thing, high in flood tide, up to the top of its banks, broad, deep, majestic, and upon a scale to which (one would have thought) mere man could never reach.

"All that!

"For two hours, hearing this thing, I was quite outside the world; and the memory of it is a possession which should endure, I think, for ever; by which word I mean, even beyond the limitations of this life. But therein I may be wrong."

That is an account by a man of letters of the first quality, who has never been so much as a hanger-on of the Theatre. Of its sort it could hardly be better. To get out of the fresh air into the region of technical jargon, it may be said that *Le Misanthrope* is almost purely a conversation piece. The curious fact that it is written in verse does not invalidate this description. If it had been submitted to the approval of a football reporter of a provincial daily, or even to the dramatic critic of a great national newspaper, it is ten to one that the expert in question would have denied its right to be called a play at all. But an intelligent layman has accepted it as a comedy, and the audience, and not the critic, is the ultimate judge.

One of Bernard Shaw's earliest attempts at a conversation piece was the play *Getting Married*. I should like to compare the two plays from a technical point of view, merely to illustrate this professional confidence of Molière's.

In the first place, Shaw explicitly and implicitly labelled his play as a conversation piece. He meant it to be a two and a half hour talk about matrimony through the mouths of actors, and deliberately purged it of any conventional plot. He did not divide it into scenes and acts, but gave his audience a rest by splitting the play arbitrarily almost in the middle of a sentence. Molière, on the other hand, cast his play in the conventional shape, deceived his audience further by writing it in rhyming couplets, and made his scene and act divisions correspond to phases of the argument, and not to phases of the action—for there was practically no action at all. So far Shaw appears to be the more daring experimenter; but it wasn't very long before, relatively speaking, he lost his nerve. A play depends, thought Shaw (the hard baked dramatic critic), on character and plot. If we discard plot we must heighten character. So he filled his play with almost Gilbertian grotesques—a Laodicean Bishop, a sentimental General, a sophisticated Don Juan intoxicated with the exuberance of his own verbosity, and a magnificently incredible Lady Mayoress. Incidentally, he imitated Molière to the extent of playing a character in his own play. He appeared as a beadle and announced Her Worship. These characters rapidly took their heads, and before he knew where he was his conversation piece was a welter of small plots. It was only after his eightieth birthday that he realized that talk was enough if the talk was good enough. He had always known this, but he had to pass the allotted span before he had the mastery to put it into practice. Molière had achieved that mastery in 1666.

As Belloc suggests, there is not a single grotesque from beginning to end of *The Misanthrope*. They are all extremely ordinary people. The plot is so simple as to be almost nonexistent and there are no subsidiary plots. I ask you for a moment to pause and consider the self-restraint of a master of grotesque characterizations in declining to play his strongest card in a very dangerous game. Molière's Theatre was a much more terrifying place than Shaw's. A number of writers of genius had shown exactly what to expect in the Theatre, and any deviation from the accepted form was not unlikely to bring ruin about the deviator's head. Molière's success in *The Misanthrope* was the measure of his complete strength and utter knowledge of what he could do with the instruments in his hand.

Before we go on to our next comparison, I should like to elaborate for a moment what I have said about Molière's Theatre being terrifying. It did not exist in a time when a few coughs during the performance or a surly notice after it would break a dramatist's heart. Once, in Molière's Theatre in Paris, the actors put up an objection to dead-heads. They thought that the musketeers, guards, Palace police, Cabinet Ministers and so on ought to pay for admission. Molière, accordingly, suspended the free list. The dead-heads replied by killing the man at the box office—each paying for admission with a stab. Young Bejart made them laugh by coming on the stage in his comic make-up as an old man and praying them to spare his life as he had so little of it left to live. The dead-heads were so pleased at this that they were content to pass the whole incident off with a light laugh. But the box-office man was dead, and the women of the company in a great fright. There was no performance that night. On the next night, to Molière's everlasting glory, he made the dead-heads pay for admission.

You will remember, then, when I come to the short passage from Molière I am about to quote, that it was written in the time of the Three Musketeers. I am going to quote a little bit of Shaw and a little bit of Molière to show you how they handle the same sort of subject. I should like you to remember another thing. Molière himself said that comedies are made only to be played. Pray visualize, during the reading, all the play of the Theatre. The incident the dramatists are trying to portray is a conversation between doctors. Most of you are familiar with *The Doctor's Dilemma.* It was written in 1906 in good King Edward's glorious days. A number of doctors arrive to congratulate Sir Colenso Ridgeon on his knighthood.

Sir Patrick Cullen is a doctor of the old school. Cutler Walpole is a surgeon. Sir Ralph Bloomfield Bonnington is a fashionable physician. Walpole believes that most illnesses are due to septicæmia; but the sepsis takes it origin in a thing called the nuciform sac, and that this organ ought to be removed by surgery. Bonnington believes in himself. Sir Patrick believes in nothing. I shall take the scene from Bonnington's entrance.

B. B.: Aha! Sir Colenso. Sir Colenso, eh? Welcome to the order of Knighthood.

RIDGEON (*shaking hands*): Thank you, B. B.

B. B.: What! Sir Patrick! And how are we to-day? A little chilly? A little stiff? But hale and still the cleverest of us all. (SIR PATRICK *grunts.*)

What! Walpole! The absent-minded beggar: eh?

WALPOLE: What does that mean?

B. B.: Have you forgotten the lovely opera singer I sent you to have that growth taken off her vocal chords?

WALPOLE (*springing to his feet*): Great Heavens, man, you don't mean to say you sent her for a throat operation?

B. B. (*archly*): Aha! Aha! Aha! (*Trilling like a lark as he shakes his finger at* WALPOLE.)

You removed her nuciform sac. Well, well! Force of habit! Force of habit! Never mind, n-e-v-e-r mind. She got back her voice after it and thinks you the greatest surgeon alive; and so you are, so you are, so you are.

WALPOLE: Blood poisoning. I see. I see. (*He sits down again.*)

PATRICK: And how is a certain distinguished family getting on under your care, Sir Ralph?

B. B.: Our friend Ridgeon will be gratified to hear that I have tried his opsonin treatment on little Prince Henry with complete success.

RIDGEON: But how?

B. B.: I suspected typhoid: the head gardener's boy had it; so I just called at St. Anne's one day and got a tube of your very excellent serum. You were out unfortunately.

RIDGEON: I hope they explained to you carefully . . .

B. B.: Lord bless you, my dear fellow, I didn't need any explanations. I'd left my wife in the carriage at the door; and I'd no time to be taught my business by your young chaps. I know all about it. I've handled these anti-toxins ever since they first came out.

RIDGEON: But they're not anti-toxins; and they're dangerous unless you use them at the right time.

B. B.: Of course they are. Everything is dangerous unless you take it at the right time. An apple at breakfast does you good: an apple at bedtime upsets you for a week. There are only two rules for anti-toxins. First, don't be afraid of them. Second, inject them a quarter of an hour before meals three times a day.

RIDGEON: Great Heavens, B. B., no, no, no.

B. B.: Yes, yes, Colly . . .

He explains that the little Prince has got well as a result of his treatment and begins to expatiate on disease, which, he says, is due to the lodgment of a pathogenic germ in the system. He cannot conceive disease existing without germs. "Can you," he says, "show me a case of diphtheria without the bacillus?" Sir Patrick says: "No! but I can show you the same bacillus without the disease in your own throat."

B. B.: No, not the same, Sir Patrick. It is an entirely different bacillus. Only the two are, unfortunately, so exactly alike that you cannot see the difference. You must understand, my dear Sir Patrick, that every one of these interesting little creatures has an imitator. Just as men imitate each other, the germs imitate each other. There is the genuine diphtheria bacillus discovered by Loeffler; and there is the pseudo-bacillus, exactly like it, which you could find, as you say, in my own throat.

SIR PATRICK: And how do you tell one from the other?

B. B.: Well, obviously, if the bacillus is the genuine Loeffler, you have diphtheria; and if it's the pseudo-bacillus, you're quite well. Nothing simpler. Science is always simple and always profound. . . .

No doubt you remember the scene. B. B. goes on piling absurdity on absurdity and the effect on the stage is very funny indeed. There is only one thing wrong with it. Doctors never in their lives talked like that to one another. If you want to know how they do talk you must jump back nearly three hundred years, and see how Molière describes a consultation in *L'Amour Médecin,* or *Doctor Cupid.* In the second act of that play Drs. des Fonandres, Thomes, Macroton and Bahys meet in consultation. They sit down and cough, and the following conversation takes place:

FONANDRES: How enormous Paris is getting! I find as my

practice improves that I have to make some incredible journeys.

TOMES: I must say I find my new Delage makes an enormous difference. You'd hardly believe my mileage.

FONANDRES: I have a Rolls, of course. I find it more worth while. Marvellous engine. It's impossible to wear it out.

TOMES: D'you know what I've done in my Delage to-day? My first visit was near the Arsenal; I went from the Arsenal to St. Germains; from St. Germains to the end of the Marshes; from the Marshes to the St. Honoré Gate; from the St. Honoré Gate to the Faubourg St. Jacques; from the Faubourg St. Jacques to the Port de Richelieu; from the Port de Richelieu, here; and after that I've got to go to the Palais Royale.

FONANDRES: I've done all that, too, and I've been to Ruel to see a patient.

TOMES: Talking of that, what do you think of the row in the Faculty between Theophrastus and Artemius?

FONANDRES: Artemius is right.

TOMES: I agree. Of course the patient died, and I think Theophrastus probably made a better shot at the diagnosis; but as things were I think he was in the wrong, and he was damned impertinent to his Chief. After all, we've got to play the game, haven't we?

FONANDRES: Of course. It's a simple matter of etiquette.

TOMES: You can't be too careful about things like that. I was called in consultation the other day and found I was expected to meet a fellow who turned out to be a damned quack. Naturally I stuck out to get things regularized and we had quite a set-to. The people of the house did what they could, but I stuck to my guns. It was a bit embarrassing, especially as the patient died during our conversation.

FONANDRES: Well, well, they've got to be taught decent behaviour—especially some of these youngsters.

TOMES: I mean to say a dead man is a dead man and that's that; but if you allow slack methods the whole profession goes to blazes. . . .

You will notice the silence of two of the doctors during this conversation. One of them, no doubt, runs an Austin and the other a Ford, and it is not for them to open their mouths when the great men are speaking; but they are heard later on. Macroton is a slow man who spreads his thoughts out carefully:

"Sir, in these matters we must proceed with circumspection and do nothing inconsiderately as the saying is."

Bahys is a live-wire who can hardly keep up with his own eloquence. He likes purging and bleeding. Macroton is all for the exhibition in the first instance of some little anodyne medicines—refreshing juleps and syrups to be given in the patient's barley-water.

I am afraid that these passages suggest a great superiority in the man of the Theatre as against the man of the world and his play on human foibles. Both were concerned to show that the medical profession was a close corporation of humbugs. Shaw took Rowlandson and Gilray as his models and attempted to use the bludgeon. Unfortunately he was not sufficiently informed as to where to hit his adversary. The dullest medical student in 1906 knew more about bacteriology than Shaw; and however ignorant and silly a doctor may be he is never a tenth as ignorant or a quarter so silly as B. B. If we attack a man for ignorance, we must be perfectly certain that we know something of the subject of which he is ignorant.

Molière, on the other hand, has all the vital spots mapped out before he begins his attack, and uses his rapier according to the laws of combat. He does not attack his doctors because they are ignorant. On the contrary, their heads are crammed with superfluous and irrelevant knowledge, and he knows it.

He attacks them for their vanity, their self-interest, their pedantry and their indifference. That is to say, he is at the advantage to which I referred earlier in this essay. He is able to universalize his creatures and to select from the incidents of their daily life only such detail as helps to fill out his picture. You must read the Doctors' scenes from *The Doctor's Dilemma* and *Doctor Cupid* yourself. All I have tried to do is to indicate that one picture is good and the other is not so good and why this should be so.

The comparison is, perhaps, unfair to Shaw. I can, perhaps, level matters up by saying that *The Doctor's Dilemma* is a much better play than *L'Amour Médecin*, which is, as it was intended to be, an amusing trifle and nothing more. It was only incidentally that Molière gave a lesson to the medical profession that still stands—a lesson they will do well not to forget.

To tell you the truth, Molière was much more concerned with amusing his audiences than with interesting them. "It is a strange business," he says, "this, of making decent people laugh." He showed people how to live by demonstration and awful example rather than by argument, although he knew very well that a play was none the worse of a good argument.

It is here that comparison and contrast become a little sharper. Molière composed most of his comedies on a central theme of love, intrigue and misunderstanding. Sometimes they revolved round a gigantesque central figure who personified greed, hypocrisy, hypochondria or some other form of monstrous egoism. If he was preoccupied with any one subject it was the love of old men for young women. He invariably made the old man look ridiculous. He himself had married a woman much younger than he was in circumstances which his enemies chose to regard as dubious. He had the rare gift of translating his own private miseries into laughter.

He shared a preoccupation with Shaw in his sympathy with the emancipation of women. Indeed, he was almost the first dramatist to show young women as individual creatures with souls to be damned and not as decorative appendages to the male sex. How he contrived to work such dangerous subjects into the traditional comedy pattern of his time is his own secret.

When we turn to Shaw's range of theme or subject it is like passing from a very deep (even bottomless) inland lake to the Atlantic Ocean. In subject alone no other dramatist has ever had such a range with the possible exception of Shakespeare. Nothing human is alien to that old gentleman whether he understands it or not. He is afraid of nothing but erotic emotion and he sits on the fence and puts out his tongue at it. He believes that every picture should tell a story and a moral story at that. He is probably the leader of the revolution against the theory of Art for Art's sake that so prevailed in the studios and garrets in the beginning of this century.

It may not be entirely meaningless to say that Shaw's journey is from the general to the particular, and that Molière's is from the particular to the general. That may be why persons facing in the opposite direction have accused each of them of lack of seriousness. Sundry dukes and marquises complained of Molière that in such a play as *Les Femmes Savantes* he was wasting the resources of the Theatre by displaying a lot of silly women in whom nobody was interested. Now, people who look from the particular to the general are very interested indeed in silly women. It is only those who look from the general to the particular who are unable to find that silly women have any cosmic significance. In the same way Shaw was reproached for treating such particulars as the family and the rites of religion with some levity. To these people, the father, the mother and the priest were objects of great importance. To Shaw they are incidents in an enormous pattern.

This difference between the two men in the matter of approach is illustrated by their treatment of the story of *Don Juan*. Molière found the story in a play by Tirso de Molina, the Spanish dramatist. The play was called *El Burlador de Sevilla y Convidado de Piedra.* I have not read the older play, nor, indeed, any of Tirso's surviving works; but I understand from books of reference that he intended the play as a study of depravity. That is to say, his approach was from the general to the particular. Molière is interested in his libertine as a man, very much as Byron was in later years. We are shown by a hundred swift economical touches the rascal's selfishness, self-possession, determination, ingenuity, knowledge of the trade of seduction and of the feminine nature, reckless courage, wit, improvisation and unscrupulousness—all highly individual qualities. We are reminded through the mouth of his servant that the man bears a very unfortunate relationship to the moral universe; but the moral universe is not the hero of the story as it was apt to become in the works of Shaw. It is the man himself who matters to Molière.

Shaw uses the Don as an instrument to drive home one of his theories about human biology. In *Man and Superman* the Don proves with unparalleled eloquence that he is merely a plaything of the Life Force, and that the Life Force inhabits not himself but Donna Elvira and the other ladies who are determined to propagate the human race and see in him a suitable agent for this purpose. Like the lady spiders, they are prepared to devour him when he has served their turn. He himself asks nothing more than to be allowed to reflect and invent.

It is here that the background of the two writers takes on some importance. Shaw's acquaintance in his younger days was chiefly among men and women who were abnormal to their times. You remember the story of the lady who wrote to Shaw inviting him to become the father of her child on the grounds that a combination of her beauty and his intellect would be something very remarkable indeed. Shaw made the obvious reply that the child might have his beauty and her brains. Molière's acquaintance was mainly among actresses, who would not have talked, or at least thought, any such nonsense. If they had, Molière would not have believed them. Such love-making belongs to the society of those long-haired men and short-haired women of whom Mr. H. G. Wells spoke on one occasion when he was exchanging abuse with Mr. Shaw. You remember what Stevenson said after reading *Love Among the Artists?* "Golly, what women!"

Be that as it may, we have here an excellent comparison of the methods of the two men, and the discrimination between their fundamental outlooks on life. Please do not think that I am decrying Shaw's powers of characterization any more than I am decrying Molière's powers of generalization. I am merely comparing their attitudes. Shaw may not have created a Tartuffe; a De Pourceaugnac, a Jourdain, a Célimène; but he has given us Alfred Doolittle, Androcles, General Gascoigne, William the Waiter, Warwick, Bluntschli, Lady Cecily, Dubedat, Shotover, Lickcheese, Mrs. Warren and Ellie Dunn and fifty more varied and living characters. His John Tanner is as good as Molière's Don in an entirely different way. I have no patience with people who say that Shaw can only create walking gramophones.

In our wanderings in and about the subject set us by the examiners we have contrived to forget a good deal of essential detail about the two men. I say that we have *contrived* to forget because we cannot find a common ground for the two men unless we neglect almost everything that is dear to historians. We must not even envisage their private social and emotional histories and environments. If we had to compare and contrast Mr. Shaw and Mr. Noel Coward—an almost impossible task—we should be confronted with two parallel lines that did not meet however far they were produced in either direction, and yet they are both distinguished dramatists belonging to the same period and working in the same workshop. Molière's workshop was usually a converted tennis-court. The stage was draped with tapestries and entrances and exits were made through curtains. It was lit by candles at the back and sides and occasionally by a four-candled candelabrum. The band was a flute and a drum or two fiddlers. The prices of admission were 5d. for seats and 2½d. for standing-room. Latecomers often walked across the stage. It is a far cry from that to the Haymarket Theatre of to-day.

It is a further cry when we examine the domestic circumstances of the two men. Molière lived the life of a strolling player with its perpetual accompaniments of sentiment, scandal and financial embarrassment. To paraphrase the celebrated old lady, "How different from the family life of our own dear Shaw." It is a long time since a dramatist was brutally assaulted by a dissatisfied Marquis. The only rewarding method is to take our heroes out of time and place and consider what they were trying to do, and how they did it. We must forget that Molière wore a huge, curly, and probably verminous wig and frills round his knickerbockers; and that Shaw wore Jaeger suits and red (and later snow-white) whiskers. We must even forget that Shaw is an Irishman and Molière was a Frenchman. We must regard them as denationalized abstractions like the Pope. The reward of this difficult enterprise is not great. We find that our two figures are both remarkable wits. We find that each of them is rash enough to bring philosophical ideas into the Theatre. We find them both lashing out at hypocrites, God-mongers, business men, and members of the Medical Profession. We find them both superior to Shakespeare but inferior to Dickens in the creation of characters—real people who suddenly came into existence without the inconvenience of being born. We find from their work that they are both great Humanists and very agreeable men. We find that they both interest themselves in Don Juan. We find them both experimenting in theatrical forms invented for them by their predecessors and also inventing forms of their own. We find them both happier in forms of their own invention or in using traditional forms to hold a content for which they were never intended. Isaac could not have felt more uncomfortable when the voice of Jacob followed the touch of the hairy gloves than Richard Mansfield felt when he tried to make head or tail out of *The Devil's Disciple.*

Many of these characteristics are common to all dramatists who are entitled to be called great. Indeed they are symptoms of greatness. Perhaps after all there is some value in our fantastic comparison. It helps to confirm a strong suspicion that Shaw is a very great artist indeed. All roads, however winding, seem to lead to that conclusion.

There is another point of resemblance that stamps both men unmistakably as men of genius. A genius is a person in whom Providence takes an intense and often capricious interest. Providence has taken a characteristic hand in the life and work of both Shaw and Molière. At the time of writing the author of *Back to Methuselah* shows every sign of having to put up with three or four hundred years of active and intelligent endeavour. Molière was struck by a terrible and fatal illness during a performance of *Le Malade Imaginaire.* This was in the noblest vein of true dramatic irony and we are safe in saying that Molière appreciated it. The joke on Shaw is a little more intellectual, which shows that Providence appreciates at least one of the differences between Shaw and Molière. Shaw himself, at any rate, sees the joke.

## LORD DUNSANY

### *A PERMANENT QUALITY*

I SAW one of Shaw's plays the other day which must have been written fifty years ago and it wore perfectly well and showed no signs of deterioration which often comes to things written in other generations like fallen leaves that do not outlast their year. This shows that his work has a permanent quality, as we all supposed it had when his plays were fresh.

He is one of those men that look at life and tell us what it is like and there are not a great many of them; all the rest take it for granted and so respect the good and the bad with equal fervour and were it not for the few writers and artists who put these things into separate heaps it is probable that nobody would be able to tell one from the other. I am sure that all of us see a little more clearly from having had Shaw to point things out for us.

## PROFESSOR J. D. BERNAL, F.R.S.

### *SHAW THE SCIENTIST*

"All problems are finally scientific problems." (Preface to *The Doctor's Dilemma.*)

WE ARE all of us Shaw's pupil's, no less the scientist than the playwright and the politician. The present and the past generation and, we hope, many generations to come have been and will be shaken out of complacency and accepted ideas by Shaw's violent common sense. In his person he has been the most expressive exponent of the revolt from the pretences of the Victorian era. But in being so he has become so much part of the intelligent background of our own time that it is difficult to write about him without the stupid reverence that he has taught us to make fun of. We cannot see Shaw's thought properly because it is already part of our own.

Now Shaw to the scientist may be two very different things: one easy and one very difficult to recognize. Shaw has often written about science, has made science the central theme of his most important plays and prefaces. In them he writes as a violent and reckless supporter of scientific lost causes, like Lamarckian Evolution, and as the enemy both to the theory and practice of methods that in the course of years have proved their truth and usefulness, like the bacterial theory of disease. It would be easy to fall into the idea that this puts Shaw among the anti-scientific minority of cranks and mystics but it would be very wrong to do so. For there is another very different and far more important side which appears, not just here or there, but in almost every word that Shaw has written: a natural, almost effortless grasp of the common-sense scepticism which is the life-blood of scientific advance: a refusal to have pompous platitudes put over him under any form or backed by any authority: a determination to accept only what seems to him simple, straightforward and fundamentally right.

Explicitly Shaw may stand out against current science: implicitly he understands it. That is why scientists are apt to count Shaw, quite as much as Wells, as one of their own, for all the abuse he has hurled at them and for all the contempt in which he holds many of their most sacred theories. For Shaw himself is more than his theories: he is the living proof of them. He is the only man of his age who has maintained a continual and active contact with the changing forces of one of the most chaotic periods in human history. He is the only man who has dared to make predictions and has not seen events give them the lie. We short-livers are no match for him. We may say we understand the present better but we cannot understand its continuity with the past so well. Even to understand Shaw we would have to have his age and his wisdom, for the understanding is that of one integral man. Forty years ago he made his hero, Jack Tanner, say in *Man and Superman* (Act I):

> "I am no more that schoolboy now than I am the dotard of ninety I shall grow into if I live long enough."

Nor is he Tanner's foil, Roebuck Ramsden, who at a much more modest age claims to be as advanced as he ever was. Shaw does grow, but he is all of a piece.

The clue to Shaw is this integral personality. His religion, his science, his politics, his way of life were all fitted together into a consistent whole. The paradoxes and the contradictions for which he earned his early reputation were in part a trick of the trade of making people interested in things that really mattered to them, and in part covered his own successful struggle to achieve that integral outlook. We cannot understand the science of Shaw without understanding the whole man. So to unravel the guiding motifs of his thought we have to go back into a past he has not forgotten but one that we never knew.

Now science has been a major factor in Shaw's life from the very beginning. He remembers, incredible as it seems to us, the pre-Darwinian era where as a small boy he heard an elderly man ask for

> "the works of the celebrated Buffoon. My own works were at that time unwritten or it is possible that the shop assistant might have so far misunderstood him as to produce a copy of *Man and Superman* . . . the celebrated Buffoon was not a humourist but the famous naturalist, Buffon. Every literate child at that time knew Buffon's *Natural History* as well as *Æsop's Fables*. And no living child had heard the name that has since obliterated Buffon's in the popular consciousness: the name of Darwin. Ten years elapsed. The celebrated Buffoon was forgotten; I had doubled my years and my length; and I had discarded the religion of my forefathers." (Preface to *Back to Methuselah*.)

The advent of Darwinism and the controversy that raged round it were a terrific formative influence, the importance of which it is difficult for us who have not felt it to imagine. Shaw reacted against Darwin violently. That reaction was not an anti-scientific one but neither was it scientific. What Shaw objected to in Darwinism was derived in part from its political and social implications and in part from a deep-seated and strongly held feeling of the community of society and the wider community of living things which had become for him the equivalent of the religion he had discarded.

There was another current in the late nineteenth century

which also drew him in. The twin star to Darwin in the scientific heaven of the seventies was Pasteur. With Pasteur and his followers, the vivisectionists and the vaccinationists, Shaw fought an unending and futile battle; futile, on one side, because doctors continued their useless and inhuman administrations and, on the other, because he himself continued to live hale and hearty without them. These two—the Darwinian controversy and the germ controversy—were Shaw's most passionate scientific concerns but they were not the only ones.

It must not be forgotten that Shaw had been a professional scientist, though for even a shorter time than he had been a successful man of business. His first hero, Edward Conolly, of *The Irrational Knot*, was not a biological but a physical scientist. He was one of the new kind of practical scientists, the electrical engineer, created from Shaw's own experience in the Edison Company's office during the first installation of the telephone system in London in 1880.

> "As I was interested in physics and had read Tyndall and Helmholtz, besides having learnt something in Ireland through a friendship with one of Mr. Graham Bell's cousins who was also a chemist and a physicist, I was, I believe, the only person in the entire establishment who knew the current scientific explanation of telephony; and as I soon struck up a friendship with our official lecturer, a Colchester man whose strong point was pre-scientific agriculture, I often discharged his duties for him in a manner which, I am persuaded, laid the foundation of Mr. Edison's London reputation." (Preface to *The Irrational Knot.*)

In *In Good King Charles's Golden Days* he shows that he has still kept alive his interest in the great physical controversies of the age of relativity. But Shaw's interest in physical science for one very obvious reason never played a dominating part;

he could never, in spite of his association with the Webbs, take a deep interest in figures. On his own admission:

> "Mathematics are to me only a concept. I never used a logarithm in my life and could not undertake to extract the square root of four without misgiving." (Preface to *The Doctor's Dilemma.*)

Nevertheless, he was able to appreciate the importance of what he could not understand and by his championship of Karl Pearson he was a prophet of the new methods of statistical analysis that have proved the major means of extension of exact science into the fields of biology and sociology.

The most characteristic scientific aberration of Shaw's was his violent reaction to the natural selection of Darwin in favour of the Creative Evolution derived from Lamarck. The whole of this he has argued out with admirable lucidity and wrong-headedness in the preface to *Back to Methuselah.* Here he shows himself a violent follower of that neglected genius of the late Victorian age, Samuel Butler. This preface is a document which should form part of every biological student's education because it shows better than any other single piece of writing both the social origins and the social effects of Darwin's teaching. Shaw is not fooled for a moment about the scientific objectivity of Darwin. He realizes that Darwin has introduced into biology what *laissez-faire* economics had long before released in public life—unlimited competition. He shows also why Darwinism was hailed as a doctrine which delivered men from the intolerable mental agony of a theology based on a personal god who, it seemed, in the light of the manifest evil in the world, must be either himself wicked or impotent.

> "We had been so oppressed by the notion that everything that happened in the world was the arbitrary personal act of an arbitrary personal god of dangerously jealous and cruel

> personal character . . . that we jumped at Darwin." (Preface to *Back to Methuselah.*)

But, as he immediately points out, the gulf that swallowed up Paley and Shelley's Almighty Fiend, was nothing less than a bottomless pit in which there was

> "a hideous fatalism, a ghastly and damnable reduction of beauty and intelligence, of strength and purpose, of honour and aspiration, to such casually picturesque changes as an avalanche may make in a mountain landscape, or a railway accident in a human figure. . . . If it be no blasphemy, but a truth of science, then the stars of heaven, the showers and dew, the winter and summer, the fire and heat, the mountains and hills, may no longer be called to exalt the Lord with us by praise: their work is to modify all things by blindly starving and murdering everything that is not lucky enough to survive in the universal struggle for hogwash." (Preface to *Back to Methuselah.*)

This passage is a clear and eloquent expression of an emotional reaction to the Darwinian theory rather than an intelligent criticism of it. Shaw recognizes this perfectly well. He admitted that Darwinism was not finally refutable, not as an explanation of evolution as a whole but as an explanation of certain small and trivial parts of it.

In its place he accepted as an infinitely more satisfying solution equally impossible to disprove, the theory of Lamarck of functional adaptation later called Creative Evolution. The basis for this preference, apart from its echo of a medieval, intelligible world order which Shaw had taken in with his cultural inheritance, was a deep, immediate sense of the unity and purpose of all created things. Shaw felt in control of himself: he felt a kinship with other living things and he felt, therefore, that they could control their own existence and their own evolution. If they did not want to evolve, they would not and if they did want to evolve, they would. He had an avowed affinity to the mystical naturalist of the type of Oken, who believed that natural science was "the science of the everlasting transmutations of the Holy Ghost and the world." (For some reason Shaw seems to have thought of Oken as a philosopher rather than the very serious and practical anatomist that he was.) The inner life, the inner drive of evolution—evolution from within—felt much more true to him than an evolution from blind external forces—evolution from without. This led him into a strange physiological theory in which all the functions of a living organism are treated as habits:

> "For instance, the very first act of your son when he enters the world as a separate individual is to yell with indignation: that yell which Shakespeare thought the most tragic and piteous of all sounds. In the act of yelling he begins to breathe: another habit, and not even a necessary one, as the object of breathing can be achieved in other ways, as by deep-sea fishes. He circulates his blood by pumping it with his heart. He demands a meal and proceeds at once to perform the most elaborate chemical operations on the food he swallows. He manufactures teeth; then discards them; and replaces them with fresh ones. Compared to these habitual feats, walking, standing upright and bicycling are the merest trifles; yet it is only by going through the wanting, trying process that he can stand, walk or cycle, whereas in the other and far more difficult and complex habits he not only does not consciously want nor consciously try, but actually consciously objects very strongly." (Preface to *Back to Methuselah.*)

Because things once striven for and learnt have become habits, Shaw argues that things which are now habits must have been at one time striven for. He recognizes, quite rightly, that there is a serious problem for Zoology in explaining the things that happen of themselves. He senses an earlier history to account for these things but he is unable to conceive of their history as other than the operation of a conscious will pervading the whole of nature. Shaw never seemed to see that there is any difference between the conscious and unconscious parts of living matter. He even attacks the Darwinians for denying consciousness to trees.

Now all this would tend to make the modern hard-boiled scientist say—we have no patience with feelings or with attitudes towards life that cannot be translated into experiments leading to predictable results. But it would be a mistake to think that that is what Shaw is after. What he looked for and what he found was a religion by which to live a most effective and fruitful life: and religion, in his sense, purged from the old social heritage of oppressive tyrant gods, is not one to be despised. If Shaw had been a scientist—and there have been many scientists who have talked far greater nonsense than he has—he could reasonably have been attacked as not distinguishing between what he wanted to believe and what he had any evidence for believing. But he was not a scientist and he made what was in his time a most penetrating and intelligent choice of beliefs.

Shaw's attitude towards evolution and his attitude towards medicine are most closely related. They both arise from the common feeling—perhaps the most deeply held of all his convictions—on the substantial unity between men and animals. Shaw never saw the reason why if an action towards a man were criminal, an action towards an animal should not be as much so; this is the logic behind his consistent vegetarianism and his implacable opposition to experiments on animals in general and to vivisection in particular.

"I am driven to the conclusion that my sense of kinship

> with animals is greater than most people feel. It amuses me to talk to animals in a sort of jargon I have invented for them; and it seems to me that it amuses them to be talked to, and that they respond to the tone of the conversation though its intellectual content may to some extent escape them. . . . I find it impossible to associate with animals on any other terms." (Preface to *Killing for Sport.*)

While admitting this feeling, Shaw does not elevate it into a dogma, nor does he try to draw impossible conclusions from it as Butler's Erewhonians did when they passed on from the refusal to eat meat to the refusal to eat vegetables. He recognizes that some animals must be killed and even that some must be eaten, but he hopes that this habit will not persist! What he cannot stand is that the sufferings of animals should conduce to the increase of man's pleasure or knowledge; he is as great an enemy of blood sports as he is of vivisection.

Shaw's attack on vivisection in the Preface to *The Doctor's Dilemma* is a very fine example of his understanding and its limitations. He begins by granting that the right to know is like the right to live. But, he goes on, the right to live is not unconditional, it must not violate someone else's right to live; nor should, he argues, the right to know. We are not entitled to kill people for the sake of knowledge: the kind of experiments that were later to be carried out in the German concentration camps were indefensible even if they had—which they did not—contributed to knowledge. Now if man and animals are fellows, the same argument will apply:

> "Just as even the stupidest people say, in effect, 'If you cannot attain knowledge without burning your mother you must do without knowledge,' so the wisest people say, 'If you cannot attain to knowledge without torturing a dog you must do without knowledge.' " (Preface to *The Doctor's Dilemma.*)

Because he feels this so strongly, he goes on to say that as the wise man does not care to learn from vivisection, there is no excuse for it at all: but still the original problem is not solved—the right to know is not exercised. Shaw has an answer to this as well, that:

> "There are many paths to knowledge already discovered; and no enlightened man doubts that there are many more waiting to be discovered. Indeed, all paths lead to knowledge; because even the vilest and stupidest action teaches us something about vileness and stupidity, and may accidentally teach us a good deal more. . . ." (Preface to *The Doctor's Dilemma.*)

Therefore if certain paths are barred from consideration by humanity, alternatives may be available and the wise man and the man of honour will choose these.

Now there are two answers to this type of argument: the first which attacks the premise that equates human and animal suffering—and I will return to that later—and the second that doubts the conclusion. If all men and all scientists were ideally wise and honourable they might have discovered what they have discovered without recourse to any animal experiments. It is certainly also true that the greater proportion of animal experiments—as the greater proportion of all experiments—prove nothing; but men being what they are, of limited wisdom and limited range of sympathy, it is too much to ask them to find by circuitous ways what they have only wit enough to find by the most direct way. If we had to learn science all over again from the start we could undoubtedly do it in a far more humane way than was actually done; the men of the past, scientist and layman alike, were hard to animals, to other men and to themselves. Now we know better and are able better to appreciate what kind of sufferings are involved in experiments and to see that that suffering is minimized and justified by a manifold decrease in suffering which the knowledge of it brings. This, of course, Shaw would have disputed and will, as far as I know, dispute still. Seeing the triumphs of science expressed in practice by the doctors he may yet and with some justification retain his scepticism and his indignation.

Parallel with his condemnation of vivisection goes Shaw's objection to vaccination and, with it, most forms of immunization. His reasons for this are more difficult to follow because they are not based on such immediately simple reactions. It is not at all certain how, in the course of his life, Shaw's attitude towards the work of Pasteur has varied. In 1911 he goes flat out and damns bacteriology as a superstition: the germ, he thinks, may be a symptom of the disease and not its cause. Later he seems to admit their partial potency. Now of course Shaw had lived in the period of the early enthusiasm and excesses of the germ theory, where scientists as much as doctors took Pasteur's work as divine revelation and thought that all disease was due to germs, could be cured only by killing them and that killing the germ stone-dead was more important than any incidental damage that might be done to the patient. If the germ could not be found, it was probably there anyhow and a vaccine of an unspecified character should be able to do for it! None of these absurdities escaped him but what does seem to have escaped him was that through this maze of exaggeration and false theory there ran a progressive thread which has emerged as the years have gone on as a surer and surer guide to the prevention as well as the cure of disease. The path of discovery has not been kind to Shaw: the viruses which were invisible in his day can now be photographed and the beneficent ones—the bacteriophages—seen at work attacking their prey.

Shaw's objections, however, are not based mainly on scientific scepticism, they are of a more positive nature. They seem to owe their vehemence mainly to his objection to the interference of the liberty of the subject rather than to any medical theory. A great deal of Shaw's objections were in his days reasonable, valid ones.

> "When, as in the case of smallpox or cowpox, the germ has not yet been detected, what you inoculate is simply undefined matter that has been scraped off an anything but clean calf suffering from the disease in question. You take your choice of the germ being in the scrapings, and, lest you should kill it, you take no precautions against other germs being in it as well. Anything may happen as the result of such an inoculation." (Preface to *The Doctor's Dilemma.*)

Further, this is the theme of *The Doctor's Dilemma* itself—that such complicated matters as introducing foreign substances into the human body is one that cannot be left either to sixpenny or Harley Street doctors who have not the time, incentive or the basic knowledge to do it properly. In this sense his criticism is fully constructive and points to the need for properly equipped scientific laboratories to take the place of the G.P.'s back surgery.

In *The Doctor's Dilemma* and its magnificent Preface, Shaw shows to the full his capacity for social understanding of the medical profession exceeding anything that has been written of it before or since. He saw, long before his time, that the chief enemy of health was poverty and not lack of medical attention; and he saw, too, that in his time medical attention, for lack of science, could do very little for people and was in fact not able to do that little because the poor could not afford the treatment and the rich could not be made to undertake it. The social solution to the medical problem that he put forward is now, forty years later, likely to become the law of the land against the protests of a generation of doctors who are unchanged replicas of those he so mercilessly satirizes. The maxims with which the Preface ends ring as true to-day as they did when they were written nearly forty years ago.

"(1) Nothing is more dangerous than a poor doctor; not even a poor employer or a poor landlord.

"(2) Of all the anti-social vested interests the worst is the vested interest in ill-health.

"(5) Make up your mind how many doctors the community needs to keep it well. Do not register more or less than this number; and let registration constitute the doctor a civil servant with a dignified living wage paid out of public funds.

"(6) Municipalize Harley Street.

"(12) Do not try to live for ever. You will not succeed.

"(13) Use your health, even to the point of wearing it out. That is what it is for. Spend all you have before you die; and do not outlive yourself.

"(14) Take the utmost care to get well born and well brought up. This means that your mother must have a good doctor. Be careful to go to a good school where there is what they call a school clinic, where your nutrition and teeth and eyesight and other matters of importance to you will be attended to. Be particularly careful to have all this done at the expense of the nation, as otherwise it will not be done at all, the chances being about forty to one against your being able to pay for it directly yourself, even if you know how to set about it. Otherwise you will be what most people are at present: an unsound citizen of an unsound nation, without sense enough to be ashamed or unhappy about it."

The major problem for scientists in contemplating Shaw's attitude towards science is how to explain his combination of natural common sense and penetrating judgment with his predilection for backing scientific lost causes and for appearing to fly in the face of the evidence of experiment and observation. The problem has an importance even greater than that of the analysis of the work of a great writer. It is the problem of a whole generation of European thought. Shaw is profoundly concerned with human betterment in his advocacy of socialism on one hand, and, on the other, with man's understanding of a changing universe in his belief in creative evolution. He has admitted and succeeded to his own satisfaction in combining these two attitudes, but he has done so in a way which has isolated him—except in general bonds of affection and respect—from active scientific and political movements. This isolation he feels to a very considerable extent himself. In one of his later Prefaces, that of *The Simpleton of the Unexpected Isles,* written only ten years ago, he even appears to turn against science altogether:

> "Religion is the mother of scepticism: Science is the mother of credulity. There is nothing that people will not believe nowadays if only it be presented to them as Science, and nothing they will not disbelieve if it be presented to them as religion. I myself began like that; and I am ending by receiving every scientific statement with dour suspicion whilst giving very respectful consideration to the inspirations and revelations of the prophets and poets. For the shift of credulity from religious divination to scientific invention is very often a relapse from comparatively harmless romance to mischievous and even murderous quackery."

If other people want to believe what he cannot believe they are credulous: and if they will believe without evidence, he seems to tend rather to their holding the old than the new beliefs. Now, of course, without the kind of education which we have not even begun to think of in this country, the vast majority of the people must be credulous: that is, they cannot possibly know the reasons for the beliefs they hold. But that does not mean that the reasons are not there. The old beliefs were metaphorical and poetical, and expressed a kind of justificatory synthesis of traditional behaviour and traditional social structure. The new, scientific beliefs express explicitly the growing material control of man over nature. If we despair of the latter by a too easy reading of the effects of human folly over the last few centuries, we may be forced to fall back on the former which, unfortunately, neither explain nor help us to control the forces that are so torturing the world to-day and are ideally suited to the support of the most reactionary policies.

Now the intellectual reason that drove Shaw to this choice is one deeply rooted in one of his most strongly held beliefs and further impressed on him by a youth lived in the middle of the evolutionary controversy. It is a belief that animal evolution and human society are explainable by the same theories, a belief now becoming to be known as biologism and one still held by many far younger scientists and philosophers. Once biologism is taken for granted the precise mechanism of evolution becomes of vital importance. If a belief in Darwinian natural selection immediately implies a justification of survival of the fittest, cut-throat competition and all the horrors of individualist capitalism, then Darwinism must go and be hanged to the evidence. Lamarck's far more human concept of evolution, making it dependent on conscious will and therefore making possible of achievement by world action a better state of affairs, is clearly a morally preferable alternative.

Biologism had another attraction for Shaw: his deep, instinctive feeling of an almost personal relation with animals. It was for this reason that he could never accept the older philosophic view finally incorporated in Christianity, that man and animals were different orders of creation, with man, alone, having a rational and, at least potentially, an immortal soul. Now in their reaction to the older theology, evolutionists of all kinds stressed the immediate kinship between man and animals, that is shown in every hair of their bodies, and overlooked the distinction that had been obvious from the earliest ages of civilization between man and animal's behaviour and social organization.

Here, strangely enough, Shaw missed or reacted against the impact of a movement which accepted both the facts of evolution, linking man and animals, and the fact of man's social organization sharply differentiating him from them. Marx and Engels, living in the England of Shaw's youth, did not fail to influence him, but their influence was purely on the political and economic and not on the philosophical side. *Das Kapital* made Shaw a Socialist but for the philosophy of Dialectical Materialism as exemplified in the other works of Marx, and particularly in those of Engels, he has only the most generalized abuse which shows that he either never read it or did not take it in. I hope it will still be possible to hear what Shaw has to say on Engels, because the thesis developed in such a book as *The Origin of the Family* shows how it would have been possible for him, if he accepted it, to reconcile his social beliefs with an entirely non-mystical and practical biology.

The Darwinian theory, after a momentary dimming at the turn of the century, is now more firmly established than ever, as its material basis in the genetic mechanism of Mendel and Morgan has at last been elucidated. We can not only observe the occurrence of new species but we can make them with X-rays. The scientist of to-day, however, sees evolution much more in wider perspective than those of the nineteenth century. He sees that the establishing of family trees is but a very small part of the work of the biologist; that by patient experiment and ever more profound observation the actual complex relations between organisms and their living and non-living environments will need to be worked out.

One of the characteristics of the development of science from the fifteenth century up to almost our own time has been taking as literal statements what the ancients had understood figuratively, and proving them to be nonsense. The task of our day is to explain what it was that the ancients were trying to express because the fact that they bothered at all about a topic showed it to be important. Thus Aristotle and Galen, and after him Aquinas discussed at length the difference between a vegetative, an animal and a rational soul, and conceived them as seated in the liver, the heart and the brain. Vesalius and Harvey destroyed this concept as a material description; the liver was a food store, the heart a blood pump and the brain a complex telephone exchange and record office. But the scientists did not attempt to get behind what the ancients meant by these distinctions, how they had used these words to strive to explain the mere growing and formative power of plants and animals, the behaviour and responses of animals and the power of abstract reasoning which was possessed by man alone. Now we are beginning to see what these mean; how the vegetative soul is the expression for the totality of all biochemical phenomena which are common to all living things and date back to the very origin of life itself; how the animate soul belongs only to mobile animals and to the few exceptional plants that have accidentally drifted into their mode of life. Sense organs, movement, desire and striving are all included in that pattern of structure and behaviour. Both the vegetative and animate soul develop through the mechanism of inheritance and organic evolution. The rational soul is different. The ancients were right. Man stands completely apart from the rest of creation; and, in their time, they were right, too, in demanding a special act to account for this uniqueness, even if they expressed it in the crude, materialistic sense of a God breathing life into moulded clay. But the ancients and with them the moderns, with rare exceptions up to the present century, missed the relevance of the rational soul. The evolutionists, both Darwinian and Lamarckian, were so concerned with proving Garden of Eden fables to be nonsense, that they were in danger of perpetrating a greater nonsense themselves: greater, that is, considering that they ought to have known better. They were so busy in seeing that men were descended from animals that they did not look for the circumstances that had made them so absolutely and qualitatively different from them—the organization and development of human society. Darwinians and Lamarckians were alike in this. The Darwinians were so certain that animals had no souls, they would not allow them to men either and tried to account for the unique position of man by granting him a larger brain. The Lamarckians, equally determined to stress the unity of creation, insisted on giving souls or creative wills to every animal because they observed that man possessed them.

In the choice between the two, Shaw very naturally decided in favour of the more humane though the less intelligible of these alternatives. He was a man of his time in thinking of evolution essentially in terms of physical inheritance and race. His Supermen and Methuselahs are to him as much the product of the evolution of the body as the dog or the oak tree. Because to expect such changes to happen by some accidental gene variative would be palpable nonsense and because Shaw instinctively and consciously felt that such changes were needed, he was prepared to argue through thick and thin against the Darwinian hypothesis, not imagining that though the problem he put before himself was a right and just one, the method of solution through evolution had already been superseded a million years ago when human society first pulled itself together in this world.

Shaw was deeply aware of the vast contradiction that exists between the limited power in space and time of our bodies and the range and time that our minds need. He was aware, in other words, of the discrepancy between the products of organic evolution and the products of social evolution. The whole theme of *Back to Methuselah* is an attempt to resolve this by the simple device of making men achieve an adequate length of life through the inner will-power of creative evolution. I am not sure how far Shaw really meant what he said there: how far it expressed literal belief or must be taken as an allegory as much as the history of the Garden of Eden. But it is clear that, allegory or not, Shaw never attempted the other solution through social rather than organic evolution.

Yet there have been few more profound analysts of our society. Shaw could penetrate its manners, bring out their latent historic and economic roots: could show us as no one has ever done so well the follies and stupidities of our own conventions. By so doing he has changed them. If the world of 1946 is a different world from the world of 1856, it is to a very perceptible extent because of Shaw's own work. More than that; throughout the vast historic changes of these ninety years, Shaw has never lost an instinctive feeling for the direction of significant social change. When others who ought to have known better derided the efforts of the struggling Soviet Union, he supported them. He had no patience with sentimental appeals to mid-Victorian liberalism. He knew it was dead, for he helped to kill it. But he did more than destroy. He has given to succeeding generations a self-confidence, a capacity to look at the world as something which men could control and improve, if men could look at it simply and clear their minds of cant. His beliefs—the new religion he made out of Creative Evolution—helped him so to see the world and so to change it. If it is not the religion of the generation of to-day and to-morrow, it is largely because he has made such a thorough job of clearing away the nonsense of the past and has given us the ground on which we can build a more rational, a more comprehensive and a more hopeful future.

## DR. W. R. INGE

### *SHAW AS A THEOLOGIAN*

MR. SHAW, one of the kindest friends I have ever had, has commiserated me on my unfortunate family history and upbringing. What could be expected of a man whose father had the offer of an English bishopric, two of whose uncles were bishops, and whose grandfather, father-in-law, and two great-grandfathers were archdeacons? If I was not born with "something consequential about the legs," I was clearly foredoomed to wear the apron and gaiters of an Anglican dignitary. It seems a long time since I discarded these certificates of orthodoxy, and now I write on the "theology" of a man who protests energetically that he is not a Christian. The word Christian has no accepted definition. Plato has often been called a Christian before Christ. Justin Martyr says that Heraclitus, Socrates, and Musonius may be called Christians, since they lived under the guidance of the Logos-Christ, who, as St. Paul tells us, followed the Israelites in their wanderings. Nietzsche thinks that there has been only one Christian—he who died upon the cross. Others have said that as Wilkes told George III that he had never been a Wilkesite, so the Founder of Christianity, if he could have known what his followers would make of his gospel, might have declared that he was not a Christian. I shall not attempt to answer the question whether Mr. Shaw would have a right to call himself a Christian if he valued the name; but I do not forget that the words "thou art not far from the Kingdom of God" were pronounced over a man who had just professed a very rudimentary creed. Personally I have no doubt that he who knew the hearts of men, and who cared so little for those who say 'Lord, Lord' and live only for themselves, would say the same of Mr. Shaw.

There are two of Shaw's writings which I think may be taken as summing up his views on religion, the Prefaces to *Back to Methuselah* and to *Androcles and the Lion.* The little book about the *Black Girl* is less important. (The Black Girl always reminds me of the unlucky schoolboy who translated *post equitem sedet atra cura* "after horse exercise the black girl sits down with care," and who probably sat down with care himself for a day or two afterwards.) Nor does the preface to *Saint Joan* add much that need be considered here.

In the preface to *Methuselah* the author shows that he has found a kindred spirit in Samuel Butler, who took a puckish pleasure in alternately shocking the clergy and teasing the solemn whiskered pundits of natural science with such awkward questions as "which came first, the hen or the egg?" The biologists, wiser than the orthodox, maintained a dignified silence.

The theory of evolution, like the emanation theory of the ancient philosophers, which is really the same thing starting from the opposite end, may describe everything but explains nothing. Natural selection eliminates; it cannot create. Most of nature's experiments are deleterious or lethal, and have therefore been rejected. Nature has extinguished the majestic dinosaurs and the apathetic dodo; it has discouraged the marsupial and the gorilla; it has vindicated the habits of the bug, the spirochaete, homo sapiens, and the cockroach. But the cause of variations remains unexplained. It makes no difference whether we call them variations or mutations. Some of the early Darwinians seem to have thought that a very small change needs no explanation, as a girl is said to have excused the appearance of a baby whose appearance needed apology by pleading that it was a very small one. But real change, whether great or small, is a mystery. It is a commonplace now that (as Kant pointed out long ago) the word evolution is used in two incompatible senses. It may mean the mechanical unpacking of what was present in germ from the first, or it may mean the interposition of new factors, in which case epigenesis would be the more correct word. I suspect that the now popular word emergence is sometimes used to cover up this ambiguity.

Shaw follows Lamarck rather than Darwin. He is a vitalist. The giraffe may have lengthened his neck by an act of will. That this is a scientific heresy is rather a recommendation than otherwise for Shaw, who like a true Irishman is always "agin the government." What he really dislikes, I think, is the theory of blind causation. Anything at all resembling the Epicurean and Lucretian theory of a fortuitous concourse of atoms as the cause of the world that we know seems to him absurd, as it surely is. The question is whether nature exhibits recognizable traces of what Paley calls prospective contrivance. It can hardly be denied that it does, even apart from the stubborn fact that the world contains minds, and that minds cannot "emerge" from chemical elements, which belong to an entirely different order. The life of nature is pervaded by prospective adaptations. The laws of physics cannot account for vital processes. We are driven to believe in the presence of mind as determining the course of events. Life discloses intelligence everywhere, adapting the present to the needs of the future.

It is worth while to remind our readers that, whatever may be said of modern behaviourists and others, the Victorians were by no means so hostile to directing intelligence in nature as is often supposed. Darwin writes: "The grand sequence of events the mind refuses to accept as the result of blind chance. The understanding revolts from such a conclusion." No one was more alive than he was to the great objection to natural selection—that an incomplete adaptation is of no use to its possessor. Helmholtz, whose disparaging remarks about the human eye are often quoted, concludes that "the result which may be reached by innumerable generations working under the Darwinian law of inheritance coincides with what the wisest wisdom may have devised before hand." Kelvin says that "we are absolutely forced by science to admit and to believe with absolute confidence in directive power—in an influence other than physical, dynamical, electrical forces. There is nothing between absolute scientific belief in creative power and the acceptance of the theory of a fortuitous concourse of atoms." Even Haeckel, the arch-materialist as he is often called, says "we contemplate the operation of God in all phenomena. To it the whole inorganic world is subject, and also the whole world of organization." As for Herbert Spencer, he ends by telling us so much about the Unknowable that whole sentences in his writings might be taken from St. Thomas Aquinas. Where these men go wrong is in assuming that evolution is necessarily a progress from a worse condition to a better, the criterion being mainly the well-being or convenience of our own species. On the contrary, the parasites often seem to have the best of it in the long run. Spencer also assumes that the "higher" is the more complicated. If we compare the first awkward flying machines with the latest jet-propulsion, we shall see how far from the truth this assumption is. The great superstition of the last century, the belief in an ineluctable law of progress, which takes such ridiculous forms in Godwin and Fourier, infected all the thought of the period, and was not without considerable influence in religious beliefs.

If we reject the theory of blind mechanism, it is by no means necessary to follow Lamarck, or to accept anything like Bergson's *élan vital*, a self-evolving, self-improving life force. If there is a God, he must be transcendent as well as immanent. There are other ways of looking at intelligence in nature. Is there unconscious racial memory? Is Bergson right in contrasting so sharply instinct and intelligence? How, if not by intelligence, did the social insects develop their ingenious and complex civilizations? May not instinct be mechanized intelligence? When a stable equilibrium has once been reached a society no longer needs citizens who think for themselves. If any such survive they will be eliminated, and nature before long takes away faculties that are no longer used. After a few generations of Marxism or Hitlerism, we should have to choose between becoming automata and being liquidated. I fear that even his admiration for the Sidney Webbs would not save Mr. Shaw from the latter fate. The social insects are an awful warning against all static utopias. They are in purgatory and they do not know it. As for our own species, it is doubtful whether we have progressed in intelligence since the large-brained Cro-Magnons, and more than doubtful whether we are morally better than the early disciples of Christ or of Buddha. If, as seems quite possible, later improvements in the atomic bomb enable us to exterminate each other, we may fancy that a future historian from the planet Venus may say that "the extinction of this noxious species is often referred to by our theologians as a strong argument for the providential government of the universe."

In the latter part of the preface to *Methuselah* Mr. Shaw comes to closer grips with religion. There is no question, he says, of a new religion, but rather of rebuilding the eternal spirit of religion, and thus extricating it from the residue of superstitions and legends that are making belief impossible. The truly religious people are those who have kept sweet the tradition that good people follow a light that shines within and above and ahead of them, that bad people care only for themselves, and that the good are saved and blessed, and the bad miserable. This does not mean that we should throw away legend and parable and drama; but woe to the Churches and rulers who substitute the legend for the dogma, the parable for the history, the drama for the religion. Who has ever refused to accept a good legend with delight as a legend? Every one of these legends is the common heritage of the human race; there is only one inexorable condition attached to their healthy enjoyment, which is that no one shall believe them literally. All the sweetness of religion is conveyed to the world by story-tellers and image-makers. Nothing stands between the people and the fictions except the silly falsehood that the fictions are literal truths.

All this sounds very simple; but those whose calling is to preach religion know that the problem is anything but simple. Religious symbols are the natural language of faith, and the creation of symbols is unconscious. Those who regard them as only symbolic, as belonging to art and poetry, not to science or history, do not as a rule really value them. They may accept them as aids to the imagination; they may even love them as associated with their best thoughts and their holiest experiences; but they are not so intimately a part of their faith that they would refuse to let them go. On the other hand, those who cling to them do not regard them as symbolic. They are most indignant if their factual reality is called in question. This attitude, which is that of simple piety everywhere, needs careful consideration. These beliefs are plainly not on the same plane as beliefs about historical or scientific facts not connected with religion. If a man finds out that I believe the English to be the lost ten tribes of Israel, or that Bacon wrote *Hamlet*, or that Christian Science will cure cancer, he will have a low opinion of my intelligence, but he will not feel moral indignation against me, or consider that as a heretic I have committed an unpardonable sin. What is even stranger, none of these beliefs has any vital connection with religion. No one, it is to be hoped, believes that Christ was divine because he was a hybrid between God and man. A mule is not perfect horse and perfect ass. If Christ rose from the tomb on the third day, that conveys no hope to us, whose bodies will turn to dust. It is abundantly plain that faith creates the belief in miracles, not that miracles create faith.

In a scientific age educated people dislike miracles, which would threaten to reduce the exact sciences to chaos. Perhaps they flatter themselves that they can do without symbols. Let them think again. If we believe in a spiritual world, where the absolute and eternal values in which God has revealed his nature to us reign in their immortal truth, goodness, and beauty, we can hardly make that world real to our imagination without picturing it either as Yonder, not Here, or as future, not present, or as changeless, not changing, or as reality, not appearance. Can any of these pictures dispense with symbols borrowed from the world of time and place, to which we know that they do not belong? Christianity frankly uses them all; its eschatology is a confused medley. But is the Intelligible World of the Platonist not equally symbolic? And does the philosopher, when he wishes to "ascend thither in heart and mind," as our collect says, like to be told that it is all poetry, or even "fiction"?

What is the reason why simple piety clings so tightly to dogmas which prove nothing that vitally concerns our human destiny, and which contradict the uniformity of nature which we take for granted in our daily life? Traditional religion is a very potent antiseptic; it preserves impartially what is of permanent value and what is out of date. The ordinary man has no urge to solve ultimate problems for himself; he doubts his own competence to do so, and he is quite right. We men living on earth are, as has been said, *amphibia*. We live partly in the world of facts, partly in the world of values. We are placed in a world of time and place, which are as it were the warp and woof of most of the pictures which we draw, and yet we are not wholly in that world; our thoughts range freely in the realm of the imponderables, as Bismarck called them. The soul, as the old philosophers taught, is the wanderer of the metaphysical world, in touch with every grade of reality from the highest to the lowest. Normally we live in a kind of dualism—time and eternity, the seen and the unseen, appearance and reality—they are different ways of expressing a felt antithesis. And a man needs to cross from one to the other. Is there a bridge? Yes; there is the authorized bridge, warranted sound by many generations of wayfarers. If it takes him across, that is all he needs. It is easy to see that to intercalate acts of God in the natural order is a simple way of bringing the two worlds into contact. But that is what science forbids him to do, science, which is bound to protect its own frontiers against invasion. Yes; but science is only an abstract study, not a philosophy of reality. It is valid within its own sphere; but it deliberately neglects the world of values, which is indisputably real. Why, in deference to this abstract study, should we clip the wings of imagination, which may be, as Wordsworth says, reason in its most exalted mood? There are many, we know, who do not wish to cross. There are the worldlings on one side and the mystics on the other. But leave us our old bridge; most of us need it.

So a traditionalist might plead, not unreasonably. Our conclusion must be that there cannot be any standardized orthodoxy, any rule of faith equally binding on the learned professor and his kitchen-maid. If some of the traditional beliefs are obsolete and untenable, they cannot be openly repudiated, for the bridge still bears; but they can be allowed to fade into pious opinions; and this is what is being done, perhaps rather too slowly. But the large majority of those who reject religion do so not because they distrust the bridge, but because they do not wish to cross.

We may now turn to *Androcles and the Lion*. It is a remarkable thing how in all the strange climates of opinion through which Europe has passed since the time of Christ, his name has been used as the banner under which the most contradictory ideas have chosen to fight. Is Christianity merely a name for the religion of people with white skins; or how else shall we find points of contact between Symeon Stylites, St. Louis of France, Thomas à Kempis, Thomas Aquinas, Oliver Cromwell, George Fox, General Gordon, Lord Shaftesbury? Have we not had lives of Christ by authors who proclaimed their nationality? Is not Renan's Jesus a Frenchman, Seeley's

Ecce Homo an Englishman, and so of other nations? It was quite to be expected that the admirers of Karl Marx should try to make Christ a communist agitator, though unfortunately, as our author says, he did not undertake the work like a modern practical statesman.

It is therefore necessary, in commenting on this Preface, to consider what evidence we have about the ministry of Jesus, and the aims which he seems to have put before himself. We must of course remember that St. Paul, our earliest witness, had no personal knowledge of Christ, and that the synoptic Gospels were not written till many years after his death. The Gospels necessarily record those parts of his teaching which made most impression on his immediate disciples, and which were found most useful for liturgical use, for instructing catechumens, and in controversy with the Jews. The Christ of history is "the Lord" honoured by the apostolic Church. Nevertheless most careful readers have found that his recorded utterances bear a strong stamp of authenticity.

Mr. Shaw's sketch of the Founder's life and death is not unlike the opinion of some reputable scholars, but it seems to me psychologically impossible. Briefly, he pictures Jesus as a wandering preacher who after a time "lost his head," and went to Jerusalem in the company of a few unarmed peasants and women, to claim divine or royal honours for himself in the presence of the Sanhedrin and the Roman governor, expecting a miracle. It is much more likely that the chief priests, wishing to get rid of him as an unauthorized and disrespectful layman, denounced him to Pilate as a Mahdi, adding that he had confessed as much himself. Neither they nor Pilate believed a word of it. Pilate was not the man to be content with one execution if he had thought there was trouble brewing. If we may judge by the inscription on the cross, he regarded the matter as a joke, and it is quite possible, as Anatole France suggests, that he never thought about it afterwards. But his disciples knew that in him God had been present among them, and that they had not really lost him.

If we wish to understand the attitude of Christ and of his disciples towards what we now call the social question, we must of course consider the conditions under which he and they lived. The Galileans were a well-educated and upstanding peasantry, whose prosperity is attested by Josephus. They were of mixed origin, and there were "Greek" towns within easy reach. Gadara, which the erotic poet Meleager patriotically called the Syrian Athens, was also the birthplace of the satirist Menippus and the Epicurean Philodemus. Two of the apostles, Andreas and Philippos, had Greek names. But there is not a trace of Hellenism in the synoptic Gospels; the Galileans were devout Jews, though out of sympathy with the Jerusalem hierarchy. The social position of Jesus and his disciples was that of superior artisans. As a wandering prophet he was of course homeless; but he associated freely with rich and poor alike, and was criticized for not being an ascetic like John the Baptist. He thought that the way of living in which he had been brought up was the most favourable for the spiritual life. Luxury and idleness he despised; money means worry, and worry is a sin. The money-grubber is called a fool, not a thief.

As a Galilean peasant he has nothing to say about Capitalism and Socialism, nor about science and art. Nothing was farther from his intention than to legislate for the distant future. Christianity is a religion of spiritual regeneration, not of social reform. It is not easy to see how projects of social reform through political action could have been thought of by the subjects of the Roman autocracy, and in fact such ideas were hardly thought of until quite modern times. The primitive Christian communities had very little to do with the social events of the time—the vulgar luxury of the Roman plutocracy, the development of slavery into serfdom, the incipient decay of urban civilization and the germs of feudalism. These changes were less marked in the east than in the west, and the lower middle class still lived undisturbed in moderate comfort. But though Christianity has perhaps always been most at home in this class, it was never a class movement. It has certainly never been a "proletarian" creed. St. Paul's epistles and the Fourth Gospel were not written for the submerged tenth; as early as Domitian the emperor's cousin seems to have been a Christian, and Pliny says there were Christians "of every class" in Bithynia-Pontus.

By its own inherent energy, says Trehtsch, the religious idea itself neutralized secular distinctions; and with this deprecia-tion of political and economic values the barriers between races and classes and peoples were also removed. "Political and social disintegration had shaken men's faith in finite ideals, and caused them to look with longing towards the infinite." The Jew symbolized the ideal as a state of future bliss, the Greek as a changeless realm of ultimate values. In the Christian Churches the former has on the whole prevailed.

In the teaching of Christ the fundamental demand is for "purity of heart," that is to say, for single-minded devotion to the highest ideals. In a sense it is individualistic; all reform must work from within outwards, from the individual to so-ciety. The human soul is of infinite value, but we must be willing to "lose" the empirical ego in order to "find" our true personality.

The Gospel is not ascetic, but it is heroic. It makes no appeal either to the classes or to the masses. No teacher has ever been so discouraging as Christ. Democratism, if it is con-sistent with itself, must abjure him altogether. "Woe unto you when all men shall speak well of you." "Narrow is the way that leadeth unto life, and few there be that find it." "The prince of this world cometh and hath nothing in me." "If they have persecuted me they will also persecute you." This is a call to heroism, to resistance even unto death, whether the power be exercised by the *civium ardor prava inbentium* or by the *vultus instantis tyranni.*

Individualism—yes; but also absolute universalism. There is a fellowship of love among those who are united in God. Love is the hierophant of the supreme mysteries, and therefore the religion of escape, so attractive in times of trouble and so seductive to the Oriental mind, is precluded for the Christian. "If a man love not his brother whom he hath seen, how can he love God whom he hath not seen?" St. Paul's immortal hymn to love in I Corinthians is in part anticipated by Plato in the Symposium. Love is the mediator between God and man. "What then is love?" Socrates asks of Distrina. "Is he mortal?" "No." "What is he then?" "He is a righteous Spirit." "And what is his power?" "He interprets between the divine and the mortal. He is the mediator who spans the chasm which separates them, and therefore in him all is bound together, and through him the acts of the prophet and the priest, their sacrifices and mysteries, find their way. For God mingles not with man; but through love all the intercourse of God with man is carried on. The wisdom which understands this is spiritual."

In the Gospel there is no thought of the State at all. Jewish nationalism is ignored entirely. The Kingdom of God is the rule of God on earth, and it is already "within us," though far from triumphing in the world. The Church borrowed from Stoicism the very fruitful idea of Natural Law, though it was compelled to recognize a relative Law of Nature, adapted to man's fallen state, which must tolerate institutions which would not exist in a perfect society. The sect-type of Christianity has often revolted against this concession.

Have I slurred over those numerous passages in the Gospels in which wealth is almost fiercely condemned, those passages which communists quote as proving that Jesus was one of themselves? The New Testament does not speak with one voice. There is one book, the Epistle of James, in which the characteristic Jewish hatred, the hatred of Marx, Trotsky, and Zinovieff, breaks out in a rather ugly form. This may be ignored; but there is also the Gospel of St. Luke. Either he or

St. Matthew has tampered with the words of the Master as he found them in his written source. Where Matthew has "blessed are the poor in spirit," Luke has "blessed are ye poor," and "woe to the rich." The two Gospels are nearly of the same date, and we cannot say with certainty which version we ought to choose. There are several other places where Luke has apparently taken the same liberty. We must remember that in the later books of the Old Testament and perhaps in Galilee in the time of Christ, the word "poor" is a designation of the pious among the people, and has no close connexion with their economic condition, though it does imply that the rich as a class were unfaithful. And though Luke, a warm-hearted man, furnishes Christian socialists with most of their texts, it is significant that he alone records the most decisive utterance of Christ on economic questions. A man asks him to arbitrate on a dispute about property between himself and his brother. Jesus answers, "Who made me a judge or a divider over you? Take heed and beware of all covetousness; for a man's life consisteth not in the abundance of the things that he possesseth."

This is the heart of the matter. Christ gives us a definite standard of values, which can be easily understood from most of the New Testament. It is a standard which rates the paraphernalia of life very low. The acquisitive capitalist and the Marxian agree in thinking that a man's life does consist in the abundance of the things that he possesseth. In the nineteenth century the rewards of success in business were so great that western civilization took a materialistic colouring. Great bitterness was engendered; both sides had much the same standard of values, a standard very different from that of the Gospels. Now that Mammon has no more prizes to distribute, we may hope that a more reasonable temper may lessen the animosity of the class-warfare. There can be no doubt that an idealistic standard of values is the foundation of Christian ethics. I hope it will not continue to be said that the Church is always on the same side, the winning side. Power, said Lord Acton, is always abused.

St. Paul is, I think, one of the greatest men who ever lived. It would be difficult to name anyone who has left so deep and so permanent a mark upon history. If his enemies had succeeded in killing him at Damascus, we might be now worshipping Mithras or Mohammed, or Hitler's resuscitated god Odin, who we supposed had long ago met his match in his predicted encounter with the wolf Fenrir. We know more about St. Paul than about any other character of antiquity except Cicero, and we know nothing whatever to his discredit. And yet several modern writers—Lagarde, Nietzsche, Renan, and now Mr. Shaw—asperse his memory with an animosity which is usually reserved for political opponents. The reasons are not easy to discover.

St. Paul was a travelling missionary, a type not uncommon at that time. He was not a systematic theologian. He grazes several heresies; his view of the heavenly Christ was not orthodox by later standards, since he believed that after the incarnation Christ was raised to a higher dignity—equality with God—than he had before. His letters were real letters, hastily composed writings which he never expected to take rank as Scripture. The letters contain specimens of Rabbinic exegesis which are now quite unconvincing; they include beliefs about intermediate spirits—the "world-rulers of this darkness" which no one now holds; but they also contain splendid passages of noble eloquence, such as Romans viii and I Corinthians xiii, which scholars have pronounced to be the finest examples of Greek prose which had been written since the golden age of Athens. The fact is that he has suffered more from his friends than from his enemies. Paul has been buried beneath a Talmud of Paulinism. No one has done him a greater wrong than Martin Luther. The German reformer has found the centre of his teaching in "justification by faith," that is to say in a subjective assurance of salvation through the imputed merits of Christ.

St. Paul, we remember, "counts not himself to have apprehended," and fears that after preaching to others he may himself be a castaway. Luther bids us have no such fears. When we add that Luther advocates complete submission to the State, on the ground that Christian ethics are purely personal, whereas the State may "hang, behead, or break on the wheel" without incurring blame, we can hardly imagine a more mischievous perversion of Christianity. The other great Reformation movement, Calvinism, is a fine manly creed, Christianized Stoicism; but since its God is, by human standards, neither just nor merciful, it can hardly satisfy those who believe that Christ came to reveal not himself but his Father in heaven.

If we read St. Paul's epistles without these presuppositions, what do we find? It is plain that the core of his religion was Christ-mysticism; "I live, yet not I, but Christ liveth in me." Mr. Shaw thinks the apostle had no warrant for identifying the spiritual presence of which he was conscious with Jesus of Nazareth. The objection perhaps has not much meaning; names are of no importance in religion. We may be sure that the Deity does not mind whether he is called God or Gott or Dieu or even Allah; he has probably forgiven Mr. Shaw's friends the Russians for calling him Bug. What is essential is that the experience was a real one. What St. Paul calls indifferently the Spirit and Christ had really made a "temple" in his soul. It is nonsense to say that these experiences, not being transferable, are of no value as evidence. If a dozen honest men tell me that they have climbed the Matterhorn, I am satisfied that the summit of that mountain is accessible, though I shall never get there myself. This is the heart of St. Paul's religion, as it has been the heart of Christianity as a living faith from that day to this.

It must be confessed that Mr. Shaw comes out of this inquiry as a very untypical theologian. His quarrel is more with the Church than with its founders, and we should all agree that Church history is a melancholy record of obscurantism, fraud and cruelty. But he admits himself that we cannot do without institutions. As Troeitsch, a Protestant, says: "the essence of all religion is not dogma and idea but cultus and communion. So long as Christianity shall subsist at all, it will be united with a cultus." Royce speaks of "loyalty to the beloved community" as the centre of religion. And yet, as I once said rather harshly, Churches are secular institutions, in which the half-educated cater for the half-converted. This must be so, unless a Church is to be either a school of philosophers or a sect of revivalists. As a semi-political corporation, a Church cannot be far in advance of the intellectual and spiritual condition of its practising members. Our rulers are blamed for not getting better men for the ministry; they have only the laity to choose from.

Christianity, we are often told—Mr. Shaw himself has said it—has not failed, because it has never been tried. By whom has it never been tried? If the majority prefer to enter in by the broad gate, that is only what we have been told to expect. But have there been no saints who have worthily handed on the torch lighted when Christ came to "light a fire upon earth"? The true apostolical succession is in the lives of the saints. The national Church to which I have the honour to belong meets with scant respect from those outside it. It is meant to be the Church of England, representing the universal Church as shaped by the character and traditions of one of the great European nations. It has and ought to have a distinctive character; in religion as in other branches of human endeavour our nation has a contribution to bring to the common effort of humanity. I believe that the Church of England has less to be ashamed of than almost any other religious body. The eighteenth century and the earlier part of the nineteenth, when "Jeshurun waxed fat and kicked," were not a glorious time; but when we think of such names as Hooker, George Herbert, Traherne, the Cambridge Platonists, Bishop Jeremy Taylor, Bishop Wilson, Bishop Andrewes, William Law and

John Keble, not to mention more recent worthies whose names deserve to be added to the list, we shall not be willing to admit that in our Church Christianity has never been tried.

Scientists tell us that the human race is still at the stage of the rattle and feeding-bottle. We may have hundreds of thousands of years before us, in which to try every possible and impossible political experiment. It is not the business of the Churches to initiate or advocate political experiments. They are concerned with the hearts of men; their hope is that the "little leaven" may do something towards leavening the whole lump. There will undoubtedly be flowering times in the history of civilization, and some dreary set-backs. *Habet mundus noctes suas et non paucas*, as St. Bernard says. The birth of the higher religions took place about the middle of the first millennium before Christ, almost simultaneously, in China, India, Persia, Palestine (under the later prophets) and Greece. The wind bloweth where it listeth; if there are any laws which determine these movements we do not know what they are. But under whatever name, the Holy Spirit will always inspire those whose hearts are open to this influence; and these are not likely to be active politicians.

## PROFESSOR EDWARD J. DENT

### *CORNO DI BASSETTO*

THE last twenty years of Queen Victoria's reign are often said to have produced the Renaissance of English music. The phoenix rose from its ashes; it is now considered to be a very handsome and resplendent bird; few people remember what a naked and helpless chicken crept timidly out of the egg to be half smothered in a very unsavory dustbin. Mr. Shaw may have known in those young days of his exactly what he wanted to do in the world, but few of his readers did. Chance made him for the time being a musical critic; most people would have described him, and with nervous apprehension, as an "agitator." Perhaps after all that is the best description of him to-day; all his life he has been doing his best to shake us up. And it was a good thing that for those few years from 1888 to 1894 he did devote himself to musical criticism, for at that moment English music badly needed a good shaking-up.

Outwardly those were the serene days of George du Maurier, when, as somebody said, England looked at life through the drawing-room window. The modern musical reader must find that era now almost as remote as that of Doctor Burney while he turns over the pages of Corno di Bassetto; but like the Countess, "I remember days long departed," with the sentimental sigh of Thomas Hood, for my own musical life was just beginning when Mr. Shaw's left off. The modern age has no use for drawing-rooms; no hotel or house-agent would so much as mention them—they are as obsolete as parlours were then. America still has sitting-rooms and living-rooms; England prefers a "lounge" and regards every room, private, public, concert-hall or theatre, as a smoking-room. In Victorian days "to lounge" was a word of sharp reproof; we were all taught to sit bolt upright and never to admit that any chair had a back to it. Mr. Shaw said (and as late as 1917) that the art of music is kept alive on the cottage piano of the amateur; but by that date the amateur had discarded his piano for a pianola and he has now discarded both for a gramophone and a wireless set. Yet we are all agreed that England to-day is a much more musical country than in 1890, and no doubt a good deal of that improvement is due to the persistent shaking of Mr. Shaw.

Those four volumes of musical criticism describe what Dr. Burney called "the present state of music," and like Dr. Burney's they are now valuable documents for the history of music and musical taste in England. As an historian I am already finding them, like Burney's, invaluable for research purposes. How thankful we may be that paper and printing were cheap in those days! Both *The Star* and *The World* were delighted to allow Mr. Shaw about two thousand words a week, and he was only too delighted to write them. Not always about music; there was not music enough to go round, and Mr. Shaw was sometimes hard put to it to find something to talk about. But after all, there was always himself, and what better subject could there be for us who read him to-day?

Mr. Shaw was brought up in a drawing-room; we have his own word for it. But he was never very comfortable there, and I was told (I cannot vouch for the truth, as I never saw him myself in those days) that when all right-thinking people wore frock-coats and top-hats he habitually went about his musical duties wearing a knickerbocker suit of yellow tweeds with a bright red tie. If he had appeared in this costume at the grand opening gala night of Covent Garden on Wednesday, 20th February, 1946, nobody would have thought it in the least unusual. In 1890 the amateur's cottage piano—there were very few drawing-rooms that aspired to a Broadwood grand—might possibly have known Beethoven's sonatas in the whatnot, but on the desk it would have had a song by Mr. Milton Wellings. The drawing-room atmosphere pervaded all music, even classical music. To begin with, there was Her Majesty's Royal Italian Opera under Colonel Mapleson, the drawing-room of drawing-rooms, already dying of Donizetti's disease; at Covent Garden another Royal Opera under Augustus Harris, just on the way to become Edwardian rather than Victorian. We pride ourselves now on having become opera-minded, and even English opera-minded; but the unchallenged supremacy of the Opera House in Victorian days ended in 1914. As to concert-halls, London in those days was almost worse off than it is now after German bombardment. There was the Albert Hall, where the Royal Choral Society under Barnby regularly performed *Messiah, Elijah* and the oratorios of Gounod. The Hanover Square Rooms had been closed in 1874; the Steinway Hall (now a synagogue) was opened in 1878, the Queen's Hall (now destroyed) in 1893, the Salle Erard (now closed) in 1884, the Bechstein (now Wigmore) in 1901, the Aeolian Hall (now closed) in 1904, the Westminster Central Hall later still. Practically the only hall for music, both orchestral and chamber, was St. James's Hall (1858–1905), with its subterranean rumble of Negro minstrels like Nibelungs in the basement, and Piccadilly before motors quiet enough for concert-goers to hear plainly and frequently the familiar tinkle of the handbell with which the itinerant muffin-man advertised his wares.

To St. James's Hall we went for everything. The Philharmonic Society, started in 1813 as a pioneer for "contemporary music" such as that of Beethoven, Clementi and Spohr, had settled down—after experiments with Berlioz and Wagner as conductors—to the leisurely beat of Cowen and Mackenzie. Henschel was conducting concerts mostly of Beethoven, Richter paid us an annual visit to propagate Wagner with a background of Beethoven, and Manns was giving popular classical concerts at the Crystal Palace for the ardent disciples of George Grove, who immortalized himself perhaps less by his Dictionary (then just appearing) than by his discovery of the long-lost music of Schubert's *Rosamunde*. The best chamber music was to be heard at Ella's Musical Union, founded in 1845 as a highly exclusively private concert club; in 1858 the Saturday and Monday "Popular Concerts"—so called to distinguish their scope from Ella's—brought chamber music to wider audiences. For the multitude there had been the Promenade Concerts of Jullien and Balfe, consisting mainly of dance music, continued later under Arditi and Sullivan at Covent Garden in the autumn; but these were languishing if not already dead in Mr. Shaw's days, so that when Robert Newman restarted them at the Queen's Hall in 1895 they were something of a new idea. Outside London there were the provincial Festivals, with their eternal round of dreary oratorio at which Mr. Shaw raged in vain. The local audiences regarded them primarily as social functions, daytime equivalents of the Italian Opera for more serious people; musicians and critics in London thought them the main opportunities for bringing out native masterpieces—which the local audiences generally detested. Yorkshire regarded it as a terrible come-down when Leeds towards the end of the century engaged a solo pianist. The Philharmonic in its very early years had refused to admit concertos to its programmes at all, and something of this tradition must have survived in the country down to the end of Victoria's reign.

Singers were in a different category. The Victorian age had been a great age of song, but to most audiences that meant either operatic arias or drawing-room ballads. German *Lieder* were practically unknown; Mr. Shaw once mentions Henschel singing ballads of Löwe at a miscellaneous concert, but the vocal recitals of Plunket Greene and others who sang large groups of Schubert and Schumann had not then begun. I remember myself the sensation which was caused by a recital at which Plunket Greene sang the *Dichterliebe* right through, and if I remember right, the *Winterreise*, to the accompaniment of Leonard Borwick, who was not a professional accompanist but a solo pianist of high distinction. It was said that you could hear classical songs at Mr. Blumenthal's private parties, but to the outside world Blumenthal was the composer of *My Queen*. Another figure whom we often meet in Mr. Shaw's pages was "Mons." Johannes Wolff, who like the Eissler sisters was a great drawing-room favourite, and a great favourite of the Queen too. But Mr. Shaw seems to have known, as just a few other people did too, that Wolff (who had a right to his French title, as he was an Alsatian) was in reality a very sincere and serious artist.

Mr. Shaw was nursed in an operatic environment; not only did he listen to his mother singing at home, but like his fellow-countryman Stanford he frequented the seasons of Italian opera in Dublin organized by Colonel Mapleson. For both of them the "retadgeds," as Stanford called them in the Dublinese pronunciation (*anglice* the Italians), were an unforgettable background to their musical lives. Mr. Shaw as a critic did his duty conscientiously by the endless procession of pianists, violinists and conductors about whom he had to write, but his reader notes at once that his real passion was opera, as it was Stanford's too. I have no idea what the personal relations between Stanford and Shaw were in those days, but they were probably quarrelsome on Stanford's side, for there were few people with whom he did not quarrel, though seldom for very long. Mr. Shaw in these pages describes Stanford as tactful—the last epithet I should have expected. But Mr. Shaw insisted all along that Stanford had a real talent for opera, and that it was utter waste of it to compose oratorios in the Mixolydian mode; and we know now that he was right—*Eden* is forgotten and Stanford is remembered by *Shamus O'Brien* and *The Travelling Companion*. It can hardly have been mere conscientiousness that drove Mr. Shaw to attend and write careful and sympathetic criticisms of all the operas performed annually by the students of the Royal College of Music. In those days Stanford was fighting for College opera against the steady obstruction of Parry and other senior members of that institution; they regarded the opera class as a waste of students' time and a dangerous distraction from their regular studies. Here again Mr. Shaw saw that the opera class was a vital necessity; it has in fact provided our stage with many distinguished singers, and it is still the main source of supply for our National Opera.

The Mapleson opera must have collapsed pretty completely after the death of Tietjens in 1877. She was typically German in her personal ungainliness, but still more so in her tragic sincerity. Like Lilli Lehmann in later years, she sang the great Italian roles such as Norma and Lucrezia Borgia not merely with technical accomplishment but with fervid devotion. As Beethoven's Leonora she was incomparable, as I myself have been assured by Stanford and other contemporaries of his who often heard her. It must have been that intense seriousness of hers—an attitude perfectly inconceivable and incomprehensible to the modern admirers of Richard Strauss and Puccini —which prepared young Mr. Shaw for the immediate understanding of Wagner. Mr. Shaw was in those days indeed "the perfect Wagnerite." The English opera-goer of to-day seems to have forgotten Wagner completely. He may be acquainted with his music in concert extracts and gramophone records, but, as far as I can judge, he has no conception of that profound spiritual experience which we derived from *Tristan*, *The Ring* and *Parsifal* in the 1890's, especially those of us who went to Bayreuth. And towards that experience *The Perfect Wagnerite* did indeed give us genuine enlightenment.

One of the best pieces of prophetic criticism is to be found in the article that Mr. Shaw wrote on the Mozart centenary of December, 1891. He pointed out, at a moment when Mozart was almost utterly neglected, that Mozart was the consummation of an epoch, and that after his death it was impossible to go on imitating him. A new departure had to be made altogether, and it was Cherubini who initiated it, followed by Beethoven, Weber and the Romantics. And he saw clearly in 1891 that Wagner too was the end of a period and not a beginning. History has shown that the Wagner imitators who were trying to continue his methods after his death were on the wrong track; they are all completely forgotten.

"Here, under our very noses, is Wagner held up on all hands as the founder of a new school and the arch-musical innovator of our age. He himself knew better; but since his death I appear to be the only person who shares his view of the matter. I assert with the utmost confidence that in 1991 it will be seen quite clearly that Wagner was the end of the nineteenth-century, or Beethoven school; just as Mozart's most perfect music is the last word of the eighteenth century, and not the first of the nineteenth. . . . *Die Zauberflöte* is the ancestor . . . of the Wagnerian allegorical music-drama, with personified abstractions instead of individualized characters as *dramatis personæ*. But *Il Seraglio* and *Die Zauberflöte* do not belong to . . . Mozart's consummate achievement. They are nineteenth-century music heard advancing in the distance, as his Masses are seventeenth-century music retreating in the distance. And, similarly, though the future fossiliferous critics of 1991, after having done their utmost, without success, to crush twentieth-century music, will be able to show that Wagner (their chief classic) made one or two experiments in that direction, yet the world will rightly persist in thinking of him as a characteristically nineteenth-century composer of the school of Beethoven, greater than Beethoven by as much as Mozart was greater than Haydn. . . . Second-hand Wagner is more insufferable, because usually more pretentious, than even second-hand Mozart used to be."

In 1892 Mr. Shaw was agitating for municipal orchestras. After fifty years we have done a little in that direction, but not anything like enough. It is amusing to-day to find that Mr.

Shaw thought that the best way to start municipal orchestras would be to begin with parish orchestras in churches in place of the organ, an instrument on which he had very unorthodox opinions. But organists may thank him even now for fighting their battle against the unmusical clergy, a battle which is still raging as fiercely as ever. "The organist is, and will always be, a slave. But if there were an orchestra in the church the organist would have to be a conductor, capable of inspiring confidence in a whole band. . . . Besides, the artistic conscience of a band is a stronger resisting force than that of an individual organist. It is always easier to say 'We object' than 'I object.' . . . As a first step . . . let everyone of musical pretensions do his best to discredit the notion that the organ is a specially sacred kind of music machine." Well, the cinema has now done that for us. But have our modern orchestras got artistic consciences?

The year 1892 was famous for the performances of Wagner's *Ring* in German by a German company which included various notable names, and a German orchestra from Hamburg under Gustav Mahler. In view of the adoration which has been lavished on Mahler in recent years it is interesting to read the scathing criticisms of Mr. Shaw. Mahler's orchestra was coarse and rough; the strings of poor quality, the wood-wind no better, and the brass "a huge tribe of mongrels, differing chiefly in size. I felt that some ancestor of the trombones had been guilty of a *mésalliance* with a bombardon; that each cornet, though itself already an admittedly half-bred trumpet, was further disgracing itself by a leaning towards the flügel horn; and that the mother of the horns must have run away with a whole military band." The Covent Garden orchestra, he maintains, could have handled the score with much greater distinction of tone and more delicate and finished execution. The Rhine sounded like "a river of treacle, and rather lumpy treacle at that"; the stage arrangements were chaotic, the singers—except for Lieban as Mime—mediocre. Yet "the impression created by the performance was extraordinary, the gallery cheering wildly at the end of each act. Everybody was delighted with the change from the tailor-made operatic tenor in velvet and tights to the wild young hero who forges his own weapons and tans his own coat and buskins. We all breathed that vast orchestral atmosphere of fire, air, earth and water with unbounded relief and invigoration."

The reader of to-day may be slightly comforted to learn that "austerity opera" existed even in late-Victorian London. Signor Lago was an enterprising manager who gave winter seasons of opera, sometimes in Italian, sometimes in English. They were as much an event as Mahler's Wagner season; Lago was the first manager to introduce *Eugene Onegin* to England, and he had it conducted by young Mr. Henry Wood. Mr. Shaw was "always tremendously down on the slovenly traditions of the old school," but he could understand "its romantic illusions and enthusiasms." He was a Wagnerite, but he could still appreciate a performance of Bellini or Donizetti that was taken seriously and not regarded merely as an opportunity for a *prima donna*'s exhibitionism. He was shocked to find that the conservatives of Covent Garden, "after years of *Faust* and *Carmen* and *Huguenots* and *Mefistofele* and *soi-disant Lohengrin*" were completely ignorant of "that ultra-classical product of Romanticism, the grandiose Italian opera in which the executive art consists in a splendid display of personal heroics, and the drama arises out of the simplest and most universal stimulants to them." That is a really notable piece of historical criticism. The operas for which Felice Romani wrote his masterly librettos were indeed both romantic and classical at the same time. (The word *stimulants* must not be taken too pharmaceutically, although Donna Lucrezia Borgia provided them in plenty, and emetics too.) The paragraph which follows must be quoted entire, for it is perhaps the author's masterpiece of vituperation.

"The popular notion of them is therefore founded on performances in which the superb distinction and heroic force of the male characters, and the tragic beauty of the women, have been burlesqued by performers with every sort of disqualification for such parts, from age and obesity to the most excruciating phases of physical insignificance and Cockney vulgarity. I used often to wonder why it was that whilst every asphalt contractor could get a man to tar the streets, and every tourist could find a gondolier, rather above the average of the House of Lords in point of nobility of aspect, no operatic manager, after Mario vanished, seemed able to find a Manrico with whom any exclusively disposed Thames mudlark would care to be seen grubbing for pennies. When I get on this subject I really cannot contain myself. The thought of that dynasty of execrable impostors in tights and tunics, interpolating their loathsome B flats into the beautiful melodies they could not sing, and swelling with conceit when they were able to finish *Di quella pira* with a high C capable of making a stranded man-of-war recoil off a reef into mid-ocean, I demand the suspension of all rules as to decorum of language until I have heaped upon them some little instalment of the infinite abuse they deserve."

An article from *The Nation* (7th July, 1917) "by a ghost from the 'eighties" has a penetrating criticism of *Il Trovatore* which follows naturally on the preceding paragraph.

"*Il Trovatore* is, in fact, unique, even among the works of its own composer and its own country. It has tragic power, poignant melancholy, impetuous vigour, and a sweet and intense pathos that never loses its dignity. It is swift in action, and perfectly homogeneous in atmosphere and feeling. It is absolutely void of intellectual interest: the appeal is to the instincts and to the senses all through. If it allowed you to think for a moment it would crumble into absurdity like the garden of Klingsor. . . .

"Let us admit that no man is bound to take *Il Trovatore* seriously. We are entirely within our rights in passing it by and turning to Bach and Handel, Mozart and Beethoven, Wagner and Strauss, for our music. But we must take it or leave it; we must not trifle with it. He who thinks that *Il Trovatore* can be performed without taking it with the most tragic solemnity is, for all purposes of romantic art, a fool."

The 'nineties were a period of truculence in journalism, and Mr. Shaw could handle the bludgeon as doughtily as any when occasion demanded. But he was never systematically truculent, like his colleague J. F. Runciman, and he wielded his weapon always with his own humorous grace. Runciman was rancorous and spiteful; his personal animosities were self-evident, and when he surprised his readers by a show of admiration, they could hardly fail to be suspicious of his integrity. Rancour and spite were of course inconceivable with Mr. Shaw; humour and good nature forced their way in even at unexpected and possibly inappropriate moments. The only fault of which one might indeed accuse him was a tendency to discursiveness and triviality. Boredom is the besetting temptation of all musical critics; one might call it their occupational disease. There is some music that one just simply can't write about—none the less, the page has got to be filled. To one who can remember those days Mr. Shaw's patience and endurance seem almost miraculous. He would sit through concerts of a type that has now pretty completely vanished—"Mr. Blank's Annual Concert, kindly assisted by——" a whole string of celebrities, major and minor—or charity concerts of similar programme. It must be admitted that musicians in those days were generous of their services, and even more generous of encores. And Mr. Shaw would conscientiously note each item, in the hopes of being rewarded by some one performance at least that could command his respect and admiration.

As to the trivialities, he has good precedent in Dr. Burney's *Travels*, which we all read with delight, often enjoying the minor incidents of everyday life more than the criticism of the music. Burney's three volumes, like Mr. Shaw's, are the picture of a period, and it is just the *accidenti verissimi,* as the old librettists would have called them, which the researcher now finds of inestimable value, because very often they can be found nowhere else. Mr. Shaw's description of the journey to Bayreuth, which covers four pages, has nothing new for readers who have taken the same sort of route in old days, but "the fossiliferous critic of 1991" will regard it, like Burney's German diary, as a classic of travel literature. Every detail of Bayreuth itself is already serious history by now. Another piece of history is a long article (*The Star,* 15th November, 1889) about a Mr. Alfred Moul, who was pianist, composer, conductor, publisher and many other things besides, never looked more than eighteen years of age, and was apparently the first man in England to stand out for performing rights. And what a wonderful description of Arabella Goddard! "She was more like the Lady of Shalott working away at her loom than a musician at a piano." She belonged to an earlier age, as Mr. Shaw admits, but she was a really great pianist, with a truly Victorian dignity of manner, and it must never be forgotten that in the 1850's she had had both the courage and the understanding to play the last sonatas of Beethoven.

In January, 1890, Mr. Shaw went to see *La Tosca,* i.e. Sardou's play. "I do not know which are the more pitiable, the vapid two acts of obsolete comedy of intrigue, or the three acts of sham torture, rape, murder, gallows and military execution, set to dialogue that might have been improvised by strolling players in a booth. Oh, if it had but been an opera! It is fortunate for John Hare that he has only the dramatic critics to deal with." And unfortunate for us that Corno di Bassetto never saw the *Tosca* of Puccini.

The only people with whom Mr. Shaw never had any patience were those who would not take music seriously, and sometimes those who took it too seriously. It is delightful to see him scoffing at the pomposities of Ruskin on music at a time when Ruskin was still alive and venerable. He was not going to stand *Don Giovanni* and *Die Zauberflöte* being described as examples of "foolishest and most monstrous words fitted and followed with perfect sound." Ruskin belonged to the generation which knew *Die Zauberflöte* only in the Italian version; and even Mr. Shaw, though he always calls the opera by its German title, always quotes the songs in Italian—though perhaps this was only a kindly concession to his ignorant readers. But he was well in advance of his time, for hardly anyone in England, at that date, understood the ethical significance of *Die Zauberflöte*. That indeed was only possible for those who shared Mr. Shaw's general attitude to what is called religion, and his outlook on music as a spiritual force.

That conception of music, not as the "handmaid of the Church," but as a spiritual force in its own right which for want of a better word I am obliged (following Mr. Shaw's own example) to call a "religion," was adumbrated in conversation by Handel, but hardly began to make itself generally felt until the advent of Beethoven. Beethoven confessed himself that he owed it largely to Handel, whom he studied thoroughly in later life, whereas his acquaintance with the works of Bach was indeed scanty in the extreme, scantier probably than Mozart's. It took the whole of the nineteenth century to bring audiences in this country to a real understanding of Beethoven; Mr. Shaw was always in advance of his time. Only in the present century have we begun, and have only just begun, to realize music as a religion; historically that may be said to date from the initiation of Sunday concerts, an institution which Miss Cons, for instance, despite all her solicitude for social welfare, thoroughly disapproved of. The whole of Mr. Shaw's musical criticism can be summed up in his observations on the Ninth Symphony.

"There must be a growing number of persons who, like myself, would rather have the Ninth Symphony, even from the purely musical point of view, than all the other eight put together, and to whom, besides, it is religious music, and its performance a celebration rather than an entertainment. I am highly susceptible to the force of all truly religious music, no matter to what Church it belongs; but the music of my own Church—for which I may be allowed, like other people, to have partiality—is to be found in *Die Zauberflöte* and the Ninth Symphony."

It was a pity that when Signor Lago did on the last night of his season in 1892 actually bring out *Die Zauberflöte* Mr. Shaw by an unlucky accident missed the performance and lost the opportunity of writing about it. But I am grateful to him for having just mentioned it, for he thus gave me an historical fact for which I had searched the files of *The Musical Times* in vain.

MAURICE DOBB

*Lecturer in Economics, Cambridge University*

## *BERNARD SHAW AND ECONOMICS*

IT IS a curious feature of Mr. Shaw's writings on economic questions that, while his ideas are inspired by Henry George and Jevons as regards their form, in their forthright denunciation of capitalist property and of income from that property they continue to bear strong traces of the inspiration of Marx. "Converted to Socialism by *Das Kapital*," but reacting against the narrow, doctrinaire Hyndman-type of Marxism which was dominant in the S.D.F. of the '80's, the author of the chapter on the economic basis of Socialism in the *Fabian Essays* of 1889 discarded the value theory of Ricardo and of Marx for the utility-theory of Jevons, which was the latest fashion of the time. References to the class struggle disappear in favour of "the necessity for cautious and gradual change" by "the transfer of rent and interest to the State, not in a lump sum, but by instalments." Revolutionary views are dismissed with a tolerant smile as the illusions of "the young socialist (who) is apt to be catastrophic in his views."[1] There is little here even about organizing a labour movement as the instrument of the revolt against Capitalism; although a good deal is said about the extension of the franchise and about municipal politics. The keynote is appeal to reason: a demonstration that the existing system is not only unjust but absurd and unworkable,

[1] These sentences are from the second essay in the collection, on *The Transition to Social Democracy*, which was a reprint of an address delivered to the Economic Section of the British Association in 1888.

which can be made to carry conviction with rich as well as poor.

Yet the generalized theory of rent upon which the economic argument is made to turn, while it is patterned upon Henry George, substantially amounts to much the same thing as Marx meant by surplus value: the product of social labour which is appropriated by a propertied class by virtue, not of any economic function they perform, but of their special position in a society divided into propertied and propertyless. This identification of what this Fabian essay calls rent with surplus value is admitted in a later work; and in the famous Maxims for Revolutionists appended to *Man and Superman* Proudhon's dictum that "property is theft" is applauded as "the only perfect truism uttered on the subject." [1] One sometimes wonders why the author should have chosen to place his conception in a Ricardo-Georgian rather than a Marxian setting, unless it was with the aim of making a more ready appeal thereby to the English radicals of the time. His denunciation of capitalist exploitation was uncompromising enough even for the taste of socialists who were proposing the "militant organization of the working classes" which the *Fabian Essays* treated as an infantile illusion. Private property, with its boast of "the great accumulation of so-called 'wealth' . . . as the result of its power to scourge men and women daily to prolonged and intense toil, turns out to be a simulacrum," he says in a characteristically telling passage. "With all its energy, its Smilesian 'self-help,' its merchant-princely enterprise, its ferocious sweating and slave-driving, its prodigality of blood, sweat and tears, what has it heaped up, over and above the pittance of its slaves? Only a monstrous pile of frippery, some tainted class literature and class art, and not a little poison and mischief." [2] Exposure of social abuses could scarcely be more unqualified

[1] *Prefaces by Bernard Shaw*, 191.

[2] *Fabian Essays in Socialism*, 1st Ed., 23.

than in those well-thumbed Prefaces to *Widowers' Houses* and *Mrs. Warren's Profession:* abuses which are emphasized as products of a system and not of the immorality or inhumanity of individuals. In connection with *Mrs. Warren's Profession* he speaks of "the alternative offered by society collectively to poor women" as being "a miserable life, starved, overworked, fetid, ailing, ugly": "starvation, overwork, dirt and disease are as anti-social as prostitution—they are the vices and crimes of a nation and not merely its misfortunes." [1] The pious complacency of the Victorian bourgeoisie met no mercy from the gall of this pen. Again, he recognized that "our present system of imperial aggression, in which, under pretext of exploration and colonization, the flag follows the filibuster and trade follows the flag, with the missionary bringing up the rear, must collapse when the control of our military forces passes from the capitalist class to the people," and that "the disappearance of a variety of classes with a variety of what is now ridiculously called 'public opinions' will be accompanied by the welding of society into one class with a public opinion of inconceivable weight." Statements like these, uttered in the penultimate decade of the nineteenth century, sound fresh and pointed more than half a century later; and Left pamphleteers of to-day could profit greatly from lessons in the power of such language.

It is again the inspiration of Marx rather than of nineteenth-century radicalism that one senses in his outspoken championing of the Dictatorship of the Proletariat in an early issue of *The Labour Monthly* [2] soon after the Russian Revolution; although in his dictum that "Mr. Henderson and Mr. Clynes can no more make our political machine produce Socialism than they can make a sewing machine produce fried eggs" he probably had something rather different in mind from the im-

[1] *Prefaces*, 230.

[2] *Labour Monthly*, Vol. I, No. 4, October 1921.

plication of Lenin's statement that "the working class must *break up* the 'available ready machinery of the State,' and not confine itself merely to taking possession of it." At the same time there were many who were surprised at the tributes which this Fabian gradualist paid to the achievements of the Soviet State (despite his references to the "mistakes" of the Bolsheviks, attributable to their habit of "despising Fabians as bourgeois");[1] and such tributes were commonly dismissed as a sign of his impish delight in the game of *épater les bourgeois* and of an undimmed flair for paradox. But most people are now sufficiently the wiser after the events of the past few years to recognize in his attitude a rare quality of realism in appraising historical situations and the process of historical change.

What some would term the eclecticism of Mr. Shaw's ideas on economic questions is responsible for much of their individual character; and his failure to adhere consistently to the Jevonian economics he espoused would be regarded by many as a saving virtue. While he accepted from Jevons (via the advocacy of the economist Wicksteed, I believe) the notion of "final utility" as an explanation of exchange value, he did not adopt the so-called theory of distribution of this school.[2] Here we have seen that he clung to the Ricardian tradition, generalizing the notion of economic rent so that it included income derived from ownership of capital as well as income derived from ownership of land. The analogy between the two

[1] *Intelligent Woman's Guide to Socialism* (1928 Ed.), 426.

[2] One reason, apparently, why Mr. Shaw rejected Mill's cost of production or Ricardo's and Marx's quantity of embodied labour as the basis of value was because he thought that this notion could be used to deny, or at least to conceal, the fact of rent. The notion that commodities exchange "in exact proportion to the labour they cost," he writes, "carries the implication that the landlords cost the community nothing." But "so far from commodities exchanging, or tending to exchange, according to the labour expended in their production, commodities produced well within the margin of cultivation will fetch as high a price as commodities produced at the margin with much greater labour. So far from the landlord costing nothing, he costs all the difference between the two." (*Fabian Essays,* 17.)

he developed in a vigorous and graphic fashion; and although this exposition somewhat lacked the rigour that economists demanded if deductive argument were to carry conviction, the substantial common sense of the conclusion contrasted boldly with the sophistries about "abstinence" and "productivity of capital," in which the analyses of economists at the time had become enmeshed. While his view bore considerable resemblance to the well-known surplus theory of J. A. Hobson, it differed from the latter in being more unqualified. *All* income from capital was surplus (whereas Hobson had treated as "surplus" only the excess over the "supply-price" of a factor of production, and regarded capital and "entrepreneurship" as having at least *some* necessary supply-price; thereby walking in the footsteps of Marshall). "Shareholders and landlords live alike," said Mr. Shaw, "on the produce extracted from their property by the labour of the proletariat." Moreover, most of the incomes of the professional middle class—the so-called "reward of ability," and especially that "artificial rent of ability inflated by snobbery and the requirements of social status"—were part of the same *genus* of unearned surplus or rent, as were also the profits of industrial management. "Private property, by cheapening the labourer to the utmost in order to get the greatest surplus out of him, lowers the margin of human cultivation, and so raises the rent of ability." [1] Monopoly gains were simply the logical extension of this type of income by methods of deliberate restriction: fruit of the natural tendency in such a society to control the value of commodities by acquiring power to limit their supply. The existence of this rent in its various forms stood exposed as the flagrant injustice at the base of the present economic system, mocking the conscience of mankind. It was also the root of the system's inefficiency, since by divorcing income from labour it stultified incentive to effort and improvement, made wealth accumulate while men decay, and simultaneously multiplied worthless lux-

[1] *Ibid.*, 197.

ury and ostentation among the rich and human degradation among the poor. "By giving all the work to one class and all the leisure to another the Capitalist system disables the rich as completely as the poor." [1]

What was essentially a social product should, in justice and reason, accrue to society as a whole; and the social appropriation of this surplus followed as a corollary which all reasonable men must accept. With regard to land, many liberals were already accepting it in their advocacy of the taxation of socially produced increment of land values (such as the rise in value of sites, due to urban development around them). But what was the point of appropriating the surplus itself, if the State could not reinvest it in the development of production? The logical outcome, therefore, of the social appropriation of economic rent must be the State acquisition of the source of that rent as well: namely, the socialization of land and capital. Thus the case for Socialism was derived primarily from a theory of distribution: as the inevitable corollary of principles of social justice to which the radicals were willing to subscribe. Socialization would proceed by stages, and at each stage there would be full compensation to the class of owners affected. What was received by way of compensation would ultimately be taken back by the State through progressive taxation which would distribute the burden equitably over all property-owners instead of lumping it on one or a few groups alone. As a first stage the municipality would acquire land necessary for urban developments, and extend industries such as road-making, housing and public utilities, probably "for the most regard(ing) their action as a mere device to meet a passing emergency"; and "as the municipality becomes more democratic, it will find landlordism losing power, not only relatively to democracy, but absolutely." [2] At the time of the *Fabian Es-*

[1] *Intelligent Woman's Guide*, 165.

[2] *Fabian Essays*, 194. cf. also *The Commonsense of Municipal Trading* (1908).

says little was envisaged beyond this stage, except for the extension of legal minimum wages. What is here called "the extinction of private property" by successive stages evidently rests on the belief that resistance to extinction will be strictly confined within the sphere of democratic institutions, and that the process even "may be anticipated by sections of the proprietary class successively capitulating, as the net closes about their special interests, on such terms as they may be able to stand out for before their power is entirely broken." [1]

The writer of these words would probably admit to-day that subsequent events in the world at large have shown this to be an idyllic picture, probably much farther from reality than the primitive "catastrophic" notions that in the late '80's he prided himself on having outgrown. In fact, in *The Intelligent Woman's Guide to Socialism*, published thirty-nine years after the *Fabian Essays*, he explicitly denies that "the inevitability of gradualness" means "the inevitability of peacefulness"; and in the light of recent events in Ireland and in Spain and Italy he admitted the possibility of extra-constitutional resistance by the capitalists to the march of Socialism. "It may quite possibly happen that even if the most perfect set of Fabian Acts of Parliament for the constitutional completion of Socialism in this country is passed through Parliament by duly elected representatives of the people; swallowed with wry faces by the House of Lords; and finally assented to by the King and placed on the statute book, the capitalists may, like Signor Mussolini, denounce Parliament as unpatriotic, pernicious and corrupt and try to prevent by force the execution of the Fabian Acts. We should then have a state of civil war, with, no doubt, the Capitalist forces burning the co-operative stores, and the proletarians burning the country houses, as in Ireland." [2] But he is sufficiently faithful to his earlier standpoint to be still concerned to stress two things. Firstly, such a revolution would not

[1] *Fabian Essays*, 199.

[2] *Intelligent Woman's Guide* (1928 Ed.), 372.

have the character of a class struggle. "The line . . . which separates those interested in the maintenance of Capitalism from those interested in its replacement by Socialism is a line drawn not between rich and poor, capitalist and proletarian, but right down through the middle of the proletariat to the bottom of the poorest section"; and he approves of Labour leaders who denounce extremist talk of class war: talk that "echo(es) Shelley's very misleading couplet: 'Ye are many: they are few.' "[1] Secondly, the manner in which this struggle for power is fought to a conclusion in no way changes the form or the gradualness with which the constructive work of Socialism must be carried through: a process in which he seems to give little place to democratic initiative, and which is apparently envisaged as essentially a civil service job, requiring considerable reorganization of State machinery and methods at the top, but deriving very little from the impetus and activity of new types of popular organization rising from below.

It is in *The Intelligent Woman's Guide to Socialism* that Mr. Shaw enunciates equality of income as a basic principle of Socialism. Here is well exhibited the essential rationalism that has always characterized Mr. Shaw's social philosophy. Socialism is something demonstrable as the only conclusion at which pure reason, if consistently applied, can arrive. This demonstration rests primarily on a critique of Capitalism as a system of distribution; and equality of income becomes the essential definition of Socialism to which the demonstration necessarily leads. The argument for equality is developed by taking in turn each of the seven alternative principles of distributing income and rejecting them as meaningless or unworkable. Since production is a co-operative effort, the separate productivity of individuals or groups of workers cannot be estimated. Division according to the amount of work done meets practical difficulties in measuring the amount, and a difficulty of principle "in attempting to compare the value of

[1] *Ibid.*, 373.

the work of a clever woman (or man) with that of a stupid one." "To each what she deserves" may mean all things to all manner of men; and "to each what she can grab" or leaving it to the play of supply and demand represents what happens to-day. Hence by a process of exclusion of alternatives, the principle of equality is left as the only satisfactory rule and as an eminently simple one. Moreover, it is the only method consistent with securing promotion purely by merit.

The simplicity of this answer unquestionably has an immediate appeal, as has also its conformity with abstract justice. But the argument by which it is reached is more summary than usual. One is left with the impression that a number of rival ninepins have been knocked over with agility without the one that is left standing being subjected to an equivalent test. In particular, the possibility that different types of work may have different "subsistence needs" seems to be too lightly passed over (at least, in the first edition of this work); as does also the possibility that the difficulties of paying according to the amount and type of work (probably on some compromise between differences that have become conventional and what the conditions of supply dictate in a particular economic situation) may be no greater than the problems which are likely to arise in practice from an indiscriminate application of an abstract principle of equality. Later, Mr. Shaw seems to have admitted that the principle of equality is inapplicable unless production is sufficient to ensure an adequate standard of life for all, including people with special needs, or accustomed to special standards, like artists and poets and mathematicians and physicists;[1] and that in the interests of raising

[1] cf. Penguin Ed. (1938) of *Intelligent Woman's Guide*, 441, where reference is made to Soviet experience as showing that, in view of the need in the early stages of a Socialist government to encourage persons of higher education and to encourage workers to acquire skill, "it (the State) must fix the distribution level at a figure which will provide for the requirements and comparative seclusion and distinction which is necessary to such persons, and then work up production until that level can be attained by everybody."

production to the required level it may be desirable to offer the inducement of a higher income to those who work harder or take the trouble to acquire skill. If it is qualified in this way, the doctrine assumes a rather different significance. It becomes an ideal standard to work towards—"a condition essential to the stability of any association of human beings" in an ideal society—as the problems of production are mastered and plenty is made to replace scarcity. But then, so also, as the problem of production is mastered, should it become possible to extend the range of things whose distribution is governed by a communist principle (since, with a higher standard of life, the demand for them will have sufficiently approached satiety to become inelastic, and their scarcity will no longer require that their use be restricted, as an alternative to rationing, by charging a price for them). To the extent that this is the case, the question of money income loses its importance and recedes into the background. If the matter is viewed in this light, income-equality becomes the goal of a socialist society rather than its essential condition; and the conception does not seem to be very different from—at least, does not seem to stand in contradiction with—the distinction made by Marx (and to-day part of accepted tradition in the U.S.S.R.) between the "first and lower stage of Socialism," where inequalities due to property-incomes have been banished but inequalities due to differences in the amount and type of work continue, and that "second and higher stage of Socialism" where a higher principle of communist equality can prevail, on the basis of a greater mastery by society over the productive forces. The difference which remains between the two conceptions seems to be that between a theory of Socialism fashioned as a theory of distribution and as a theory of production. With the former as one's starting-point, it seems logically necessary to define Socialism in terms of some principle of distribution which will contrast it with the present order; and it has apparently been this starting-point which has placed Mr. Shaw under a sense of obligation to postulate in unequivocal fashion the principle of distribution on which the society of the future will be based. But if one is willing to treat as crucial the social ownership of the means of production, and the liquidation of the old class relationships, resting on private property, then one will feel less constrained than Mr. Shaw has apparently felt to be dogmatic as to the precise pattern of income-distribution that a Socialist State (which may operate in a variety of historical contexts) must adopt to justify its name. Marx's well-known phrase about social justice, that it can "never rise superior to the economic conditions of society and the cultural development conditioned by them," well illustrates the distinction between an historical approach and a purely rationalist one.

But it is probably as a mode of exposition, rather than as a systematic construction of novel economic doctrine, that Mr. Shaw's economic writings ought properly to be judged in any attempt to estimate the influence they have had on their age and their enduring importance. The brilliant lucidity of style and mastery of language, which we have all come to associate with his writing, is part, but not the whole, of the impelling quality that has fascinated the minds of three generations of readers. The unlaboured elegance of his choice of language; the gift for memorable epigram seasoned with paradox, and for the apt example; the power of denunciation and the nimble Irish wit are, again, part but not the whole of it. Even more, it is the penetration and deftness of thought, lying behind the style and the telling aphorism, which can reduce an opponent's thesis to a few terse propositions, and then demolish them as self-contradictory or flagrantly untrue to reality, not by tortuous train of argument, but by adroit encirclement and by saturation with a cumulative series of pointed examples. And when one has said that, one is conscious that it is still not the whole story, and that there is some quality in the fastidiously fashioned structure of his thought and exposition which has eluded description.

Perhaps the best example of his success in polemic is his famous controversy with Mr. Mallock, which first appeared in *The Fortnightly Review* in April, 1894 (when Frank Harris was its editor), and was reprinted as a Fabian Tract (No. 146) in 1909. At least, this example is one to which the present writer is particularly attached, if only because it stands out in his memory as an early formative influence on his own ideas. Here the arguments of Mr. Mallock, which only since then have been widely seen to be ridiculous as they stand and have been generally discarded by intelligent apologists of Capitalism, were dissected with the touch of a master, and were severally disposed of, each in a single consuming phrase. The main claim on which Mr. Mallock had relied was that profit and interest on capital were the reward of superior ability. To this Mr. Shaw opposes "the obvious fact that the interest on railway stock is paid mostly to people who could not invent a wheelbarrow, much less a locomotive"; and he proceeds to ridicule, as "rustic ignorance of economic theory" and "incredible ignorance of society," "the notion that the people who are now spending in week-end hotels, in motor-cars, in Switzerland, the Riviera and Algeria, the remarkable increase in unearned incomes noted by Mr. Keir Hardie have ever invented anything, ever directed anything, ever even selected their own investments without the aid of a stockbroker or solicitor (or) ever as much as seen the industries from which their incomes derive." To the argument that greater equality of income would leave no one willing to go into the learned professions or take positions of responsibility in industry he retorts: "If an ordinance were issued to-morrow that every man from the highest to the lowest should have exactly equal pay, then I could quite understand difficulties arising from every man insisting on being head of his department. Why

Mr. Mallock should anticipate rather that all the heads would insist on becoming subordinates is more than I can reconcile with the intelligence for which he is famous." To the argument that Socialism would abolish all incentive to production, by making the State "an organized conspiracy" to rob men of their incomes, he replies: "My impression hitherto has been that the whole history of civilization is the history of millions of men toiling to produce wealth for the express purpose of . . . meeting the State-enforced demands of landlords, capitalists and other masters of the sources of production. . . . Are not those very rents and dividends over which Mr. Mallock has so ingeniously gone astray, produced to-day by workers of all grades, who are compelled by the State to hand over every farthing of it to 'drones'?" The long and short of it was that "Mr. Mallock has confused the proprietary classes with the productive classes, the holders of ability with the holders of land and capital, the man about town with the man of affairs." Was there really anything more that needed to be said?

What must have repeatedly struck those concerned with the advocacy of Socialism, and contributed to a steeling of their hearts and minds, is the absence in any of Mr. Shaw's economic writings of the least trace of an apologetic note. Throughout there is the austere *hauteur* of tone which derives from a writer's supreme assurance of the rightness of his case and of his own ability to confound his opponents in verbal argument, without descent to evasions or personalities. This tone is part of the same pattern as the cogency of his exposition and the *bravura* of his polemical style. It is the invigorating language of confidence in ultimate success and of dauntless iconoclasm: language which always breathes the spirit of attack.

# A. S. NEILL

## *SHAW AND EDUCATION*

OF ALL men Shaw is the most difficult to write about, to explain, to analyse, because . . . but the answer lies in a reminiscence. In 1913 a friend of mine wanted to write a Life of Shaw, and wrote asking the author's permission to quote from his works. The permission was given on a postcard: "But why write a book about me? Why not write a book about yourself, if you've got a self, and, anyway, who wants to know what you think of me when they can read what I think about myself?" And thirty-odd years later it is still true. Shaw has explained so much, so patiently, so incisively, so brilliantly, that one is inclined to cry impatiently: The man has said all there is to say; no use trying to interpret an interpreter. And there is the personal psychological difficulty in writing about Shaw. When I first discovered his plays and prefaces in my student days, a new world was opened up to me. He was the oracle. When he addressed the students of Edinburgh University I recall trembling with fear when I got up to ask a question, and blushing with shame when the answer poked a little fun at me, and I don't expect that I am the only one to feel himself a country bumpkin in the presence of his wit and wisdom. So that to write of Bernard Shaw is rather like writing about the New Testament: a Calvinistic youth made me incapable for ever of judging the New Testament without bias and warped judgment, and my enthusiasm for Shaw many years ago must still have some bearing on my valuation of the old man of to-day. I had and still have a G.B.S. complex, and what I write now should be considered in that light.

The *Parents and Children Preface* dates back to the year

1910, that is to the time when Freud was unknown, when psychology was to most people a peddling science, divorced from all that was dynamic. Freud's discoveries led to a new attitude to the child and its education, and it should be valuable to learn whether Shaw anticipated the modern outlook, approaching it from a different angle, a conscious rather than an unconscious angle. So far as I can read, Shaw has not been influenced by Freud and the new psychology at all. If this is so, what he says about education must be judged, not by standards of to-day, but by standards of yesterday. In 1910 education was accepted by the great majority as a moulding of character and a training in academic subjects with a few side lines of the freehand drawing and basket-making type. Narrow-minded pedants were arguing about compulsory Greek. Bernard Shaw, at that time famous for his cap and bells, suddenly launched a bombshell in the pedagogic and parental world. Hark at the man:

> "Nobody knows the way a child should go. All the ways discovered so far lead to the horrors of our existing civilizations. . . ." (*Misalliance.*)
>
> "The vilest abortionist is he who attempts to mould a child's character." (*Maxims for Revolutionists.*)

These sayings do not sound shocking to-day, but getting on to forty years ago they were most shocking, for they cut at the root of the whole question of children and homes and schools; they in effect cried: Stop talking about Greek and grammar and geography, and realize that education is life, not school, moving, not sitting docile at desks. They put character high above school certificates, but not the kind of character that the schoolmasters and prefects claimed (and claim) to produce; Shaw's idea of character was something deeper and better and freer than any moulded character. Hark at him again:

"Every child has a right to its own bent. It has a right to be a Plymouth Brother though its parents be convinced atheists. It has the right to dislike its mother or father or sister or brother or uncle or aunt if they are antipathetic to it. It has a right to find its own way and go its own way, whether that way seems wise or foolish to others, exactly as an adult has. It has a right to privacy as to its own doings and its own affairs as much as if it were its own father." (*Misalliance.*)

That was heretical in 1910, and I fear it is heresy to many teachers and parents to-day. It ignored the school and its discipline and study, it by-passed things pedantic and scholastic, and went straight to the open road of life, the road one follows from the time one leaves school at fourteen or seventeen until one dies of old age, a road our schooling does little or nothing to prepare us for. Shaw put pedagogics in their right place—far down the ladder of education. How many 1910 dons or headmasters would subscribe to Shaw's: "The child should spend most of its time at play"? How many 1910 (or 1946) parents could accept as right his: "The true cry of the kind mother after her little rosary of kisses is 'Run away, darling.' It is nicer than 'Hold your noise, you young devil: or it will be the worse for you': but fundamentally it means the same thing." Shaw says hundreds of wise things that any modern child psychologist would accept as true, for just as Shakespeare in *Hamlet* told the story of the Œdipus Complex centuries before Freud analysed it, so did Shaw, decades before the Child Complex was consciously known, tell much of its story by simple intuition linked with intellectual penetration. And if he often nodded he wasn't the first great man to nod. He nodded when he gave too much moment to his own boyhood experiences. They coloured his outlook too much. Because he was a brilliant child, picking up his education in spite of his teachers and their school-books, he is too ready to assume that every child can do what he did. In his young days every child's mind was a blank slate on which the teacher wrote what he considered best for the child's immortal soul. Shaw's slate was pretty well scribbled on before his masters had time to reach for their chalk, and he seems to make the mistake of thinking that all children are little G.B.S.s with partly filled slates. He scorned the teachers' chalk on his slate, yet it is clear that he did not escape entirely free from the influence of the teachers. Certainly they failed to mould his character, but they had some success in moulding his opinions, for at heart, he over-values the learning, knowing, thinking side of life at the expense of the doing side. The old man who loves chopping wood now, never to my knowledge advocates the working in wood that every boy loves as being as important as—say—maths or chemistry or grammar or Latin or what-not. He wants children to *hear* the best music, see the best pictures, *read* the best books, because as a boy he loved the trinity—music, art, literature. He does not believe that it is better for a child to compose a bad limerick than to recite by heart the whole of *Paradise Lost*. His best books, music, pictures are in their way just as dangerous as the dominie's worship of school subjects and university degrees; one can acquire a "culture" without ever doing a creative thing in life, a truth that becomes apparent if one dines with a university senate or with a headmasters' association.

The fact is that Shaw is scared by children. Intellectually he is all for them; he is on their side against the moralizing or beating adult, but emotionally he fears them. One of his headings in a preface is *Children as Nuisances*, a tell-tale heading indeed. "A child is a restless, noisy little animal, with an insatiable appetite for knowledge, and consequently a maddening persistence in asking questions." Again: "People of high character and intelligence cannot be plagued with the care of children," a statement that makes me a moron, for I've been "plagued" with them for getting on to fifty years.

The complaint about the child's constant questioning dates Shaw as a writer on education. I take it he was a great asker of questions at a time when some very important questions were answered with lies or evasion or both. The modern child does not seem to ask many questions . . . in my school I have been asked only two in the last week, "What time is it?" and "When is pocket-money to be given out?" . . . and most modern educationists take it that the child who asks many questions is a problem who is seeking some deep information about his birth or his parents' morals or his sex or his fearsome God. If you give a child an environment in which he has no scope to do things he will ask questions, far too many questions. Free and busy children ask only the important questions . . . Got any nails? Got a cycle pump? How do you hard-solder copper? That is, they ask questions that have an immediate aim, whereas the little highbrow who wants to know all about the stars is likely to have been schooled in the young Shavian manner of absorption, not creation.

It is when he speaks of child behaviour that Shaw betrays the conflict between his intellectual conception of children and his human reaction to their movement and noise. All very well for him to say that children are noisy and must be allowed to make a hell of a noise, for he cancels this out with his: "If the child is to remain in the room with a highly intelligent and sensitive adult, it must be told, and if necessary forced, to sit still and not speak." That he goes on: "which is injurious to its health, unnatural, unjust, and therefore cruel and selfish beyond toleration," does not disprove the fact that Shaw loves the theoretical idea of a child better than he loves the actual factual brat that disturbs his peace and blunts his axe, and as one who is always having his axes and saws blunted by children, I have every sympathy with him. I think, however, that he is evading the issue when he plumps for nurses and boarding-schools and indeed any school or person that will take the child away from sensitive men who might get headaches. I also want boarding-schools for all children, not because they are damned nuisances but rather because their parents are.

No, it is Shaw the teacher who is dangerous. He who can, teaches; he who cannot, writes about teaching. In 1910 he wrote: "Children must be taught some sort of religion." In 1944 he wrote: ". . . the child must be taught a morality as a religion . . .", and more than once in his prefaces he says that a child must be taught to sit quiet, to be mannerly, etc. Taught, taught, taught. It is this teaching business that relegates Shaw to the pre-Freud era. He even lauds the teaching of Jacques Dalcroze at Hellerau, near Dresden, apparently seeing in the new Eurhythmics the beginnings of a new education where pupils "walk to music, play to music, live to music. . . ." I was a director of the Schule Hellerau from 1921 to 1924, and although the Eurhythmics taught may have varied a bit from those taught by Dalcroze, I saw no evidence that this type of education helped pupils to become more balanced or sincere or complex-free; my chief memory is of some very neurotic girls who wept after every success and specialized in Dances of Death. Not that Dalcroze Eurhythmics are of no value. They are wonderful, fascinating, but only as minor factors in education, for it is possible to be an expert in walking six beats to a bar, waving one arm four beats and the other seven, while the head beats out three, and at the same time be a hopeless neurotic who can't face life. Eurhythmics, yes, but with a plus. What is that plus? I call it freedom, but what does Shaw call it? Knowledge? If knowledge, would he write thus: "It seems that the State must tell its children lies of some sort to keep them in order, and that the lies must vary according to their ages: for a boy or girl of ten will not be afraid of the cock coming down the chimney"? And what sort of a man is he to write about sex lies: "Instruction in sex is as important as instruction in food"? He cannot have it both ways, telling the truth about sex but telling lies about cocks and witches to keep brats in order.

Shaw always sees the child in relation to the adult; he does not see it as a child among children, living for most of the time among its peers, and only incidentally among the grown-ups at meal and bed times. Thus he has little faith in the ability of children to organize their own lives: he would teach them manners, not realizing that the manners they evolve through give and take living together, are infinitely better than the taught variety. That he does not know children through experience is shown in his distrust of children. . . . "Child life should be so organized in its successive age groups as to create a strong collective opinion among children that there are certain things everyone must learn and know. Public opinion, far from being non-existent among children, is so tyrannical that it needs restraint rather than release." That is true of children who are caned and made fearful and insincere and mannerly, and God knows what in State and Public Schools (and no doubt private ones also), but it is not true of children who have not been made to say Nay to Life by religious or moral or hateful teachers. I find a jury of children more charitable to an offender than their elders in a jury would be. Again Shaw is ignorant of children when he says they ought to do so much community work a day. I question if anyone ought to do community work until the age of twenty or maybe forty. There must be some self interest in everything we do, that is if we are to be pleasant about doing it. Children know this well. When I call for volunteers to gather potatoes many a child looks pained and disinterested, and my staff and I have to do the donkey work, but to-day, after five years' military occupation of the school, children from seven to seventeen are working valiantly and happily to restore the rutted playing-field to condition. Childhood is playhood, as Shaw has said again and again, and he can't make it adulthood without using external authority, that is, the type of authority that is akin to that of Hitler and Goebbels and the Drill Sergeant and the dignified Headmaster. I fancy Shaw believes that blood-poisoning in nearly every case comes from inside, from a poor condition of the blood. This is the main difference between the naturopath and the allopath; the former believes that disease comes from inside, bad feeding, etc., while the allopath attributes it to the outside germ or poison. Shaw is all for the naturopath system in physical illness, but in education he is an allopath, feeding the little rascals with just enough dangerous drugs to keep them quiet little adults who will behave themselves and fear the village policeman.

Take this paragraph from *Everybody's Political What's What* which dates from 1944: "Learning should bring, not book prizes and medals, but privileges and liberties, status and earnings; for in this way only can children be educated as citizens." This pre-last-war stuff in the post-present-war world! Most caning dominies would subscribe to the unpsychological offerings of this dictum. The only way to learn to be citizens is to live as citizens, and when a girl of seven at my school meeting moves that the breakfast bell be rung again ten minutes later "cos I often don't hear the bell" she and her peers are experiencing citizenship and directing it, while the poor child who has to listen to a lesson on citizenship is gaining nothing of any value to him. And why should it be learning that brings privileges? Why not make sport the criterion, or richness of vocabulary, or humour or beauty? Because this old man, who has spent his life creating, feels in his bones or unconscious that he has created because he has learnt much. That is why I claim that his educational theories are ultimately derived from his own schoolmasters, and are therefore of no great value. But when he gets away from all theory, he says the most delightfully penetrating true things about children, things that cancel out most of what he considers his educational creed. His creed says that a child must be taught manners and some sort of morality so that he may fit into life generally. . . . "Somebody must teach the (moral) codes to the children . . . they must be imposed somehow, or the human world will be an Alsatian madhouse." But Shaw the creator says: "Children should be educated to live more abundantly, not apprenticed to a life sentence of penal servitude." He is a philosopher, not a psychologist, so that when he talks of children his philosophy very often fails to guide him. "It is important to put the happiness of the child rather carefully in its place, which is really not a front place," he writes. The first demand of child psychology is that a child should have a personality as free from conflict and fear as possible, and most moderns would judge a school by the degree of happiness (or misery) registered on the faces of the pupils. To be free from moralists and educators and disciplinarians is the first requisite if a child is to be happy, and here I quote Shaw saying: "The preoccupied person is neither happy nor unhappy, but simply alive and active. . . ." If my child is happy, and Shaw's is alive and active, they have this in common, that they are free to be creative or destructive without having to explain things later to teacher or father or God, and neither Shaw nor I can determine whether the bright, fearless look of pleasure in life that is the sign of a free child is happiness or activity or what-not. That look should have front place, and Shaw the creator knows it.

What a pity it is that Shaw ignored the unconscious of the child, or for that matter the unconscious of the grown-up. He gives the impression of believing that a child can be good or mannerly or industrious by taking thought. He does not see the child as a creature with dim phantasies and fears and loves and hates, and a good problem-child would drive him crazy, for he would be utterly at a loss to understand what the little devil was aiming at. He sees education as something that should be dynamic, but he does not see the child as dynamite. Indeed, if there is any symptom of dynamite in a child, Shaw will hastily shove him out of the room, hence, what he says is of more value to the class teacher than to the psychologist. The former deals with class-work and outward behaviour and heads, and Shaw's bombshells about schools and schooling should stimulate him when they don't make him furious, but the child psychologist finds Shaw a desert, because the psychologist must deal with feelings, and motives and inner fears. If the emotions are right, the intellect will look after itself. If Shaw agrees with this he somehow fails to get it across the footlights. A post-Freud Shaw would surely realize that emotion must come first in the education of children. To-day, because our education neglects the emotions, a child leaves school with a small amount of intellectual training, but his emotions are completely untouched, and naturally seek an outlet in cheap films and illustrated papers, dog-racing and dart-playing, watching games and fanning jazz-band leaders, and Shaw's brilliant plays and prefaces do little to counteract the waste of emotion, whereas a balanced education would raise the culture of the masses in a generation. And by an emotional education I do not mean listening to Bach or gazing at Botticelli; I mean an education in which the child is free to express its emotions in language (however obscene), in creating and destroying, in playing with work, and, most importantly, in self-determination, ruling its life as fully as possible in company with its peers, free from all moralists and moulders and religionists and politicians. And when adolescent he should be free to express his love interest, just as he should be free to do so from the age of one.

What message has Shaw for the million proletariat youth whose emotions are forced into smutty jokes about sex and unsatisfactory adventures in dark passages? If Freud "saw sex in everything," Shaw sees it in nothing. Certainly he says, tell them the truth about sex, but his old friend Frank Harris knew the truth about sex, and it did not prevent his writing his banned and adolescent book *My Life and Loves*, in which his schoolboyish, guilty value of sex is his boasting of his unbelievable potency. It isn't knowing that matters; it is feeling, being aware innerly, and education should aim at giving opportunities for feeling and inner awareness to have play. "The truth shall make you free." It won't unless it is accompanied by feeling, and in psycho-analysis it is a fallacy that knowing the root of a complex automatically cures it; it doesn't unless the memory of the first cause is accompanied by the emotion that was attached to the first cause.

I scan Shaw's latest pronouncement on education in *Everybody's Political What's What* to find any sign of his having altered his 1910 views in the light of modern psychology, and I can find no sign at all. He is too conscious a writer. Not that being unconscious as a writer necessarily means helpfulness. Barrie was almost unconscious as a writer. His plays are filled with a symbolism that he did not understand. Homer Lane told me that he once sat beside Barrie at a dinner party, and, having a brilliant theory on the symbolism of *Peter Pan*, Lane said: "Sir James, have you any idea of the symbolism of *Peter Pan?*" Barrie gave him a terrified look, said: "Good God, no," and turned his shoulder to Lane during the rest of the dinner. Barrie, the famous creator of children, throws no light on the inner child; his Peters and Wendies are but second editions of his Sentimental Tommy. I mention Barrie because one often hears it said that while Shaw stands for head, Barrie stands for heart. Barrie only stood for sentimentality, that is, giving a swan emotion to a goose. There is no sentimentality about Shaw; his geese are geese, geese that cackle insistently. One Mary Rose is more dangerous to humanity than all the characters in Shaw's plays, for like her brother Peter Pan, she lures men to a regressive infantility, tickling their buried phantasies of all-powerfulness and security and the omnipotence of the childish wish. Shaw is never regressive; his feet are always flat on the ground; he does not fly over the treetops of Kensington Gardens. He sees children for what they are . . .

to his conscious eye. Barrie saw the inner child that he wanted to see, the egocentric Tommy, the always-a-baby Peter, the pseudo child-mother Wendy; he did not see the common, so-called ugly side of childhood. His children were little toffs with nurses and prams in Kensington Gardens, nice children whose fathers wore tall hats and kept big dogs. Shaw sees children as brats with snivelly noses and clumsy manners and noisy steps; he does not identify himself with children as Barrie did, usless in his vague yearnings to Beethovenise them all. And possibly this is what is wrong with the man. Genius, said Barrie, is the power of being a boy again at will. If it is Shaw is no genius, at least in his understanding of children. He cannot stoop to their level . . . no wonder the Scottish boys threw stones at him as he walked along the beach: they knew, yes, they spotted the grown-up man who could only see children from a distance. Children have a special sense, so that every bastard knows or feels he has something odd about him, and every son of parents who call each other darling at the dinner-table and who hate each other in the bedroom, knows that there is something much amiss in his home. Yes, they stoned the right man, and I say it even although friends have told me of Shaw's romping in a nursery like a two-year-old. I dare say he did, but I am willing to wager that they were good little children, well brought up, and not jammy and demanding and strident. Shaw cannot identify himself with a child because he abhors the rawness of a child, the primitive drive that makes childhood something almost entirely different from adulthood. It isn't a disgrace not being able to identify oneself with a child, but it is a handicap when one discourses on children and their education. The true educational reformer is the man who has never grown up, not the Peter Pan who fears life and responsibility, rather the man (or woman) who can recapture the emotions felt in childhood, and, recapturing them, can share them with a child, and approve of the child. Shaw can be only what the child Bernard was, but a Homer Lane can be every child. That's why Shaw writes and why Lane ran The Little Commonwealth. When a delinquent girl indulging in phantasy said to Lane: "Do you remember the time you took me to London and we went to the theatre and had dinner at a posh hotel?" Lane replied: "I remember, the Ritz." She laughed and cried: "Oh, you liar; I've never been to London." Lane identified himself with the child because he knew that he must; he played the game that she kicked off with. Genius—the power of being a boy again at will.

All this amounts to is that I am unfairly asking too much of Shaw. One Little Commonwealth (the most outstanding educational demonstration of the last thirty years) is worth a library of books about children, Shaw's books, my books, anybody's books. My pupils once had a debate on the motion: "It would be good for humanity if all books were burnt." The amendment was carried: "Burn all books except technical ones telling how to build houses and dig gardens, etc." Priggish children might have exempted Shakespeare and Shaw. They didn't even exempt my own books, which shows what my pupils think of me as an author anyway.

Here I pause and have to confess that the foregoing is the only criticism I can apply to Shaw. I feel that by and large his philosophy about children hardly differs at all from the post-Freud psychologists' theories about children, and certainly what he says is infinitely more readable than most psychological textbooks. I say by and large, for few child psychologists would subscribe to his: "A child may be strongly repelled by the multiplication table and pence table, which nevertheless has to be drummed into it at all costs. But let the child be convinced that not only can it never hope to be given pocket-money until it knows its tables, but that the mastery of them will result in the possession of its first shilling, and it will go through its task without being hurt by it." Some psychologists would be inclined to tell the child that if they found him looking at the multiplication table there would be a proper row.

The great fact about Shaw is that he is constantly looking ahead of the school. His school method may be poor, but his school philosophy is rich in that it sees education as a lifetime process, a fact that is evident in the way he has of digressing suddenly from the child to the adult. But what effect he has had on education in general it is impossible to judge. No Training College to my knowledge prescribes his *Parents and Children Preface* as a textbook instead of Macdougall or Percy Nunn, or for that matter Froebel or Pestalozzi, yet a sane Training College Head might well be of the opinion that Shaw is one of the big educational reformers of our time. His words are a clean, strong wind that could blow a few cobwebs out of those Training Colleges that see education as a matter of school method, and class-room discipline, and school subjects. Yet when I lectured in South Africa in 1936 the Calvinists who disliked my views thought that the biggest condemnation they could make was to call me "a disciple of his master, Bernard Shaw," . . . which wasn't very fair to G.B.S. or myself. To-day I question if it would help a teacher to get a job if, in his interview with the Board of Governors, he confessed to being a believer in Shaw on Education. The danger would be that one of the Governors might be enlightened enough to declare: "Why, then, you would abolish our schools, would you?" Which wouldn't be such a bad thing in the long run.

Here I wonder what Shaw would advocate in place of abolished schools. And here one must realize that Shaw is a writer, that is a neurotic, for no active, sane man would write. I have always been rather critical of Jesus because he left his carpenter's bench to lecture, and assuredly people would not have messed up his tables as effectively as they have messed up his teachings. Shaw is redeemed because he at least chops wood, but when he uses his axe to chop down some of our old family estate oaks, I am not so certain about him, for, however skilled he may be in felling stupid ideas, he has not shown any evidence of being a skilled planter. His ideas are manifold, but ideas don't build schools. I write this with a bias, for I built a school empirically, saying: I don't know what children are; I'll watch them and see what they do and what they want and what they love and what they hate. Then I wrote books about what I saw or thought I saw. I talk and do, while Shaw talks and—er—chops wood. In this context alone do I feel myself superior to him. (Here I go criticising the old man again, tut, tut!) But it is legitimate wondering rather than criticism. True, it looks as if I were condemning Freud because he sat in a consulting room in Berggasse, Vienna, instead of painting pictures or making model engines in half his time, or Charlie Chaplin for acting the fool instead of making refrigerators three days a week. Maybe I am; maybe I feel that every job should touch hand and eye and foot if it is to be broad enough. I always liked to hear that the late Kaiser Wilhelm followed the national custom of Germany by sending each of his sons to learn a hand trade, although the fate of Germany isn't a very good advertisement for its system of education. I have a complex about hands, for I like to potter about with nuts and bolts and furnaces, and I am possibly talking through this complex. Shaw hasn't got this complex which might be termed the Hand or Head Complex. I say Hand *and* Head. Learning and Making; Knowing and Creating. I had a university-trained teacher in my school and he could not hammer a nail in a wall. He was uneducated. Another teacher I had (M. A. Hons) could chop wood, but when I saw him trying to fit a Whitworth Nut on to a Metric Thread I knew he was only half educated. We are now some distance away from the days when culture meant a library and quoting Latin tags and, in general, the education of the country squire; we are now in the age of radio and airplanes and machines, and the new culture will include nuts and bolts and heads and hands. And

I wonder if Shaw will appreciate this new culture. No man can keep up-to-date. When I have to listen to modern jazz it all sounds a raucous noise to me, but to everyone I know under twenty-four it is music as divine to youth as Beethoven was to the young Shaw. No propagandist can be immortal because by the time he dies the iniquities he preached against are often done away with, and my private opinion is that Shaw's only chance of immortality lies in his few plays that leave out propaganda . . . like that lovely little gem, *How He Lied to Her Husband*. But who wants immortality anyway? Certainly not G.B.S.

So that, to return to the point, Shaw as an educator is or will soon be dated. He can tell us a thousand things that are wrong with education, but it would be risky to allow him to be . . . well, say, Minister of Education, although personally, I'd jump with joy to see him try the post out. Too much head. Yet those who keep saying that he has no heart are short-sighted. Most of his characters are heartless or sound so, but Shaw the man is full of heart. (I never met him but I remember his kindly, twinkling eyes of thirty years ago.) He is the super, awful example of the hearty man whose head ran away with him. Let me play with the phantasy of G.B.S. as Education Minister. I see him sending out stern dictates to teachers, breaking their pedagogic hearts with his sane demands for child freedom; I see a distracted teacher fearfully approaching the Minister in Whitehall, ready to bolt at any moment, and then completely bowled over by Shaw's smile and sympathetic pat on the shoulder. A Jekyll and Hyde he is. He puts all his worse side into his writing and his best side into his human relationships . . . and this is a guess, for I know not the man, but I do it myself and conclude that he does. Again I tell ye that writing is a neurosis, a criminal one at that.

I conclude on this note of Shaw's heart, his soft-hearted love of humanity. Why he got the reputation of being a sayer of violent, dangerous things I do not know. I cannot think of one quotation from his works that would shock a spinster; this Jekyll plus Hyde always takes the sting out of the tail of his aphorisms, so much so that often he isn't nearly dogmatic enough. I think that may be one reason why his influence on education may have been less than it should have been. He is too ready to see both sides of a question, ignoring or discounting the assumption that truth is best found when two protagonists each see only their own point of view and thresh it out in public. Shaw will tell us what his father said about—say—the Bible, but we are often left to infer what Shaw thinks of his father's judgment. He diagnoses much but seldom prescribes. The doctor's dilemma. Ah, got it at last. G. Bernard Shaw, M.D. The most brilliant diagnostician of the age. The best M.O.H. of schools in these broad lands, an M.O.H. who doesn't believe in drugs and medicines. No, I take back the Ministry of Education offer; the sphere is far too narrow for him. Education and its blemishes are only a small part of life, and to tinker with schools is to begin at the wrong end. This doctor is a very wise physician who sees that no chemist's shop and no drug prescription will help an atom, nay, they will do harm. So that to dwell on his chapters on children is quite wrong. His big message is: Put this civilization in order and then talk about educating children. His Cabinet job should obviously be Minister of Health, somatic, psychic health. One should then recommend any teacher (or anyone else) to read, not *Prefaces on Children*, but just Shaw, Shaw passim, Shaw the man who believes that education is as important at ninety as it is at nine.

## ALDERMAN A. EMIL DAVIES, J.P., L.C.C.

### *G.B.S. AND LOCAL GOVERNMENT*

WHEN, in the year 2056, the bicentenary of Bernard Shaw's birth comes to be celebrated, some schoolgirl in her essay might write:

> "George Bernard Shaw was noted as an authority and pioneer in regard to municipal affairs. He was a London Borough Councillor and wrote a book entitled *The Commonsense of Municipal Trading* which has become a classic. He also wrote some plays."

That hypothetical essay will not, however, be written in those terms, for Shaw, the greatest dramatist of the age, overshadows all the other Shaws, among whom, however, the advocate of municipal enterprise has always been insistent.

Few people realize that for six years, viz., 1897 to 1903, this great iconoclast put in a mass of constructive work on the St. Pancras Vestry, which subsequently became the St. Pancras Borough Council, part of the complicated system of London Government. He served on the Public Health, Parliamentary, Electricity, Housing and Drainage committees. His election was due to a deal with the Tory majority by his friends, the Phillimores, themselves members of the Vestry, whereby only a sufficient number of candidates to fill all the seats was put forward, and contests were avoided. This may be the origin of Shaw's oft-repeated opinion that the best people are not elected by popular vote, but are otherwise arranged or selected, a sentiment which, as an alderman during the whole of my twenty-seven years on the London County Council, I am not inclined to dispute.

The advent of so unconventional a person in their midst must have caused a sensation among the councillors. I have heard Shaw relate with gusto how shocked they were when he suggested that some women should be members of the committee concerned with public conveniences. This suggestion was thought most indelicate, and this opinion was not modified when the innovator made the reasonable remark that, as women use these places, they should have some say in their management.

While Shaw was a considerable influence on the Council, his experience there had a lasting effect upon him. It may be interesting to "place" this period of practical municipal work in relation to his literary work. His Fabian tract, *Socialism for Millionaires,* appeared one year before he became a vestryman, and his first play, *Widowers' Houses,* was produced at the end of 1892. In the following year, *Mrs. Warren's Profession* was written but not produced (the Censor having prohibited its presentation); *Arms and the Man* in 1894, whilst in 1897, the year in which his municipal life began, *Candida* was produced. Then followed *The Devil's Disciple, Cæsar and Cleopatra,* and the other plays. It is evident that his attendance at the Town Hall—and these were two and three a week, lasting some hours—did not affect Shaw's output of plays.

Shaw's influence on municipalization, however, began some years before his practical work as a councillor. In 1889, the year which witnessed the birth of the London County Council, there appeared a Fabian Tract, written anonymously by Sidney Webb, entitled *Facts for Londoners,* and this was immediately followed by *London Programme,* in which Webb, Shaw, and other leading Fabians worked out a detailed programme of administrative reforms to be made the basis of a consolidated Progressive Party. This included the municipalization of milk, gas, pawnbroking, and slaughterhouses, the creation of municipal hospitals, a municipal steamboat service, and the right of women to become members of the Council. In 1892 Webb and a few other Fabians secured seats on the Council, and influenced its policy in several directions, so much so, that in an address in November, 1894, Lord Salisbury described the Council as "the place where collectivist and socialist experiments are tried . . . where the new revolutionary spirit finds its instruments and collects its arms." The Radical wing of the Progressive Party agreed largely with the Fabian programme, but wished profits from municipal undertakings to be utilized in relief of rates: but the small band of Fabians in their ranks, prompted by Shaw, wanted the abolition of the profit motive altogether, and municipal services to be run at cost, as in the case of the drainage system in all our cities. This point has always been urged most insistently by Shaw, and although even to-day the cogency of this concept is not generally admitted, it works out that way in practice, for, as he points out in Chapter IX of *The Commonsense of Municipal Trading:*

> "When the Electric Lighting Committee makes a profit it tries to keep it by crediting it to the reserve fund. A proposal to apply it to the reduction of the rates usually comes from the Finance and Rating Committee. . . . If the amendment is carried, the Electricity Committee considers that the Finance Committee has plundered it and takes care, next time, to reduce the price of current to the consumer so that there shall be no profits to be seized upon. Thus the theoretically right course is taken even when the councillors do not understand the theory; and the practice is to avoid profits by keeping the prices down to cost. The absence of profits is, in fact, a proof of the proper conduct of the enterprise. Such absence in a commercial company would be a proof of incompetence."

This difference between ordinary commercial and community values is emphasized throughout the book, which is Shaw's classic work on the theory of municipalization, and is as good reading to-day as when it first appeared. Indeed, most of it is still topical, as witness the following few apothegms:

> "Until the municipality owns all the land within its boundaries, and is as free to deal with it and build upon it as our ground landlords are at present, the problem of housing cannot be satisfactorily solved."
>
> "When the absurdity of the present municipal areas forces us to reconstruct our whole scheme of local government, there will still be a place for local committees to deal with the small change of municipal life."
>
> "Independence of thought and character is not strangled in municipal public life as it is in the House of Commons. ... If he (the recruit) values useful public activity and freedom of conscience, he will find a municipality enormously superior to Parliament, unless his political talent or family influence is of a very unusual order."
>
> "The balance sheet of a city's welfare cannot be stated in figures. Counters of a much more spiritual kind are needed, and some imagination and conscience to add them up, as well."

Another example of Shaw's prescience is contained in a chapter of *Fabianism and the Empire* (1900), entitled "Municipal Trading," which concludes with the words: "The water areas of the country will have to be delimited, and vested in responsible authorities, probably the County Councils."

In 1904, following upon Shaw's six years' experience of local government, the celebrated *Commonsense of Municipal Trading*, already referred to, appeared. In the spring of that year Shaw stood as a candidate for the London County Council, a fact that is not generally known even to some of his greatest admirers. He stood in company with a Liberal, Sir William Nevill M. Geary, Bart., for South St. Pancras, the constituency he had represented on the Borough Council. Shaw's habit of uttering unpalatable truths is not an electioneering asset, and one of the most prominent men in the Conservative Party in St. Pancras tells me that just prior to the election, Shaw had said publicly that the dairymen of that borough were poisoning its inhabitants by the contaminated fluid they were serving. As a result, that trade used all its influence against him. On asking my informant (Sir David Davies), who is probably the sole surviving contemporary of Shaw on the St. Pancras Borough Council, how G.B.S. was regarded by his colleagues on that body, he said that they respected him enormously for his earnestness and industry, were somewhat amused at his constant endeavours to obtain publicity, but were not aware that they had a genius among them.

One of my treasured possessions is the election address of the two Progressive candidates for the London County Council, South St. Pancras division, the wording of which leaves little doubt as to its authorship. About one-half of this address deals with the subject of religious instruction in schools, and much of it would have been valid in 1944, just forty years later, when yet another Education Bill was under discussion. Here are some extracts from this address:

> *The Education Bill*
>
> "There is no doubt that the question which will be uppermost at the election is that of the administration of the London Education Act by the new Council. On that question we stand for Education and for Tolerance. We are personally ready to work, and to work ungrudgingly, for the education of the children of London, without asking whether their parents be Established Churchmen, Free Churchmen, Roman Catholics or Jews. We recognize that

without perfect toleration, public education is impossible. If you elect us you may depend on us for one thing at least, and that is, that however strongly the citizens of London may differ from one another on sectarian questions, the children of London shall not suffer for it if we can help it."

*The Church Schools*

"What is it that we feel most strongly about the Church Schools? Is it that the children are taught the Church catechism? Not at all. What concerns us is the fact that the children in the Church schools seldom win the County Council scholarships, that the school buildings are often inferior and insanitary, that there are not teachers enough, that what teachers there are are always underpaid and sometimes unqualified, and that the clergyman is forced to beg, often literally from door to door, to make both ends meet. The Education Act gives the London County Council for the first time the power and the means to make an end of this; to have the schools rebuilt and fully staffed, the teachers properly qualified, well paid, and raised to the rank of public servants, the clergyman relieved from his dependence on the purses of a small minority of his parishioners, and the children given the same advantages for their start in life as the Board School children now possess."

Here also are a few more Shavianisms from this address:

"May we remind you in all earnestness that there is nothing more dangerous than the conscience of a bigot."

* * *

"We need not say that we are in favour of economy. We have never yet heard of candidates who were not."

* * *

"A vigorous County Council, spending money freely on public health, convenience, and safety, saves the ratepayer more than it costs him. It is better to pay a shilling more to the rate collector than a couple of pounds more to the doctor."

* * *

"At present the rates are not only heavy, but they are assessed on a wrong principle. Nothing can be more unfair than to levy full rates on a shopkeeper when the costermonger outside his shop—who is sometimes a richer man—pays nothing. Nor is the rating fair as between one man of business and another; because one man may make very high profits in a very small shop or office whilst another may make very small ones in a business which takes up a great deal of room and consequently pays much more in rates."

* * *

*Taxation of Ground Values*

"Then there is the eternal question of the worker and the idler. We are ourselves owners of property, and therefore not likely to be indifferent to the interests of property; but we sympathize entirely with the growing claim that those ratepayers who work, whether as men of business or professional men, should contribute less than those who simply live on the rents earned by the activity of our shopkeepers and householders. The ground values of London must by this time amount to nearly twenty millions a year; and the interest paid out of London business on capital that has been lent out of ground rents and not out of fair earnings, is incalculable—it is certainly not less than another twenty millions. All this ground rent and interest on unearned capital saved out of ground values is recognized by Parliament as a proper subject of taxation by special schedules of the Income Tax, heavy death duties, and the like. We venture to say that it is quite as proper a subject for special local rating; and we shall advocate not merely the election cry of 'Taxation of Ground Values,' but the complete exemption from rating of our real poor householders and shopkeepers, the partial exemption of those a little better off, and the heaviest possible rating in those cases, few but flagrant, where monopolists who do no productive work at all enjoy incomes amounting sometimes to much more than a thousand pounds a day. Considering that every pound we spend on houses and shops, and every addition we make by our energy to the goodwill of our businesses, falls in the long run—or the short run; for long leases are things of the past in St. Pancras—to the owner of the ground, it is not too much to ask that as long as London belongs to the ground landlords they shall pay for keeping it in order."

* * *

*Conclusion*

"In conclusion, may we ask you to consider this long pamphlet as something more than an ordinary election address? We do not believe that either we ourselves or the Progressive Party have a monopoly of honourable intention, public spirit, and political capacity; and we offer these pages to voters of all parties as a help to the understanding of the main questions at issue in the election—questions which are practically never handled by the newspapers without a strong party bias. We do not ask you to vote for us: you must vote according to your judgment; but we do earnestly beg you not to leave your vote unused. If no more votes are counted this time than three years ago, the successful candidates will represent only a minority of the ratepayers; and upwards of 3,000 votes will be wasted. Later on we shall send you clear instructions as to what to do when you go to the polling station, so that if you have never voted before, you will know exactly what to do. Voting is as easy as buying postage stamps, and costs nothing.

"We need hardly add that if we are returned, we shall consider ourselves charged with the interests of the whole constituency, and not merely with those of our supporters at the poll."

It is painful to reflect how much of the foregoing is true to-day, and it need hardly be added that the voters of South St. Pancras did not do themselves the honour of electing to the L.C.C. the greatest British man of letters since Shakespeare, the result being as follows:

| | | | |
|---|---|---|---|
| W. H. H. Gastrell | (Municipal Reformer) | .. | 1,927 votes |
| F. Goldsmith | " " | .. | 1,808 " |
| G. B. Shaw | (Progressive) | .. .. | 1,460 " |
| Sir W. Geary | " | .. .. | 1,412 " |

Shaw has never ceased to preach the importance of freeing municipal trading undertakings from the profit-making incentive. In his most recent political work, *Everybody's Political What's What* (1944), he again urges in most emphatic terms that such services should be supplied at cost price.

So far as London is concerned, various utility undertakings have passed into public ownership through the creation of public corporations, e.g., water, docks, passenger transport, and throughout the country generally more and more services are being municipalized. The striking socialist victories in the November 1945 elections were not the outcome of a sudden *volte face*, but the cumulative result of thousands of speeches and publications during the past few decades, in the making of which Bernard Shaw's numerous Fabian Tracts and other works, particularly the classic already mentioned, have played an important part.

## DR. DANIEL JONES

*Professor of Phonetics, University College, London*

### *G.B.S. AND PHONETICS*

ONE of G.B.S.'s outstanding characteristics is his versatility. And what can illustrate this better than the fact that this remarkable man, known to most people as a playwright and author, and to some as a musician, is an enthusiast for a subject which some may consider outlandish—phonetics? His interest in this subject dates from long ago, and has always taken a practical and constructive shape. He is an expert shorthand writer, and it was presumably the phonetic principles involved in shorthand that opened his eyes to other possibilities offered by this science.

So convinced did Shaw become of the valuable potentialities of the subject, that some twenty-eight years ago he conceived the idea of making the general public aware, by means of a play, of what phonetic science is and what can be done with it. Hence his *Pygmalion*, which he tells me is the most popular of his plays. One of the purposes of this comedy was to show up the somewhat disagreeable fact that under present conditions people's manner of speaking has much to do with their success or failure in life (in the material sense). A second was to call attention to phonetics as a means of enabling a dialectal speaker to change his accent. In *Pygmalion* phonetics is represented as providing a key to social advancement —a function which it may be hoped it will not be called upon to perform indefinitely. Those who have seen the play and have given thought to the principles demonstrated in it will no doubt have inferred that the methods of phonetics are of more general application—that they enable a person with a definitely local accent to speak, if he so desires, with a pronunciation more widely current and not necessarily that of a particular social class, and that they give us a means of learning to pronounce foreign languages far more intelligibly than was possibly in pre-phonetic days.

Mention must be made here of services in the phonetic line which Shaw has rendered to the B.B.C. For several years he was chairman of a special committee charged with the duty of making recommendations for the guidance of announcers. These recommendations related to uncommon words of which the pronunciation was doubtful, to words which are pronounced in more than one way, to English proper names which announcers might not ordinarily be expected to know, and to suitable anglicizations of foreign words and names which either had occurred or were thought likely to occur in the news. Information relating to these words was collected by specialists in phonetics appointed by the B.B.C., but the last word concerning difficult points lay with this committee. Shaw's task as chairman was not always an easy one, since many of the pronunciations which came up for discussion gave rise to considerable controversy. However, under his guidance much good work was achieved, as the remarkable series of booklets *Broadcast English* shows.

Shaw is apparently very keen on time-saving, and has recently pointed out that the use of a phonetic alphabet for the ordinary writing of English would effect an enormous economy in this direction. He is aware that many systems of reformed spelling have been invented during the last 100 years, the two best being probably Sir Isaac Pitman's *Phonotypy* which involved the use of forty letters and the *New Spelling* of the Simplified Spelling Society which does about the best that can be done with the letters of the present alphabet. One would have thought that at any rate the Pitman system approached fairly closely to what Shaw would consider to be ideal, except that it is short by two letters of what Shaw would like to see. But he will not have this or any other existing system, though I have not been able to discover why. This, by-the-bye, illustrates a way he has with him: he propounds something in general terms, and leaves other people to find out what he really means and to work out the details—a proceeding which may be distasteful to many, but which is good pedagogy nevertheless. In the present case I think Shaw must have in mind an entirely new alphabet without any particular connection with our present Roman, or, as he prefers to call it, Phœnician system.

However that may be, Shaw makes out that all spelling reformers hitherto have been on the wrong track, and that in particular they have neglected in their propaganda to emphasize what he regards as the most outstanding advantage presented by phonetic spelling—the time factor. He has pointed out that the time spent every day by hundreds of millions of people writing, typewriting and printing English words with many more letters than are really needful can only be measured by astronomical figures, and he maintains that the cost of a change-over to phonetic spelling—including the scrapping of most of our existing printing plants and typewriters and the manufacture of new ones, and the reprinting of all important books—very great as this may seem, would soon be compensated for over and over again by the time saved by everybody who has to write English.

This is not the place to discuss the possibilities of reform on these lines. I would, however, record Shaw's contention that the matter is not one that phoneticians or spelling reformers of the old school are competent to deal with. He holds that it is a matter primarily for statisticians, mathematicians and psychologists. If they can succeed in producing figures to show what manner of saving would be effected by taking proper account of this time element, he considers that the advantages will prove to be so colossal that educational authorities would be obliged to consent to spelling reform on the lines he advocates.

In concluding this short account of Shaw's activities in the phonetic field I would express thanks to him, firstly for myself who as a phonetician by profession much appreciates aid rendered to my subject by so eminent a man in a different walk of life, and secondly on behalf of countless numbers of the public who without the stimulus applied by Shaw might never have learnt anything of the value of phonetics, or might even never have known that such a science exists.

J. C. TREWIN

*Literary Editor of* The Observer

## *SHAW AS A WIT*

CARTOONISTS used to have the odd idea of personifying Ireland by a comic peasant: a grotesque figure—all Pat, peat, and poteen—brandishing a shillelagh and making truculent noises. In some quarters the notion seems to linger still. No harm in it, say the tolerant. Yes, by Saint Patrick, but there is, Horatio. Traditionalists to whom John Bull's other island is even now a wet western quagmire filled with jigging aborigines, offer a sharp insult to the endearing conversation-piece that is the city of Dublin—Dublin of the swords, where the wit of the Irish sparks and glitters beside the dark-flowing Liffey. The talkers' Dublin is indeed a city of light. Its admirers may grow as wearisome in its praise as the cartoonists with their yellow pictures of Paddy O'Flynn (Begorra and bedad!), but we cannot undervalue a city that first nourished the savage wit of Swift and the prickling, leaping wit of Shaw. Wilde polished his impromptus elsewhere, but he—like Sheridan—was Dublin-born. At the beginning of the eighteenth century George Farquhar, new-come from Dublin, was in London with a flask of canary at his elbow and his Irish humour dancing. And we do not forget that although Congreve was a Yorkshireman by birth—a curious county for this mannered playwright—he was a student of Trinity College, another in Dublin's galaxy of University wits. (Add, too, the name of Oliver Goldsmith.) So the catalogue runs in splendour. In our own day there is Sean O'Casey, genius from Dublin's lesser streets, whose wit is not so much a considered thrust of steel as a "gold embroidery of dancin' words."

They have always cared for words in Dublin. No doubt they have squandered them, cast them about recklessly, but they have ever delighted in texture and lustre and rhythm, in the sway and lift of a sentence or the honing of a phrase to a razor's edge. To be a Dubliner, it would seem, is to be copious in argument, exuberant in attack, and if not inevitably a Sheridan, at least a colourable semblance. First in the constellation, though long absent from his birthplace, is Bernard Shaw, great Irishman of English letters, and in play and pamphlet the Chief Wit of his time: one, that is, who can "give sudden intellectual pleasure by the unexpected combining or contrasting of previously unconnected ideas or expressions." The dictionary offers this sad mouthful. Why not define wit as a high levity, the flash and outbreak of a fiery brain? You must be wise to be witty—the fashionable phrasemonger remains a mere journeyman—and none can say that Shaw, of all dramatists, is green in judgment.

Since his early days in London, as a venturer from Dublin bent on annexing the greater capital, Shaw has had an easy command of wit in all its form and moods and tenses. He can find the line effective in the theatrical situation—for instance, Prossy's "I'm only a beer teetotaller, not a champagne teetotaller. I don't like beer," or Gunner's "Rome fell. Babylon fell. Hindhead's turn will come." Equally he is ready with the line that tingles both on the stage and in the text (Lady Britomart's "Cannons are not trade, Stephen. They are enterprise"), or—when he wishes—with the wit that is not verbal but visual (the waltzing exit of Androcles and the lion). Then there are the swashing blows of the pamphleteer as he chivvies idea and argument, fallacy and fad: "Statesmen are afraid of the newspapers, of the profiteers, of the diplomatists, of the country houses, of the trade unions, of everything ephemeral on earth except the revolutions they are provoking; and they would be afraid of these if they were not too ignorant of society and history to appreciate the risk." Shaw's form of blarney is a cheerful candour. He wheedles with the sword-point. As Keegan says in *John Bull's Other Island:* "My way of joking is to tell the truth. It's the funniest joke in the world." Frequently, as G.B.S. phrases it, the wittiest. "When a stupid man is doing something he is ashamed of, he always decides that it is his duty," says Apollodorus. "Martyrdom," observes Burgoyne, "is the only way in which a man can become famous without ability." "If history repeats itself, and the unexpected always happens, how incapable must man be of learning from experience!" (Maxims for Revolutionists). "Beauty is all very well at sight, but who can look at it when it has been in the house three days?" (Ann Whitefield).

Shaw's better jokes have an enviable staying power: devouring time blunts not this lion's paws. His belief in covering his plays wherever possible (and impossible) with a top-dressing of farce may sometimes exasperate. We sigh a little when the slapstick comedian shoulders aside the wit, or when, as in certain scenes of *Too True to Be Good*, Shaw is thwacking around with the flat of his sword. Like Charles Lamb with his Mr. H., he has always trusted fondly in the spell of the comic name (Ftatateeta, Brollikins) and in the facetious nickname or diminutive (Ricky Ticky Tavy), and he will repeat his favourite jokes without scruple or mercy apparently on the principle that what he tells us three times is true. "My reputation is built up fast and solid, like Shakespeare's, on an impregnable basis of dogmatic reiteration." His gibing at the Anglo-Saxon attitude is the best example. No one has found so much relish in laughing at the Englishman: it is Dublin's revenge. Britannus is the type ("He is a barbarian, and thinks that the customs of his tribe and island are the laws of nature"). Then Broadbent: "After all, whatever you say, they like an Englishman." So to Edstaston in *Great Catherine*—

one of the short plays that have fallen like dewdrops from the lion's mane—and to de Stognumber: "How can what an Englishman believes be heresey? It is a contradiction in terms." There is no slander in an "allowed fool" and this happy mocking will always go well in the theatre, as Shakespeare found in *Hamlet*. But it is not wit's finest flower, and G.B.S. has let it cover too much ground.

The plays—as I have said elsewhere of *Too True to be Good* —remind one now of the chasm of *Kubla Khan*, with its ceaseless tumult seething and huge fragments vaulting like rebounding hail, and, less often, of the river "five miles meandering with a mazy motion." (*Too True to be Good* is on the whole a minor play in spite of the molten lava of its sermons. Why, alas, has not Shaw treated Judgment Day in such royal prose as this—meet for apocalyptic thunders—instead—instead of putting us off with the fantasies of *The Simpleton?*) In most of his work the prose is unmatched in our time. The dialogue, strong and supple, is a union of steel and shot-silk. Moreover, it is admirably speakable. The long sentences, as actors will confirm, are balanced to a hair. What other dramatist at the age of eighty-three has written dialogue so wise and so perfectly cadenced as that of *In Good King Charles's Golden Days?*

Shavian wit is a stream of fluent persuasiveness. It comes trippingly off the tongue. "Now if I said that," comments Hesione Hushabye to Mazzini Dunn, "it would sound witty. Why can't you say it wittily?" Shaw, we realize, can always say it wittily and richly, with style but without agonized resort to hammer and gouge and chisel. Too often, as we know, a "sparkling comedy" in the commercial manner is either carefully careless, achingly laborious, or frozen into a pattern of frigid epigram. We have come to dread the self-consciously clever utterance of a Good Talker, a label that all too probably hides a Good Bluffer. Shaw merely talks on in Dublin's best English, now with a mellifluous chuckle, now flippantly, with a candle-power unattainable by the dim bulbs of a later day, and now with a sudden flash and sting. At those moments when inspiration sags, as in the debating chamber of *Getting Married* or in the mazes of *Heartbreak House*, we can comfort ourselves by recalling the Disraelian figure who rather liked bad wine; one got so bored with the good.

Probably it is wrong to snatch any passage from its context, but Shaw at his wit's meridian should be sought in the Don Juan in Hell scene which is usually, and regrettably, omitted from the stage presentation of *Man and Superman*. The speeches here have a high voltage, and Shaw at any point will flick off such phrases as "Hell is full of musical amateurs; music is the brandy of the damned"; or (the Devil speaking) "At bottom the Universe is a constitutional one, and with such a majority as mine I cannot be kept permanently out of office"; or, in the expected Shavian mood, "Englishmen never will be slaves: they are free to do whatever the Government and public opinion allow them to do." Take a more sustained passage, one of Don Juan's. It should be read aloud:

> "Hell is the home of the unreal and of the seekers for happiness. It is the only refuge from heaven, which is, as I tell you, the home of the masters of reality, and from earth, which is the home of the slaves of reality. The earth is a nursery in which men and women play at being heroes and heroines, saints and sinners; but they are dragged down from their fool's paradise by their bodies: hunger and cold and thirst, age and decay and disease, death above all, makes them slaves of reality: thrice a day meals must be eaten and digested: thrice a century a new generation must be engendered: ages of faith, of romance, and of science are all driven at last to have but one prayer, 'Make me a healthy animal.' But here you escape this tyranny of the flesh; for here you are not an animal at all: you are a ghost, an appearance, an illusion, a convention, deathless, ageless: in a

word, bodiless. There are no social questions here, no political questions, no religious questions, best of all, perhaps, no sanitary questions. Here you call your appearance beauty, your emotions love, your sentiments heroism, your aspirations virtue, just as you did on earth; but here there are no hard facts to contradict you, no ironic contrast of your needs with your pretensions, no human comedy, nothing but a perpetual romance, a universal melodrama. As our German friend put it in his poem, 'the poetically nonsensical here is good sense, and the Eternal Feminine draws us ever upward and on'—without getting us a step farther. And yet you want to leave this paradise!"

Any leisurely reader of the Shaw Folio will find glints that a playgoer must miss, however well a piece has been interpreted. (Shaw, very reasonably, is the best director of his own work; he is not only witty in himself but the cause that wit is in his actors. Blest the producer that can use the author's notes or persuade him to take the stage. "It is an education as well as an experience to hear Shaw read one of his plays," says Mr. Harcourt Williams in *Four Years at the Old Vic.*) A reader in the study has to be his own producer but he has the benefit of the stage directions, and none can be more agreeable than Shaw's. Certainly many of them are unorthodox. In the Don Juan in Hell scene we learn that the Devil "begins in the French manner." In *The Devil's Disciple,* after Richard's line, "I never expect a soldier to think, sir," we have the note: "Burgoyne is boundlessly delighted by this retort, which almost reconciles him to the loss of America." We are told of B. B. in *The Doctor's Dilemma:* "Even broken bones, it is said, have been known to unite at the sound of his voice," and of Mrs. George in *Getting Married:* "She proclaims herself at the first glance as the triumphant, pampered, wilful, intensely alive woman who has always been rich among poor people. In an historical museum she would explain Edward the Fourth's taste for shopkeepers' wives." *Pygmalion* by way of epilogue has an entire essay in which those of us who are given to wondering how Jacques fared with Duke Frederick, and whether Beatrice and Benedick skirmished to the last, hear just what happened to the new-minted Eliza. It should be read after all performances to let the audience know that Eliza married not Higgins but Freddy Eynsford Hill, and that they have a flower-shop "in the arcade of a railway station not very far from the Victoria and Albert Museum." We learn, among other things, that "Freddy, like all youths educated at cheap, pretentious, and thoroughly inefficient schools, knew a little Latin," and that "Galatea never does quite like Pygmalion: his relation to her is too godlike to be altogether agreeable."

The reader, it is only fair to say, will have his moments of agony when he tries to cope with some of Shaw's phonetic renderings. It is like crawling through barbed wire to come to terms with Burgess in *Candida* ("I thort you wouldn't get a hearl's nevvy visitin' in Victawriar Pawrk"), Drinkwater in *Captain Brassbound's Conversion* ("Sir Ahrd ez erd witnesses to maw kerrickter afoah"), and Bill in *Major Barbara* ("Well, if Aw cawnt settisfaw you one wy, Aw ken anather"). Wit in phonetics is for the ear, not the eye.

Naturally a reader will not rest until he has met the Prefaces, those tracts, fanfares, sermons, encyclicals, which Shaw wrote—"eking out a penn'orth of play with a pound of preface"—because they offered extra elbow-room. (More power to the elbow.) Here a bushel of chaff is hid in many bushels of wit. Shaw again makes provocative use of the magnifying-glass, the coat-trailing exaggeration, the beard-jutting assertion. For a taste: "Self-denial is not a virtue. It is only the effect of prudence on rascality." Again: "Imprisonment, as it exists to-day, is a worse crime than any of those committed by its victims."

Dramatist, pamphleteer, critic. Leave Corno di Bassetto,

scourge of the concert-halls, and remember G.B.S., and his dramatic criticism, that candid-camera record of our theatre in the 'nineties. Shaw was never merely a conscientious mosaicist, using his notices as a base for the inlaying of precious fragments. In criticism, as in pamphlet and play, he spoke right on, and whether in defence or the probings of a Grand Inquisitor his pen was keenly tempered. Here, for example: "Mr. Jones (in *Michael and His Lost Angel*) has got beyond the penny novelette conventions which are actable in our theatre. I fear there is no future for him except as a dramatic critic." Or in this: "For the most part, one has to listen to the music of Shakespeare—in which music, I repeat again and again, the whole worth and charm of these early plays of his lies—as one might listen to a symphony of Beethoven's with all the parts played on the bones, the big drum, and the Jew's-harp." And finally, in this, from a consideration of "the piece founded by Augustin Daly on Shakespeare's *Two Gentlemen of Verona*": "A man who, having once seen cypresses and felt their presence in a north Italian landscape, paints them lettuce colour, must be suffering either from madness, malice, or a theory of how nature should have coloured trees, cognate with Mr. Daly's theory of how Shakespeare should have written plays."

Any note upon Shaw as a wit must turn, as this has done, into an anthology. The writer comes to praise and stays to quote. To borrow the passage Shaw himself used for Daly, one goes like Mrs. Todgers "a-dodgin' among the tender bits with a fork, and an-eatin' of 'em." No dramatist, critic, pamphleteer, sociologist, has been more magnificently bountiful. One last quotation: "I am ashamed neither of my work nor of the way it is done. I like explaining its merits to the huge majority who don't know good work from bad. It does them good; and it does me good . . . I leave the delicacies of retirement to those who are gentlemen first and literary workmen afterwards. The cart and trumpet for me."

And happily so. If this magnificent trumpeter had never sounded his Reveille—in preface as well as in play—how immeasurably poorer would our stage have been, the whole traffic of British life and letters, and, not least, the high lustre of our wit.

## SIR WILLIAM HALEY

*Director-General of the B.B.C.*

### *THE STRIPLING AND THE SAGE*

*"And that's how it all began, my dears,*
*And that's how it all began."*

IT IS amusing to cast back to the first conjunction of the greatest social force of this century with one of the few seminal and most incisive minds of our time. The initiative came from the newcomer.

10th March, 1924.

*G. Bernard Shaw, Esq.,*
*10, Adelphi Terrace.*

*Dear Sir,*

*The British Broadcasting Company, which from its earliest days has included at least one informative talk in its nightly programme, is advised from many quarters that these talks are amongst the most popular features. The Company accordingly believes that the time is ripe to strengthen its programmes in this direction by arranging to broadcast simultaneously from London through all Stations, a steady series of addresses (of an entertaining though informative character) by the most eminent and best-known persons.*

*We would welcome your assistance in this development. The talk we have in mind should be one of about twenty minutes' duration; it should be free from highly controversial matter, including politics and religion. The manuscript should be approximately 1,200 words in length.*

*The hour favoured for such a talk is 9.15 P.M., which we believe is the hour of our maximum audience, but owing to the difficulties in dovetailing our several programmes, at least a month must elapse between the final arrangements for an address and its actual delivery. . . .*

Stimulating and beneficial for broadcasting as Shaw's impact was eventually to prove, it took some time to bring about. Not until October, 1924 could the Director of Programmes write: "It was so exciting having you down here really standing in our Studios that I have not got over it yet. Still less can I believe that you have agreed to broadcast." Shaw looked upon the affair—a reading by him of *O'Flaherty V.C.* as "rather a lark." The B.B.C. solemnly said it was "an artistic event of the greatest importance" and promised that not only would it be broadcast "over the whole of the British Isles, from Aberdeen to Plymouth," but "also from our High Power Station which is heard regularly in Morocco." The broadcast was a great success, many people thinking it was "uncanny that a playwright should be able actually to sing 'Tipperary' and assume three or four different voices as well." Shaw genially took the Director of Programmes to see a silent film, *Warning Shadows*, with exactly what motive I do not know. At any rate the B.B.C. man came away feeling he "would like to take the screen story and make it into a play." A strange foretaste of what was to come, with the talkies still some years off.

In order to appreciate the nature of the relationship which thereafter gradually developed between G.B.S. and the B.B.C., it is necessary to remember their respective positions at this point. The British Broadcasting Company was an infant prodigy of barely two, still tentatively feeling every step of its way; Shaw was established and famous, a veteran of sixty-eight, whose work was known and performed in almost every country in the world. It is not fair to say that it was the old master who had all the young ideas. Shaw was exhortative, impetuous, impatient, ardent. His criticism, always good-natured, generally over-stated, arose from his rapidly widening perception of the immense possibilities of the new medium. In many fields of its broadening endeavours he goaded Broadcasting on. No one at Savoy Hill was in danger of being complacent while the Organiser of Programmes could report (of a conversation in 1925), "His opinion of the plays we broadcast was expressed in the one word 'damnable.' When I asked him if he thought it really was as bad as that he said he thought it was even worse." The great merit of such stimulus was that Shaw kept it up. He did not just say his say and pass by. I do not wish to give the impression Shaw was for ever at it. In actual numbers his contacts with the B.B.C. have not been great. His broadcasts have been fewer than many of us would have liked. But on and off through the B.B.C.'s first two decades he has returned to the charge. Like many a spouse he remained faithful—and nagging. Four or five years after the incident I have just related he was commenting on a broadcast of one of his own plays, "Its infamy was such that I hereby solemnly renounce and excommunicate everybody who had a hand in it. . . . Apart from the artistic side of the question the selection of 9.25 as the hour for raising the curtain, thus deferring the end until midnight, would have been a studied insult if any such thing as study had entered into the wretched business." Then he proceeded to go into a host of illuminating, critical details. It is not paradoxical to think that the value of such blasts was enhanced rather than diminished by the B.B.C.'s hurt revelation that the broadcast had occasioned a number of favourable Press notices, a host of most appreciative letters, and not one single other complaint! (One interesting note that persists in the friendly exchanges down the years is the B.B.C.'s belief that the great merit of Shaw's plays for broadcasting lies in their dependence on the brilliance of their dialogue and Shaw's insistence on the visual side of his drama.)

In many fields it is fair to say that G.B.S. was demanding of broadcasting that it should run before it could walk. At times he *was* ahead of practical possibilities. But even on such occasions it did the B.B.C. no harm to be reminded that the day was coming when running would be possible. And with all his occasional extravagances, Shaw was generally on the side of the angels. Quite early he was declaring that "until the B.B.C. has a company of wireless specialists for dramatic broadcasting and ceases to be dependent on ordinary theatrical companies" he would hold his hand in the matter of allowing broadcasts of his plays, thus envisaging the eventual founding of the B.B.C.'s Repertory company. There were, of course, a few occasions when he was wrong.

When it came to political and controversial broadcasting he was naturally even more vehement. It was perhaps injudicious of the B.B.C., when it conceived a "Modern Symposium" series of talks to approach Shaw to take part, attaching a proviso:

> "Probably it would be almost essential that the individual talks should bear some relation to each other, and to some extent at any rate follow on, and refer back to the previous ones, but it is not intended that they should consist of argument or controversy so much as an expression of opinion."

But the year was only 1929, the field of controversial broadcasting, comparatively recently opened, had not yet widened to its later dimensions, and all the compiler of the series was trying to ensure was that the talks should not degenerate into an unconstructive dog-fight. But to G.B.S. any such limit was a gross provocation. Broadcasting should be generating disputation, anything to the contrary was "nonsense." "Until that childish absurdity is dropped finally and without compromise Mr. Shaw will not take the B.B.C. seriously."

Fortunately he hardly ever kept his threats. And so the highly valuable comedy went on; Shaw from time to time admonishing the B.B.C. for the good of its soul; the B.B.C. admiring its tormentor and never failing to come back for more. Now and again there were mis-hits on both sides, the B.B.C. asking G.B.S. to act as chairman in a broadcast discussion ("Listeners-in cannot see me sitting and do not want to hear my silence"), and Shaw proposing he should contribute a General Election broadcast "viewed from the extreme Left." On the other hand one must for ever regret that the 1935 project of a "Shaw-Churchill" broadcast debate did not materialize.

Shaw has made practical contributions to Broadcasting, from his work as Chairman of the Spoken English Committee to his occasional appearances at the microphone. But his greatest benefaction is to have been at the height of his vigour and powers in Broadcasting's first formative years, to have become firmly seized of what the newcomer could eventually accomplish and never to have been satisfied with less than full attainment (which to all time must lie ahead); to have been impatient without ever losing patience; and to have held fast to the B.B.C.'s eventual power for service and good when so many others have become lost in irrelevant trivialities. And all this he has done in a manner so gaily outrageous that it could only encourage and never dishearten. The B.B.C. on his ninetieth birthday salutes its Grandest Inquisitor.

# VAL GIELGUD

## *BERNARD SHAW AND THE RADIO*

IT MAY seem a queer and somewhat graceless thing to say about one, who has consistently proved himself the youngest man both of his age and of his time, that he was born too soon. None the less, I cannot but feel that one of the greatest tragedies in connection with broadcasting lies in the fact that Bernard Shaw did not come into this world some twenty or thirty years after the date of his actual birth. I fear that it is no more than the truth to say that not only the generation to which Mr. Shaw belongs, but the generation immediately following it, have consistently failed to take broadcasting altogether seriously. The majority of these generations first laughed at it as a toy; then wondered at it as a child wonders at a conjuring trick which it cannot understand; objected to it strongly as a mixture of private corruption and public nuisance; accepted it finally as just one more of those inevitable modern inconveniences. They even contribute to it, and continue to contribute to it, in a corresponding frame of mind. For them a concert implied a concert hall and a play implied a theatre. Broadcast versions of these things might have a certain value owing to the immense size of their potential audiences, and on the grudging principle that half a loaf may be better than no bread. But that to listen to an item in a broadcast programme can be both an experience complete in itself, and artistically and æsthetically satisfactory, was for the most part beyond their ken and almost beyond their comprehension. It is an attitude of mind from which broadcasting, and those responsible for broadcasting, have suffered inestimable loss. And this is particularly the case with the plays of Bernard Shaw.

It is impossible to imagine that, had the flowering of Mr. Bernard Shaw as a playwright coincided with the achievement of maturity of broadcasting, Mr. Shaw would not have been radio playwright number one and *par excellence*. Of all modern playwrights Mr. Shaw has shown himself least inclined to be trammelled by conventions purely theatrical or by the cramping "unities" of the stage. Of all modern playwrights Mr. Shaw has proved himself a master of words, of dialogue, and of the stage-play as a medium for the verbal expression of opinions and points of view. He has confessed that he has made use of dramatic form for the "putting-over" of opinions which the average man or woman will not bother to read in books. He has, I think, implied that he is more interested in conveying his opinions to mankind, and in conveying numbers of mankind to these opinions, than in what is commonly called "commercial success." In plays specially written for broadcasting Mr. Shaw would have found an unrivalled medium for the handling of language to give dramatic expression of points of view; for the achieving of the largest audiences possible for such plays. Unfortunately, when Radio was born, Mr. Shaw's allegiance had already been given. Not that he has proved unwilling that his plays should be broadcast. But he has been adamant on the point that they should be broadcast precisely as they were written for the stage.

There has been a curious contrast in this connection between the attitudes of Mr. Shaw and Mr. Somerset Maugham. The latter, while expressing a certain mild surprise that anybody should feel inclined to transfer to one medium what has originally been conceived in terms of another, has never shown the least objection to the adaptation of his work to the exigencies of broadcast presentation. Mr. Shaw has repeated with unwearying consistency that what he has written he has written; that every word must be broadcast—or the play left to the theatre for which it was designed. It hardly needs pointing out to people at all familiar with the difficulties of broadcast programme planning that this has raised a barrier in many cases insuperable to presentation of Mr. Shaw's plays at the microphone. The problem of the quart and the pint pot is commonplace at Broadcasting House. It is exemplified most vividly in the problem of fitting almost any full-length play of Bernard Shaw's within the confines of an evening's broadcasting, particularly when that programme is already, to some extent, "in irons," owing to such immutably fixed points at the Nine o'clock News and Parliamentary Report.

On the other hand, again unlike Mr. Somerset Maugham who, having given permission for his works to be translated, takes no apparent interest in the result, Mr. Shaw has given typically striking evidence of being by no means the least attentive listener, whenever his plays have been broadcast. One of his famous postcards invited the producer responsible for an early broadcast of *Captain Brassbound's Conversion*, towards the end of 1929, to borrow a revolver and use it upon himself! I received—and value highly—letters of most pertinent criticism and comment upon productions respectively of *St. Joan* and *The Millionairess*. Indeed, in writing of *St. Joan*, in which Miss Constance Cummings gave what I thought to be a notably brilliant performance—one which, incidentally, made history from the broadcasting point of view as it was given without a script—Mr. Shaw showed for the first time a tendency to withdraw from his absolute standpoint. He admitted that certain references, such as those to the Visions in the last act, could have been cut as being aurally ineffective, and that certain other emendations—which he specified—in the text would have been desirable. It is one of my most cherished hopes that, when the time comes for the B.B.C.'s third programme to swing into active operation, giving programme time unlimited by fixed points, a series of Mr. Shaw's plays will be prominent amongst the programme's activities. If that hope should be realized I hope it may also be possible to persuade Mr. Shaw to make emendations and cuts along the lines which he suggested with regard to the *St. Joan* performance. Dramatic broadcasting, no less than the cinema, could not fail to profit immensely from the active co-operation "on the floor" of the most remarkable and vital literary figure of our age.

Of Mr. Shaw as broadcaster I can speak only in the capacity of the average listener, but I am inclined to assert, without much fear of contradiction, that he belongs to that small and select band who have been born with a natural aptitude for the microphone—an aptitude shared by such personalities as Gladys Young and James McKechnie amongst actors; Gillie Potter amongst comedians; Compton Mackenzie amongst writers; and perhaps pre-eminently the late 'A. J. Alan' amongst story-tellers. Precisely wherein this aptitude consists it is difficult to define. I seem to remember that I once heard Mr. Shaw say himself over the air that he could always tell from the voice of a good broadcaster exactly what he had had for dinner. What I think he meant, and what is undoubtedly true, is that the one most essential quality of microphone work is an absolute sincerity. In this medium all the trimmings and trick-work so beloved of the practised platform orator are useless. Mr. Shaw's approach is altogether simple, and equivalently convincing. Add to this the winning charm of a great personality and the richness and range of a voice naturally beautiful, and it becomes obvious how magnificently equipped he is naturally for outstanding microphone accomplishment.

# SIR KENNETH BARNES

## *G.B.S. AND THE ROYAL ACADEMY OF DRAMATIC ARTS*

### BERNARD SHAW, MEMBER OF THE R.A.D.A. COUNCIL

ON THE death of Sir William Gilbert in 1911, the Council of the R.A.D.A. unanimously decided to invite George Bernard Shaw to fill the vacancy. At this date the Council was limited to twelve members, and the eleven from whom the invitation came were Squire Bancroft as President, Arthur Pinero, James Barrie, Herbert Tree, John Hare, George Alexander, Johnston Forbes-Robertson, Cyril Maude, E. S. Willard, Edward Terry, Arthur Bourchier—all men! I had not met Bernard Shaw personally, but fully realized the stimulating influence he would exert if he accepted this invitation. I felt he might take the view that the Academy, founded by Tree in 1904, was a somewhat conventional institution, and, on that account, uninteresting. This apprehension was ill-founded; I remember the first meeting he attended, when he criticized the wording of the Council's letter. He had been asked to join because he stood for a section of the theatre-going public not hitherto represented on the Council. He reminded the members that a play of his had just been produced at a music hall! From the first, having consented to become a member of its governing body, there was no doubt about his intention to take a real interest in the work of the institution.

There were four women students to every man; so he immediately fastened on the anomaly of a council, controlling an institution composed mainly of women, without a single feminine member! During 1912 there were five meetings, and three times Mr. Shaw returned to the attack! It was evident that the majority of the existing members feared that the introduction of a woman into their midst would create discord! He could not, however, be put off by opposition, and when a vacancy occurred on the death of Edward Terry, the Council decided to let him have his way and Irene Vanbrugh, my sister, was elected as the first woman member. I could not have been more pleased, as I had always favoured Mr. Shaw's view, and one of my first reforms was to make the tuition fees of women teachers equal to those received by men. I cannot pretend that some of G.B.S.'s criticisms of my management of the Academy did not disturb me at the time. He considered the deportment of the students, as he had seen it at a prize-giving, deplorable! He described the premises as "The Gower Street lodging-houses." This gave me my cue to seek his help towards the building of the theatre in Malet Street, and he was present at the laying of the foundation stone in 1913. By now I had begun to realize the policy which he had in mind. The Academy was to be a public institution, in which speech, deportment and acting could be taught, and for which, ultimately, Government recognition could be sought. At one meeting he stated that it was our duty to give the students as liberal an education as possible, in subjects required for an Arts degree at a university. His influence was a bracing one and emphasized the need for an institution in London which could form a link between the discordant worlds of Education and the Theatre. Just as matters were being undertaken on broader and more ambitious lines the 1914 war caused a five-year interruption. During this period I was away on foreign service, but the Academy did not close its doors in spite of financial difficulty; the meetings of the Council were held and the minute book shows that the most regular attendant was George Bernard Shaw.

My sister, Irene Vanbrugh, saved the financial situation by arranging a film which included most of the stars of the Stage, and also Mr. Shaw himself, who went, with other councillors, so that a meeting could be filmed, as a prelude to the performance of *Masks and Faces.* G.B.S. refused to submit to make-up for the filming, because he assured the Director that if the members of the Council were not made up, they would come out better than the actors who were made up! This indeed turned out to be the case when the film was shown!

In 1913, before I left for the war, the Academy had been incorporated, and when I returned to my duties in 1920, the time was ripe for a Petition to the Privy Council for a Royal Charter. The status which a charter confers on an institution was in line with the policy which Bernard Shaw had always advised. He was pleased when we were able to obtain London County Council Scholarships for Dramatic Art, and supported the establishment of a Diploma in Dramatic Art by the University of London. Through his influence the constitution of the Council was broadened. The number of its members was increased to twenty, and it was made representative, not only of the Theatre, but of the Crown, the Church and the educational world. The Earl of Cromer, who was then Lord Chamberlain, the Bishop of Chichester, who had always shown a great interest in religious drama, Professor Gilbert Murray and Viscount Burnham joined as members. Royal Patronage was conferred on the institution, and the theatre in Malet Street was completed and opened by the Prince of Wales in 1921. I mention these facts because I wish to emphasize the breadth of view which Mr. Shaw always shows in connection with the R.A.D.A. He wanted the institution to be of use to the Theatre and the British public, and he realized that such lay representation on the Council would create confidence, and put the Academy on the same footing with the public as the Royal Colleges of Music. There was one important point of difference: Music was recognized at law as a fine art by an

Act passed in 1843, drafted, as Mr. Shaw surmised, by the Prince Consort. Premises used for the advancement of Science, Literature and the Fine Arts were held to be exempt from the payment of the General Rate. We determined to appeal against this payment on the grounds that acting was a fine art; the application having to be made to the Registrar of Friendly Societies, after the granting of the Charter in 1920. The Registrar, however, decided that acting was not a fine art within the meaning of the Act, and that the Charter of the Academy permitted the teaching of voice production, dancing and fencing which could not be said to constitute the teaching of acting. It was pointed out to the Registrar that these subjects were merely subsidiary and part of the training of the actor, and that the regulations of the Academy prevented any student from taking anything less than the whole course. He, however, was adamant and turned us down.

In 1921 Mr. Shaw was one of those members of our Council who attended at the London County Council to hear an appeal made by Sir John Simon against the judgment of the Registrar. This committee was doubtful about the status of acting as a fine art, but turned down the appeal on the technical point of the wording of the Charter. It looked as if we had been beaten, but we returned to the charge. The wording of the Charter was altered by the consent of the Privy Council; the judgment of the Registrar and the L.C.C. was overruled and eventually, in 1930, acting was legally recognized as a fine art! The interest which Mr. Shaw took in the complicated legal procedure, which went up to the Divisional Court, and the support he gave to Sir Charles Russell, our Hon. Solicitor, was a great help in securing a result in which tenacity had been essential. In a Minute of the Council he was responsible for this resolution, "that an appeal be made to the L.C.C. against the judgment set up by the Registrar, that acting was not a fine art; and that, if necessary, the matter should be taken to a court of law."

In 1924 Sir William Joynson Hicks, Financial Secretary to the Treasury, received a deputation from the Council of the R.A.D.A. to consider our application for the same grant-in-aid, £500 a year, annually received by the Royal Colleges of Music. When our case had been set out, "Jix" asked Mr. Shaw if he would like to speak. When he consented, and began by stating that any Government giving a grant to an institution connected with the Theatre would immediately run the risk of being turned out of office, I must say I felt apprehensive, not having discerned the characteristic insight which prompted Mr. Shaw to take this line. He went on to say that if the R.A.D.A. were to install an organ on its premises, the Government might then consider making a grant, but an organ would be an expensive investment on the chance of its being considered to endow the R.A.D.A. with respectability! Sir William replied, "Why not try a harp, Mr. Shaw?" and laughter rang through the vasty spaces of the Treasury Room, and the result was that the grant-in-aid was voted.

The time had come to pull down the two houses which comprised the Gower Street part of the premises, and to put up a new and commodious building, which with the Malet Street Theatre would afford premises of greater dignity and usefulness. The main difficulty was to collect enough money, as at least thirty thousand pounds, and probably more, would be needed if the plans prepared by Mr. Geoffrey Norman, and approved by Mr. Shaw and other members of the Council, were adopted. Every effort was made to collect funds, but twenty thousand pounds was still needed. At a meeting in 1927 Mr. Shaw promised five thousand pounds when the remaining fifteen thousand was forthcoming. As he left the meeting I thanked him warmly and said that I was afraid it would be a long time before I should be able to call upon his generous offer. He must have sensed my despondency, and, being the great friend that he is, he sent me, on the following morning, a cheque for five thousand pounds! This turned the scale, and sufficient money, augmented by a loan, became available. In February, 1930, Mr. Shaw proposed that the work of rebuilding the Gower Street premises should be started next April. At this same meeting the legal judgment that "acting was a fine art" was announced. Dame Madge Kendal said that she regarded this as most opportune, as it would "differentiate acting from the mechanical art of the cinema." Mr. Shaw, realizing that the future possibilities for the Talkie films would be vast, replied that he still hoped to make a cinema 'fan' of Dame Madge. The new building in Gower Street was opened by the Duchess of York, accompanied by H.R.H. The Duke of York, now our King and Queen, in November, 1931.

G.B.S. had always been the most regular attendant of all the members of the Council at its meetings, and the Academy benefited through the years up to the last war by his sagacity and practical sense of what could, and what could not be done in an institution which had to make its way against prejudices from opposite directions, both lay and professional. His name on the Council has brought more *réclame* to the school than any other name could have done, and all those who know anything about Bernard Shaw recognized that whenever he gave his name he was prepared to give his time and great abilities as well. The granting of Leverhulme Scholarships in 1932 and our association with the B.B.C. were undoubtedly advanced by the presence of Bernard Shaw on our governing body.

When war broke out in 1939 and the blitz started, owing to the small number of students willing and able to continue, a serious financial position resulted. Our friend immediately offered a loan of a thousand pounds, and added that he did not expect to be repaid! He was strongly against closing the institution, as he had been in 1914. He had made up his mind to see it through. In 1941 our Malet Street Theatre was reduced to rubble by a land-mine, and direct hit. He came to see the damage and was, I think, astonished at its extent. He looked silently at it for half a minute, then turned away and said to me, "Well, they made a good job of it."

In 1928 the whole Council had tried to persuade Mr. Shaw to become their President, and this effort was renewed later on, but he always refused. He thought that position should be occupied by an actor or actress. When, on his eighty-sixth birthday in 1942, he retired from the Council, he was asked to allow himself to be called Honorary President of the Academy, but he replied that he thought no good purpose would be served, although he appreciated the honour. He wished to indicate that his interest in our work had not ceased by remaining as one of the Associate Members. This has enabled me to keep in touch with him in connection with the direction of the R.A.D.A. but also to realize how greatly we have missed his presence at our meetings.

### His Practical Interest in the Students

Although he took such a sustained interest for thirty years in the Academy as an Institution, the basis of this interest was a warm, practical sympathy in the welfare of young people who were determined to devote their lives to the Theatre. It is a fact that I never received a refusal when I asked this famous dramatist to superintend rehearsals of any of his plays that were being studied for performance by our advanced students. He usually consented to come for two hours on these occasions, but always ended by staying for three hours and coming again a second and even a third time, when he felt the students so keenly appreciated the unique opportunity of rehearsing under his direction. During these long rehearsals, even when he was over eighty years of age, he hardly ever sat down, but watched every movement and listened to every intonation with his amazing power of concentration. No detail was regarded as unimportant and his comments were gems of lucidity and humour. He had a power of bringing the best out of young people that I have never seen equalled in a long experience. The courtesy with which he treated students was wholly delightful, but of course his critical faculty and prestige assured that no liberty was taken. These rehearsals by Mr. Shaw at the R.A.D.A. remain in my mind as the most significant episode in our working days. At rehearsals he not only explained the dialogue but demonstrated the characters in action; never because he knew he could do this very well, but only if he felt that demonstration would convey the point he wished to make. He regarded good speech as the first and most important qualification for an actor, and he came down hard on mispronunciation and careless diction. A sense of rhythm in speaking dramatic dialogue, an accuracy of timing, were constantly being inculcated. The individual personality of every student was estimated and imitation was never encouraged. He used to imply that acting is full of tricks that the professional performer is bound to know and use, but never to the detriment of sincerity of expression, which meant a keen sense of interpretation of the character drawn by the author.

Every year the annual public performance by the students found G.B.S. in the same gangway seat in the front row of the dress circle. Below in the stalls the audience was largely composed of well-known people of the Theatre, as this event has always been recognized as a kind of meeting-place for actors and managers. The most distinguished person in the house never stirred from his seat and watched the three-hour programme, made up of extracts from plays which included, on many occasions, some act or scene from one of his own plays with which he had helped the performers at rehearsal. I think he rather liked the eclectic character of the programme, as he once told me he thought it would be a public attraction for additional matinées. I used to visit him half-way through to find out whether he was satisfied with the work of the students, and was greatly cheered when he said to me, "This is a good show." He realized how items had to be cut in order to give the eligible students their chances, and he allowed short extracts of his plays to be done. On one occasion I suggested that the curtain could be brought down at some rather incongruous point in a scene from *Back to Methuselah*. Knowing that this would not make a good curtain he wrote some dialogue which brought the passage to a dramatic climax.

In 1941 he suggested that the students who had earned a Diploma and were leaving the Academy should be given a little book embodying the advice of various members of the Council, which would be useful to them when they entered the ranks of the profession. I obtained twelve contributions but the most valuable part of the book is the introduction written by Mr. Shaw himself, although he refused to have his name attached to it. I quote the opening paragraphs:

> "With your Diploma as a graduate of the Royal Academy of Dramatic Art you now pass honourably into the ranks of an ancient and famous profession. Your personal reputation and your professional achievements are henceforth bound up with the credit, not only of the Academy, but with that of the standing of theatrical art in the civilized world. The road is open for you to the utmost that your ability can command, or your ambition desire, including a celebrity and popularity equal to and sometimes greater than that enjoyed by the most eminent statesmen, scholars, soldiers, divines, or great public servants of whatsoever degree.
>
> "Such a position has inestimable privileges; but it has also its strict obligations; and it is in respect of these that we must not leave you to face them without a word or two of counsel on points of conduct for which the technical skill and practice we have given you may leave you unprepared.
>
> "Unless you have given some consideration to this, your

first impulse may be to say that your private conduct is your own affair. This is not so: you are now a public servant in the widest sense; and in direct proportion to your success will be the publicity given to the most intimate events of your life off the stage. A successful player has no private life."

The recipients of this book, which Mr. Shaw named *The R.A.D.A. Graduate's Keepsake and Counsellor*, were urged to join British Actors' Equity and to observe strictly the etiquette of the Theatre, and *esprit de corps* amongst members of the profession. He had five hundred copies of the little book well printed and bound, and when that number has been distributed we shall have another edition. I know that this *Keepsake* is greatly valued by our ex-students. Last year he presented to the Academy a bust of himself, sculptured by Rodin when the sitter was fifty years of age.

The influence of Bernard Shaw on the young generation of players is very remarkable; not only are they always anxious to have his plays chosen for rehearsal and performance, but a great number of passages selected by students themselves for diction tests are taken from Shaw's works. He has understood the young modern mind, especially, I think, the feminine side of it, more thoroughly than any other great writer of our day; and I feel sure his influence will be a lasting one and will tend to cultivate a healthy appreciation of the values of life, and the discipline needed for developing a personality that is intelligent and free. Those who are unable to find the wisdom and read the serious lessons of life behind the Shavian fireworks and wit will never understand the author. His mind scintillates and startles with opinions apparently contradictory, but, as with the diamond, the central light does not shift. Satirist he is, but not cynic; provocative, never careless; moreover, time has proved and will prove him a prophet. For reasons which I have never fully understood this large-hearted man of genius determined to help the R.A.D.A. and its Principal in his work there, and accomplished this end with a thoroughness and ability that has laid me for ever in his debt. It is indeed rare to meet such a firm hand for guidance and friendship. May I offer him my admiration and affection on his ninetieth birthday?

## ROY LIMBERT

*Director of the Malvern Festival*

### *THE INSPIRATION OF SHAW*

"IT IS not a usual thing to wish a man many happy returns of the day on his eightieth birthday; if it comes to that, it is not a usual thing for a man to have an eightieth birthday at all." So wrote the lamented John Drinkwater in the Malvern Festival Book of 1936—and he went on: "But Mr. Shaw, in this as in so many other things, is different. There is no discernible reason why his vigorous eighty years should not in due time become a vigorous hundred. And so we can all wish many happy returns of the day to a dramatist who has enlivened and enriched an age, and to a man who has on countless occasions shown that he can be the most gracious of friends."

*The most gracious of friends.* No less than John Drinkwater can I personally testify to this. For it is not as playwright, as philosopher, or as man of letters, but rather as collaborator and as active, moving spirit in the life of the theatre, that I have to speak of G.B.S. Quite apart from the works of his genius, without him as a man, without his human interest, encouragement, and driving force, there could have been no such monument to him as now exists in the Malvern Festival.

When the Festival was first established, neither Sir Barry Jackson nor I could foresee its growth into a national—indeed, an international—institution. A cycle of Shaw plays had been planned, to be performed in a single fortnight of 1929, simply as an act of homage to our greatest dramatist; with this a duty would be done—and the future could be left to itself. But here, as was quickly discovered, not enough account had been taken of the extraordinary magnetism of Shaw. Popular demand compelled an annual recurrence of the Festival, and four years later Hugh Walpole was writing, in an introduction to the printed volume of the plays given in 1933:

> "The Festival has resemblances to Ben Jonson's Bartholomew Fair. Everyone becomes a little transmuted. I don't know whether the band in the gardens is an especially good one, or whether human beings during that one week are more amiable than at any other time of the year—I don't *know* what the reasons for the excitement and expectations are—it *can't* be because Mr. Bernard Shaw is in knickerbockers on the terrace!—it remains true that this week has magic in it."

Yet to a large extent, I believe, it *was* because Mr. Bernard Shaw was himself so much in evidence at the Festival. Nowhere else could one go, either in England or abroad, and find the Master alive and present—and not only that, but still zestful and creative as ever, taking a full share in all the activities of the Festival, and ready more than once to produce new plays for it. A few other men besides Bernard Shaw have become legends in their lifetime; to him alone, through his mind and personality combined, has it fallen to inspire the homage of a permanent annual Festival years before his cessation from life and work.

In this lies one of the secrets of the Malvern Festival, which both in scope and in atmosphere differs radically from all other institutions of the same nature. From the very start—from that tentative, experimental fortnight seventeen years ago—it showed itself a living thing, expanding and growing in all kinds of unexpected directions. For its "*genius loci*" was not merely a memory—the congealed, if also, in Milton's phrase, "the precious life-blood of a master spirit"; it was G.B.S. himself, G.B.S. in the flesh, sitting in the theatre to enjoy, with as much savour as the whole audience, his own sparkling plays; G.B.S. striding over the Malvern Hills; G.B.S., genial and approachable, strolling on the terrace amid throngs of visitors from all over the world; G.B.S. with, for all anyone could tell, yet another new play in his head, or possibly even up his sleeve, earmarked for first performance at next year's Festival.

It is in itself a tribute to Shaw that the Malvern Festival, whose programme originally consisted entirely of Shaw plays, should so soon have a stage for Drama in general. The greatest minds feel no jealousy of others, and in consequence G.B.S. could willingly see not only classics of the past, but also the work of contemporary, and in some cases of comparatively unknown, authors presented side by side with his own, and by the same company. No matter how slightly Shaw himself might be represented in the programme—on two occasions, indeed, in 1931 and 1933, no Shaw play was given at all—the Festival still bore the stamp, as it enjoyed the presence, of G.B.S.

None the less, the Shavian contribution on the Malvern stage has been gigantic. Of the sixty-five plays presented in the eleven seasons 1929–1939, no fewer than nineteen—or, if we include each production of those given in more than one season, twenty-two—were by Shaw, the earliest of them, *Widowers' Houses*, written in 1885, and the latest, *In Good King Charles's Golden Days*, in 1939. The Malvern presentation of the work of one still active brain thus covers a span of fifty-four years; eventually it may well exceed sixty years, and provide a veritable Diamond Jubilee. Sophocles, it may be remembered, won his twenty-second prize for drama at the age of ninety; and it is hard to believe that G.B.S. will not to-day regard this as a challenge to himself.

In the Festival Book for 1936, Shaw wrote modestly of that

year's programme that there was too much Shaw in it—although, in fact, only three of the six plays were by him.

"The ideal programme for Malvern would be of new plays by new men. Here am I, by no means a new man, offering one play 23 years old which every playgoer in the universe must have seen a dozen times, and another 12 years old and nearly as hackneyed as *East Lynne*. . . ."

Then, with characteristic generosity, he proceeded:

"If you want to flatter me, you must not tell me that I have saved your soul by my philosophy. Tell me that, like Shakespear, Molière, Scott, Dumas and Dickens, I have provided a gallery of characters which are realler to you than your own relations and which successive generations of actors and actresses will keep alive for centuries as their *chevaux de bataille*.

"Take *Pygmalion*, for example. In 1913 its extraordinary success in London was not the success of my Eliza and my Higgins, but of Mrs. Patrick Campbell's Eliza and Beerbohm Tree's Higgins. What you see at this year's Festival is Miss Wendy Hiller's Eliza and Mr. Ernest Thesiger's Higgins, both entirely new and more interesting than most new plays; for Thesiger is an actor of great distinction whose range obviously exceeds that of the parts his cleverness as a comedian often condemns him to play, whilst Miss Hiller's sensational spring to the very top of the tree in London in *Love on the Dole* makes her appearances as St. Joan and Eliza theatrical events of the first magnitude. This is as it should be; for the Malvern Festival would be nothing if it had not a tradition of great acting as well as interesting dramatic literature. Sir Cedric Hardwicke established this tradition from the beginning; and Gwen Frangcon Davies, Edith Evans, Phyllis Neilson-Terry and Curigwen Lewis have given performances which have made the Festivals memorable quite independently of the authors who were lucky to find such interpreters. With that to fall back on, I need no excuse for myself. My old plays and Garrick's old comedy will do as well as the next best to shew what Malvern acting can do."

These words of Shaw reveal, perhaps more clearly than anything else could do, the spirit with which, from the start, he viewed the Malvern Festival. There was no Olympian aloofness, or pretence of impersonal detachment, in his attitude; he would aid in the rehearsals, and follow all details of the productions, with undisguised relish, treating himself as one of the Malvern team. True, he might write, as he wrote in the 1937 Festival Book:

"I am a booster of festivals because they are markets for my plays. I have actually planted a municipal mulberry tree in Malvern, and thereby created a general impression that I was born there. In course of time visitors will be shewn for sixpence the room in which my first cries were heard. Thus will I become a source of wealth to Malvern in return for the extent to which it is at present a source of wealth to me. As the festival habit grows from the seed sown in Malvern I hope to plant many mulberry trees, and end by having as many birthplaces as Homer."

But this was only a piece of Shavian persiflage, concealing a real belief in the Festival and a real affection for Malvern. He had, in fact, with some ceremony planted a mulberry tree in the Priory Park in the previous summer. During the same month, the Festival Company wished to send him a present for his eightieth birthday, but Shaw let it be known that he would infinitely prefer individual gifts, not one of which was to cost more than sixpence—a request which led to a raid on the local branch of Woolworth's, and produced various light-hearted offerings. Shaw himself, however, declaring that he owed far more to the actors than they to him, sent £100 to the Actors' Benevolent Fund so that he should "know his place." Such have been the touches that endeared him to every Malvern Festival Company, evoking a loyalty and enthusiasm which did much to create that magic of which Walpole spoke.

But long before Shaw suggested that eventually the belief would grow that Malvern was his birthplace, a visitor to the Festival—Miss E. M. Barling—had played with a similar idea, and written in 1931 an "extravaganza" entitled, *Back to G.B.S.* This purported to be a description of the Shaw Tercentenary Celebrations at Malvern, A.D. 2156, by which time truth and fable had become so intermixed that certain scholars of the day held the name Shaw to be a *nom de plume* covering the dramatic productions of H. G. Wells, "the only mind of that period possessing the necessary breadth and vivid imagination to write the plays. Being of a shy and retiring disposition, and disliking the limelight of the theatre, what more natural than that he should seek out a young and struggling dramatist who would lend his name to the plays and get all the glory?" This little skit, in addition to being published and sold for the delight of Festival visitors, was broadcast by the B.B.C. in 1932.

Yet, for all the fun and good humour that it called forth, the serious purpose of the Festival grew apace. Lectures by university professors drew large attendances, even on hot August mornings, and showed how keenly visitors desired to get the utmost from their nights at the theatre. But, though authoritative, the lectures were in no sense narrowly didactic; and when the programme was composed of historical plays—that is to say, "a play from a different century for each night of the week"—they did undoubtedly assist the audience towards a full appreciation of the pieces. Dr. F. S. Boas, Professor Allardyce Nicoll, Mr. Bonamy Dobree, Principal A. E.

Morgan, Professor Ifor Evans and the late Lascelles Abercrombie came year after year to pour out at Malvern the treasures of their learning, while G.B.S. would act as a lecturer in print, and write in the Festival Book articles of wit and wisdom on the current programme.

Indeed, for an author who is commonly supposed to rank among the keenest business men of his time (this, of course, being but another aspect of his myriad-mindedness, and one, moreover, which he shares with Shakespeare), Shaw always displayed a truly astonishing liberality towards me. Many of our dramatists contributed to the Festival Book in years when a work of their own was in the programme; but from G.B.S. I could count on two or three pages even if no Shaw plays at all were being performed. That one who can sell at a handsome price a whole volume of prefaces *minus* the plays that they were written to introduce—a feat which to ordinary mortals must seem like the achievement of the Cheshire Cat—that such a magician should give freely of his time and pen to enhance and embellish the productions of others is surely worthy of grateful and appreciative record.

Not only his pen, but his voice also, was at the service of the Malvern Festival. Thanks to the peculiarly energising effect of Malvern upon its visitors, plays and lectures and garden parties, social club, and "after-theatre" supper dances soon proved not enough; the appetite grew by what it fed on, and demanded still more mental vitamins. So Tea-Time Talks were inaugurated—informal gatherings, held twice a week, at which distinguished figures of the stage, literature, and the arts would speak on the theatre in general. Needless to say (after what has gone before) G.B.S. took his part in these, and coruscated over the tea-cups in his best Shavian vein. I recall, among other things, his telling the assembly how his secretary always dragged him to plays which were having a long run in London—and to which he obediently went "in order to learn how the trick is done."

It is, perhaps, worth mentioning here that side by side with the Festival proper a Pageant of British Film was run at Malvern, and that here also Shaw was represented.

*How He Lied to Her Husband, Arms and the Man,* and *Pygmalion* were all exhibited at one time or another during the Festival period, and visitors were able to read in the Festival Book Shaw's own comments on the film productions.

In 1938 the management of the Malvern Festival underwent a change. For nine years it had been carried on jointly by Sir Barry Jackson and myself in association; but at length Sir Barry felt impelled to withdraw, and it became my lot to keep the flag flying alone. Although in every respect that really matters the Festival had been successful beyond anticipation, the times had been difficult past all precedent owing to world conditions. The protracted economic slump which began in 1929, coincident with the birth of the Festival, and which was followed by constant unrest and alarm over the international scene, could not fail to affect us adversely. There was doubt whether the Festival could continue.

To many minds, as well as to my own, such a demise would have seemed little less than a tragedy. For here was a national institution, fast gathering the most enviable traditions, and already well on the way to occupying a place in world esteem equal to that of Salzburg or Bayreuth. That it differed widely from either of these—although music had been added to its attractions in the form of weekly concerts with renowned orchestras and soloists—only emphasized its individual and British character. Visitors from many countries—and particularly from the United States—had been loud in their praises; and year by year, as the duration of the Festival was extended—from a fortnight to three weeks, and then from three weeks to a month—its importance and its fame were growing. The municipality and the private residents of Malvern alike had thrown themselves wholeheartedly into the Festival, and by means of both public and personal hospitality on the most

generous scale had given to guests from overseas a new impression of England. Thus, quite apart from the artistic side of the question, it was impossible not to fear that a national asset was in peril of dissolution. Accordingly, I resolved on all grounds that the Malvern Festival must be maintained.

In this I was nobly aided by G.B.S. Already, in the past, he had written five plays for the Malvern Festival, viz: *The Apple Cart, Too True to Be Good, The Simpleton of the Unexpected Isles, On the Rocks* and *The Millionairess;* and now he made available the new work, *Geneva,* characteristically writing a note on it in the following terms:

> "*Geneva* is a title that speaks for itself. I hope our Malvern pilgrims this year will be reasonable about it. The critics are sure to complain that I have not solved all the burning problems of the present and future in it, and restored peace to Europe and Asia. They always do. I am flattered by the implied attribution to me of Omniscience and Omnipotence; but I am also infuriated by the unreasonableness of the demand. I am neither Omniscient nor Omnipotent; and the utmost I or any other playwright can do is to extract comedy and tragedy from the existing situation and wait to see what will become of it."

A play like this, having all the rich promise of a Shavian disquisition upon the League of Nations, was alone sufficient to give a *cachet* to the 1938 Festival. The cast included Eileen Beldon, H. R. Hignett, Norman Woolland, Ernest Thesiger, Cecil Trouncer and Donald Wolfit. But, in addition to that, *St. Joan* was in the programme—and so was Elisabeth Bergner, as the Maid. With such a piece of casting we had, in effect, two new Shaw plays—and since all the other plays were new as well, it may fairly be said that in 1938 the Malvern stage was better served than ever. Certainly a very difficult bend had

been safely negotiated—and but for the interruption of the war the Malvern Festival would have continued to take place annually from that day to this.

There was, however, to be one more Festival before the black-out descended, and again G.B.S. came forward with a new play. *In Good King Charles's Golden Days* was the *pièce de résistance* in 1939—in its cast were Yvonne Arnaud, Eileen Beldon, Anthony Bushell, Alexander Knox, Herbert Lomas, Ernest Thesiger, Cecil Trouncer, Irene Vanbrugh and others —and from a splendid reception in Malvern it moved to a successful presentation in London. It is interesting now to recall that at the Festival in that year Gabriel Pascal gave one of the Tea-Time Talks, and that his subject was, "My Shaw Pictures and Their Cultural Significance."

Bearing in mind that I am but one contributor among many to the present symposium, I have deliberately confined myself to G.B.S. in relation to the Malvern Festival. That is because I desire to portray him in one special aspect—namely, that of a man of action—knowing that it is for other and more scholarly pens to write of him as leading dramatist, literary Titan, political controversialist, or metaphysical thinker. It would, indeed, be doing him scant justice to let it be imagined that he furnished the Malvern Festival with nothing but his plays —that he was the impassive, inert demigod of a Worcestershire shrine. He was—and for that matter, he still is—the grand inspiration of a very living movement.

To enumerate all the distinguished figures—whether as playwrights, novelists, actors, speakers or merely visitors—who have taken part in the Malvern Festival would lead me far beyond the limits of this article. That their name is legion is due, once again, to Shaw, for his intellectual company is something that none, afforded the opportunity, could possibly forgo. I must content myself by saying that the standard of our endeavour was set, inevitably, by G.B.S., and that with him as

a beacon we have been magnificently supported. The words below, which I take from the Festival Book of 1939, illustrate well the course of development:

"Fortunate in the privilege of its close connection with Bernard Shaw, the Malvern Festival is strengthened yet further in having Sir Cedric Hardwicke as Associate-Director. It is, indeed, not too much to say that the success of *The Apple Cart*, with the triumph of Cedric Hardwicke as King Magnus, gave the Festival such an initial impetus ten years ago that a tentative experiment offered assurance at once of becoming a permanent institution. Since then, six new plays by Shaw (including the present *King Charles*) have had their first performances at Malvern, whilst in addition thirteen of his older works have been presented. Only his unavoidable absence in America prevents Cedric Hardwicke from acting in our current programme. That both the greatest dramatist and the foremost actor of our day should be thus closely identified with Malvern necessarily lends the Festival an importance of which both Company and Management are fully sensible. With such forces to encourage it the explanation of its success is not hard to find, for behind leaders like these all concerned are bound to give of their very best."

Among the leaders from 1938 onwards were three second only to G.B.S. himself as rallying-points—James Bridie, J. B. Priestley and H. K. Ayliff. Five years previously, Bridie had written *A Sleeping Clergyman* for Malvern, and he now gave us *The Last Trump*, while Priestley came in with *Music at Night*. In a single programme we thus had three new plays by dramatists of the highest standing—and we had, too, a master-hand in H. K. Ayliff to direct them. Except for a break during the years 1934–37, Ayliff had produced all the preceding Malvern Festival plays, and he had no equal for experience

of, and skill in, this exacting task. The loyalty and devotion which brought him back to Malvern under the fresh dispensation form yet another example of the centripetal force exercised by G.B.S. In 1939, when again there were new plays by Shaw and Bridie, Ayliff was once more producer of the entire programme.

Several names are mentioned in these pages, not for the sake of drawing attention to a distinguished gallery, but for the purpose of showing how powerfully, and in what an effective way, G.B.S. has been both a focus and an exemplar of effort. The cold, disembodied intellect, the austere, self-contained critic, the harsh satirist who is a combination of Swift and Voltaire—these are not Bernard Shaw at all. If the march of time appears neither to dim his eye nor blanch his cheek, it succeeds even less in subduing his humour and dulling his good spirits. By ordinary standards, he was old when the Malvern Festival began—yet for nearly twenty years his presence and his personality have been at hand to infuse vitality and vigour into it. Nor can I see any reason why two decades should not become at least a quarter of a century.

Macaulay said of Dr. Johnson that it was the memory of Johnson that kept his works alive. No historian of the future will be able to say such a thing of Bernard Shaw—for the works, in this case, have too throbbing a life of their own. Yet of Shaw as a man the memory surely will endure—and Malvern will remain a less static memorial than Lichfield. For even when Shaw himself departs, and when it shall be that "the beacon light is quench'd in smoke, the trumpet's silver sound is still," the Malvern Festival will be—and continue to be—"Dedicated to Bernard Shaw."

With this I must leave an enthralling subject. To have worked so closely and so harmoniously with Bernard Shaw has been for me not only a high privilege, but also a personal revelation. The great commanders, from Alexander to Kitchener, from Marlborough to Montgomery, have exerted some mysterious charm which calls forth the utmost from those around them; and that faculty G.B.S., also, possesses to the full. It is the kind of thing about them which is never forgotten, which sets a tradition, and which acts as an inspiration. Hence the title of this article; hence too, I think, much of the veneration in which those who know him must ever hold Bernard Shaw.

# GABRIEL PASCAL

## *SHAW AS A SCENARIO WRITER*

"Life becomes as the stoics more than once tell us, like a play which is acted or a game played with counters. Viewed from outside, the counters are valueless; but to those engaged in the game their importance is paramount. What really and ultimately matters is that the game be played as it should be played. God, the eternal dramatist, has cast for you some part in his eternal drama and hands you the role."

SO STARTS Professor Gilbert Murray in one of his most important essays on drama. From my early youth, I too regarded the world as a stage belonging to me; I became, as a young cadet, member of the Imperial Theatre of Vienna at the age of eighteen; but after two years of acting, a terrific boredom overcame me and I decided to select my parts in Life and play them without the usual cue from fellow-actors or help from any prompters. After long years of erring and searching, as it was predicted to me by a Hindu "Perfect Master," I arrived one day in the spirit of playing my Life's part at G.B.S.'s flat at Whitehall Court. I told him that I was his Richard Dudgeon and I believe that he himself was convinced that I was the materialization of his "Devil's Disciple."

What was my aim? To persuade G.B.S., in spite of his first unfortunate experience of pictures, to entrust me with the difficult task of adapting his plays through the medium of the screen for a world-wide audience? Or was it the desire for fame, for success, for material gain or the attempt to enrich the medium of the screen with a new style, new formula, new inspiration? Or was it a desire to serve the G.B.S. doctrine as a faithful disciple? It was none of that.

I am one of those strange puppet players you find on the island of Java or in South China, carrying their cut-out puppets in a little case, travelling from city to city, putting up their white backcloth on the walls, then playing their shadow plays.

It was my predestination when I had nothing else in my pocket but my ticket to China, to go to G.B.S. and tell him that I *am* his Richard Dudgeon.

It would have been very easy for G.B.S. to say to me: "You are a fool, a phantom or a shadow of your own imagination and nothing is real in you." But he is one of the few like Gilbert Murray who know that the whole "*Divina Comedia*" is only a human game.

When finally, after that certain Friday, the 13th December, which he called: "Auspicious day in the history of Art," we became friends and partners in the great venture to conquer the millions of the world with the screen version of his plays which during the last fifty years had been reserved for a few ten thousands of the so-called intelligentsia, I realized that I must stop playing the role; that I must do the job and henceforth let others play.

I realized the terrific responsibility which I had undertaken; G.B.S. is a man who can read your mind before you open your mouth, he knows everything about you the moment you enter his room. Very quickly I learnt that it was better to work with him in complete simplicity and faith.

I had worked, before I met G.B.S., with many great writers on the Continent, and I had found that when they started to work on a picture scenario, through too much respect for the so-called technique of the shooting script, they lost their own personalities and artistic integrity and became like mumbling children. Like the great actors in the silent picture days, who, when they were placed on the set for the first time, became completely confused and made the most childish mistakes.

Not so G.B.S. He had no respect whatever for the so-called technique of the cinema. He told me, what in my subconscious I already knew, that nothing matters but the story itself; and the duty of the producer is to tell this story simply and faithfully, keeping to the author's intentions.

Thanks to G.B.S. I returned to my original profession of directing pictures, which I had abandoned, to become a great impresario and God-knows-what. As he put limitless faith in my artistic ability, it was my duty to ask him for several supplementary scenes which I needed for adapting his plays to the large audience of the screen.

G.B.S. would have been the greatest scenario writer for the screen if I had met him twenty-five years earlier, but even at this late stage he started his new career as scenario writer with terrific fervour, enthusiasm and unbelievable visual knowledge. During my career I have never found a great playwright with as much genuine instinct for camera angles and as much rhythmical sense for movie continuity. Certainly, when I first asked him in *Pygmalion* to write me the reception and bathroom scenes he was stubborn about them because our understanding was that I should put his plays on the screen as they were, without any of the elaborate Hollywood "beauty parlour" treatment. Nevertheless he wrote those two scenes in no time and they have the same freshness and vigour as the rest of the play. For *Major Barbara* he wrote sixteen new sequences for me. I was only able to use six of them for lack of screen time. For my latest picture, *Cæsar and Cleopatra,* I needed only three short sequences as transition-scenes to avoid sudden jumps in the action and G.B.S. was very generous, permitting certain cuts to be made which I thought necessary for the screen adaptation.

These few facts characterize only the week-by-week routine of our collaboration during his scenario work. But the great point in G.B.S. as scenario writer is not only in his writing but in his steady inspiration which he gives to me, his producer, during the whole preparation and making of his picture.

I showed him the still photos weekly and he immediately recognized with his critical eye the development of the characters by the players, he saw the slightest faults in their make-up or in their portrayal, or the slightest stylistic error in sets and *décor*, and he became my second artistic conscience, which for a producer-director is more important than formula, tradition and technique, of which Hollywood is so proud.

It is unbelievable how much a great author who is interested in the realization of his works can help a producer. The present system of picture making in my opinion is utter nonsense. They buy a story from a great author and give it to another writer who has as much to do with the original as I have to do with the Stock Exchange. This literary family doctor becomes the *spiritus rector* of the whole picture. The poor author who developed in his brain and his heart the structure of his human comedy over a period of years must instead of facing the white-heat furnace of his producer, leave it to a foreman, not even selected by himself, to supervise the casting of his bronze statue.

Something is basically wrong in this system adopted by nearly all major production companies of Hollywood.

G.B.S. gave me the backbone to fight these methods and remain an independent interpreter of his works.

It was a hard road we started together, but I feel it is only the beginning. His *St. Joan, Devil's Disciple, Man and Superman, Blanco Posnet, Candida, Arms and the Man, Androcles and the Lion, The Doctor's Dilemma, The Apple Cart,* and his other plays are all waiting for rebirth on the screen.

It will take at least ten years to bring to the screen all the works mentioned, and if, as we all hope, he will continue his invaluable work as scenario writer and inspirer, the world can expect some surprises in the young art of the screen.

I am proud that through the faith of G.B.S. in me, I was

able to give an example to the world with *Pygmalion* of how a masterpiece should be handled by the producer.

Maybe it would be of some interest to the world to know that G.B.S. is not only the great living playwright and brilliant scenario writer but he is a great actor and an even greater director who knows his timing better than anybody I have ever met.

He also knows the right timing on the world stage. Let me tell you about the last hour of that remarkable episode which has been commented on in so very many different versions, how he gave me the rights of *Pygmalion*. After several visits we became friends, he was convinced I had something to say in the artistic world. But I knew that if I did not do something drastic, our short and delightful relationship would go on for months without getting down to brass tacks.

I had nothing in my pocket but an invitation to make pictures in China. I therefore said to him, on the 8th December, 1935: "Look here, G.B.S., if you don't give me your rights, I am leaving 15th of this month for China, but I am ready to wait until Friday, 13th, four o'clock—which would be an admirable day to sign a contract."

He said to me: "What! Is this an ultimatum?"

I said: "Yes, an ultimatum."

I did not hear from him for five days and the 13th came. I was living in a little flat in Duke Street, I cooked my own luncheon. A guest of mine, a charming lady from India, brewed Turkish coffee and at three o'clock she said: "Gabriel, your Irish Pope has let you down."

I replied: "Not at all, it is not four o'clock yet." But certainly I felt despondent.

It was a quarter past three . . . it was half-past three . . . it was a quarter to four . . . still no telephone call, no contract. At a quarter to four I started to pack my toothbrush and some imaginary luggage; imaginary because I had nothing. My Hindustani friend was delighted that I was going to the East and declared triumphantly a few minutes before four o'clock: "You see, he has not understood you, he has not believed in you."

Suddenly, Big Ben struck, and the door bell rang. A messenger boy entered:

"Are you Mr. Gabriel Pascal?"

"I am." And just as Big Ben was sounding the fourth stroke he handed me a big envelope. I opened it. It was the contract of *Pygmalion* and the photo of G.B.S. signed and inscribed: "Auspicious day, Friday, 13th December."

He proved that he is not only a great scenario writer but a great *metteur en scène* of Life. . . .

## S. I. HSIUNG

### *THROUGH EASTERN EYES*

WHEN I first came to this country my greatest ambition was to meet three persons: Galsworthy, Barrie and Shaw. Galsworthy died within a month of my arrival in London; Barrie was seriously ill and confined in a nursing-home; and Shaw had just gone to China. Had he gone there to see me, my disappointment would have been more than compensated; but when we met upon his return to England, he told me quite frankly that the chief aim of his trip to China was to see the Great Wall. Once I told a friend that I could hardly get over the fact that Shaw went to China not to see me but the Great Wall, adding that I ought to be more dissatisfied as there were over four hundred million people in China, and surely there must have been one or two of them more interesting than the old Wall. My friend comforted me with the philosophical view that it certainly indicated that since I was in London, there was no one in China worth seeing.

That, of course, would greatly gratify my vanity if there is but a grain of truth in it. How could there be? I soon heard from a number of my friends at home telling me about their interesting meetings with Shaw. They claimed to have held most original conversations with the great man. They adored him and reported many of their discussions to me. When I asked Shaw whether he remembered meeting this famous Chinese author or that prominent Chinese professor, Shaw sadly shook his head. In fact he told me that the only person who had made a deep impression on him was a very polite fellow who presented to him a pirated copy of one of his plays: it was a bilingual edition, the man being the translator. Shaw said he was greatly impressed by the man's impudence. Mrs. Shaw was by his side as she always was. She added promptly that that was in Japan—not in China—and the man a Japanese. She was sure that no Chinese could be so impudent.

There is another person in China Shaw should remember, but it was not from him I heard of the encounter. At a reception given in Shaw's honour, a famous professor was presented to him. On being told that the professor was a great educator, Shaw, while shaking him cordially by the hand, exclaimed with deep feeling: "God help you!" This little incident has been very carefully described to me by a number of my friends. I deduce from that that it is known almost in every educational circle in China. I wonder whether Shaw would remember this man at all.

One of the penalties of being famous is that everybody knows you or about you while it is utterly impossible for you to be in the same position with but a fraction of them. The fact that they really do not know you though they think they do does not help you in the least. Indeed it is much worse. Shaw's position is the worst in the world because there are dozens of books written about him—including a dictionary and an epitaph. As for articles on him in newspapers and magazines, they are far beyond count. But those writers who have published scores of books and yet have to write their autobiographies are far from enviable. I hear that some of them have to engage publicity agents. Now, in China, there used to be a sure remedy. When a very rich and successful man wanted immortality, he could always get himself into the works of his contemporary distinguished men-of-letters. He could commission the author for a full-length biography of himself just as one could commission a modern master for a full-length portrait. Since it is for a pen-portrait, he could, instead of sitting for it, furnish the writer with the desirable material carefully prepared by himself, his children or anybody whom he chose. With this material the man-of-letters rewrote it in his excellent style and future generations read and recite a masterpiece of biography. This practice went on until a writer produced a biography by composing only one sentence of his own. He said that the life of so-and-so, according to the draft submitted, was as follows. He then quoted the paper in full without comment. He did not claim to know the man at all. If Shaw is commissioned in the same way by some successful man to write a biography, I wonder whether it would be printable. But I am sure the man will get his money's worth.

There is a saying about a certain great man to the effect that all the people in the world could be divided into two groups: those who know him and those who don't. But to Shaw this is hardly applicable. It would be more true to say that they are divided into those who like him and those who don't, as it is difficult to find anyone in the world who doesn't know him. It is also quite understandable that when one has read some forty or fifty plays of his, one feels one could call him by his first name. His friends call him G.B. or G.B.S. and the public likes to follow suit. It is good to see a certain popular columnist, who calls everybody by his first or pet names, always refers to him as his good friend G.B.S. Although Mr. Churchill is always "Winnie" and Lady Astor "Nancy" to him, he never once wrote about Shaw with the name "Georgie" or "Bernie." Even such a man has some respect for Shaw.

Once Barrie asked me rather abruptly: "Do you often see the Shaws?" I was for a moment puzzled, and could not decide whether by "the Shaws" he meant the shows of the West End. But his next sentence was very illuminating. He added: "I imagine Shaw, waking up in the morning, would raise his arms and say 'Hurrah, I'm Shaw!' " However, this remark is not so extraordinary as it sounds. Many a friend of Barrie's would say that they would imagine Barrie making the same exclamation. After all, anyone tends to feel like that when he realizes he is at the top of the world. And if there is someone among us who finds himself constantly at the top of the world and feels like this, certainly that is nothing against him.

Of course I cannot ignore the amount of unkind things said about Shaw. Perhaps he enjoys a greater amount than any of his brother authors. There is, among books written about him, his "epitaph," which very few living persons are privileged to have. To attack Shaw, many writers have found out, is to attract instant attention. And if you are lucky enough to draw a rejoinder from his pen, your fortune in the literary world is almost ensured. Unknown authors consider this their infallible short cut to establish themselves. Public speakers, too, find the name of George Bernard Shaw a great boon to them. If they notice that the audience is becoming a little restive and needing some brightening up, all they have to do is to bring in one or two witty sayings by their good old friend George Bernard Shaw. The quotation may be incorrect or even pure invention, but the name never fails to be a refresher.

In the literary world there seems to exist one or two of what we may call brotherhoods which, though without any formal organization behind them, generally function very smoothly all over the world. Sometimes one wonders whether it is a conspiracy. The left-wing writers, for instance, invariably slap each other's backs and join together, even though they do not know each other's work, to attack their critics and enemies. Well-established authors of the left recommend without reserve and protect vehemently new ones. Irish authors—a much smaller number of them—also stand very stoutly together. Some of the big shots launch their debutants from time to time in every branch of the arts. They praise and defend each other as no others do. In some cases the works so boosted are justifiable. But there are quite a few whose books, though magnificently recommended by their well-known compatriots and their blind followers, are an agony to read. Indeed I have made a rule that if a certain author's writing has been praised too much by another, especially by one whose name spells fame, I shall always take the greatest care to avoid his books. But Shaw is an exception. He has never been one of their protégés, nor does he try to nurse one—at least I hope he will not do so merely for the sake of patriotism. On the contrary, some of his countrymen have passed very devastating remarks about him and some of his sallies at his brother authors are unforgettable. Not that I like to encourage civil war, but such exchanges of thrusts, in the form of expert criticism, have been the best reading I can remember.

Unless you know the author, it is often dangerous to take his writing at face value. It is even misleading to grasp their subtle meaning between the lines. After you have read Shaw's remark about Shakespeare and himself, you would naturally think that he is arrogant and conceited. Simply because he has lived much longer than Shakespeare, he regards the works of the Bard immature. Most people would think that to say Bacon or some one else wrote Shakespeare is excusable, but to claim to be better than Shakespeare is utterly unbearable. But when I met Shaw for the first time, I was astonished by his polite manners and attractive courtesy. It would be more than permissible for a young guest to look after his much older host, but with Shaw this would never do. Let the guest be as young as his junior by half a century, he insists on opening the door for him, seeing him to his chair, or helping him into his coat.

Neither does he talk all the time as he does in his plays. I am not so great an admirer of his *St. Joan* as of his other works. I find that he has given the Maid of Orleans, who was a woman of action rather than of words, only one thing to do on the stage, that is to talk endlessly and to talk exactly like Shaw. It was a great relief to me to see her choosing the stacks. And if you expect Shaw to be always monopolising the conversation as some of his immortal characters, you are very much mistaken. Least of all he talks about himself, and if you ever succeed in egging him on to tell you a little about himself, you will find that he is surprisingly modest. Once at Malvern, where annual dramatic festivals were held in his honour until war broke out, we were fortunate enough to get him to tell us a little about his early struggles. He confessed frankly that all his attacks on Shakespeare and the established drama were nothing but trying to get a living for himself. "Of course we have to attack the old drama for all we are worth, otherwise where do we find a stage for our own plays?" he told us candidly. When someone said wasn't that giving himself away, his reply was even more frank than before. "That's nothing. I have not told you half of our tricks."

His wit and humour, so abundant in his work, however, never leaves him for a moment in his conversation. Once I took my old friend General Kwei to see him, and as usual, the guest started to voice his admiration for Shaw, for his impressive beard, his sparkling eyes, his prominent forehead, his nose and mouth, and even his teeth. That was going a little bit too far, and Shaw stopped it in a very humorous and friendly way. "Do you really admire my teeth?" he asked. "Well, you could do so at closer quarters," and he took them out of his mouth and offered them on his palm to Kwei.

Kwei wanted to know how did Shaw manage to be so young in so advanced an age, Shaw replied that that was quite simple. You must not smoke, drink, eat meat, nor have anything to do with women until you are fourteen.

It was Shaw's turn to ask Kwei a question or two, and he wanted to know what Kwei, as head of the Chinese military mission to this country, intended to do during his sojourn in England. Kwei said the supreme aim was to promote Anglo-Chinese co-operation. "That," answered Shaw, "you will find easily achieved. Great Britain is extremely good at co-operation with other countries provided that the co-operation is a hundred per cent to her own advantage." When Kwei went back to see Chiang Kai-Shek, it was one of the gloomiest periods of the war and Shaw's remarks were the only things which made the Generalissimo laugh heartily as he had never done for a very long time.

Some people say that Shaw has a very perverse temper; others say that he is a man of moods: you never know what mood he is in when you meet him; and there are those who think that he likes to stand purposely upside down doing antics to shock and provoke you. Before I came over I was greatly impressed by a cartoon of Shaw standing on his head. Perhaps because I am a great admirer of Max Beerbohm I used to believe that Shaw would say and do whatever is opposite. Our first meeting nearly bore out this belief of mine. He told me that he had been to some classical Chinese theatre in Peking and I was anxious to know what impressed him most in that traditional house. On an old-fashioned Chinese stage, there are a hundred and one things, conventional and praiseworthy or otherwise, to attract a stranger. I was looking forward to hearing some sharp attack on our theatrical custom. His answer staggered me: it did not come from the sphere where I expected. He said that the most impressive sight in a Chinese theatre was nothing on the stage done by the players, but the throwing and the catching of bundles and hot towels deftly performed from great distances in the auditorium by the ushers. I could only conclude that he must have been sitting most of the time with his back to the stage.

I often ask: Has Shaw really got a perverse temper? No; far from it when you really get to know him. Is he a man of moods? Neither could I say yes. I have always found him in a good and almost charming mood. I remember that when I had my first offer for my maiden English work, I instantly went to him for advice, and it was sound and practical advice which was given to me. Incidentally, when the production of my last play (the word last here is not misused, and I hope nobody will ask me again when I am to write another play) was in negotiation, it was also Shaw who told me what to do.

I do not think it was sheer topsyturvydom of a man to pay special attention to trifles and ignore important things of the world. One's point of view differs so much from that of others. Much depends upon one's philosophy of life.

Shaw is above all a great philosopher and thinker. In fact I consider him a much greater philosopher than a dramatist. Most of his recent plays are almost unactable and certainly unacceptable to the public if they were signed with any other name. But they are very interesting philosophical discussions. You find kings and queens, clergymen and rogues, scientists and soldiers, all talk as eloquently, wittily and humorously as Shaw himself. As he sees things slightly more philosophically than most of us, it is natural that we find all his characters slightly eccentric, and we think the author more so.

Before he was accepted as a great author, his struggles had been doubly hard compared with other writers. It was in those early days when he wrote the best of his plays. In more ways than one, they could be regarded as masterpieces of dramatic art. And for nearly a quarter of a century nobody would take him seriously. If it were not for the banning of one of them which instantly created a sensation, people might be unable to see his plays even to this day. And when he has grown tired of sticking to his mastery of stagecraft and is indulging in long philosophical ramblings on the stage, everyone acclaims him the greatest dramatist of the age.

I must now disclaim my responsibility of writing this to be put among the contributions of so many illustrious men of my time. Indeed I have deliberated for a long time before I put my pen on paper. There are only three reasons for anyone to be anxious to read a thing. The most proper one is that it is well-written. Failing that there is still a demand for it if it bears the hall-mark of some very distinguished author. But should it be badly written by some totally unknown person whose name nobody could pronounce, it is still worth reading provided that the subject has never been touched by anybody else. As in the present case, it is utterly impossible for me to induce the reader to believe that this composition could come under any of these three groups. All I could do is to ask the reader to view it with the greatest indulgence, which has been so well cultivated during those long years of war.

## ALDOUS HUXLEY

### A *BIRTHDAY WISH*

ERASMUS was the best-seller of the sixteenth century; all Europe read Voltaire; all the world has read or listened to George Bernard Shaw. Works of art having a reasonableness-appeal can, if good enough, achieve a popularity almost equal to that accorded to sex-appeal and sect-appeal. The fact may seem surprising. But *homo*, after all, is *sapiens* as well as *amans, credens* and *bellicosus*. When an enormous talent places itself at the service of sweet reasonableness, the sapient and æsthetic sides of human beings respond with enthusiasm. As artists, the apostles of rationality are admired and loved; as practical teachers, alas, they are ignored. If people had been content not merely to read Erasmus's books, but to take his advice, there would have been no wars of religion, perhaps no revival of polytheism in its form of nation-worship; if they had done what Voltaire so brilliantly implored them to do, there would have been no French revolution, no Napoleonic imperialism, no universal military conscription; and if, instead of just applauding Mr. Shaw's plays and chuckling over his prefaces, we had also paid some serious attention to his teaching, what remains of our civilization might not now be lying under sentence of death. But, as usual, *homo amans, credens* and *bellicosus* has proved to be a great deal stronger than *homo sapiens*. Reason continues to be used, in the main, as the instrument of passion. Science and technology are still the servants, not of truth, or liberty or happiness, but of nationalistic idolatry and the lust for political or economic power. As in the past, first-rate minds proclaim by their actions that they are ready to forward policies of unspeakable silliness and wickedness. According to the investigating psychologists at Nuremberg, Messrs. Schacht and Seyss-Inquart have IQ's of over 140 and must therefore be placed in the "genius" category. Field-Marshal Goering is a close third, with a score of 138. Like patriotism, intelligence is evidently not enough. Then what is enough? Let us all wish Mr. Shaw as many happy returns of the day as will suffice him to distil his ripened wisdom into the answer which our world so desperately needs.